SIXTY MILES
OF BORDER

SIXTY MILES OF BORDER

An American Lawman Battles
Drugs on the Mexican Border

TERRY KIRKPATRICK

BERKLEY BOOKS, NEW YORK

THE BERKLEY PUBLISHING GROUP
Published by the Penguin Group
Penguin Group (USA) Inc.
375 Hudson Street, New York, New York 10014, USA

Penguin Group (Canada), 90 Eglinton Avenue East, Suite 700, Toronto, Ontario M4P 2Y3, Canada
(a division of Pearson Penguin Canada Inc.) • Penguin Books Ltd., 80 Strand, London WC2R 0RL,
England • Penguin Group Ireland, 25 St. Stephen's Green, Dublin 2, Ireland (a division of Penguin
Books Ltd.) • Penguin Group (Australia), 250 Camberwell Road, Camberwell, Victoria 3124, Australia
(a division of Pearson Australia Group Pty. Ltd.) • Penguin Books India Pvt. Ltd., 11 Community
Centre, Panchsheel Park, New Delhi—110 017, India • Penguin Group (NZ), 67 Apollo Drive,
Rosedale, Auckland 0632, New Zealand (a division of Pearson New Zealand Ltd.) • Penguin Books
(South Africa) (Pty.) Ltd., 24 Sturdee Avenue, Rosebank, Johannesburg 2196, South Africa

Penguin Books Ltd., Registered Offices: 80 Strand, London WC2R 0RL, England

This book is an original publication of The Berkley Publishing Group.

Copyright © 2012 by Terry Kirkpatrick.
Cover photos: Shutterstock. Cover design by Gerry Todd.
Interior text design by Laura K. Corless.

PUBLISHING HISTORY
Berkley trade paperback edition / July 2012

Library of Congress Cataloging-in-Publication Data

Kirkpatrick, Terry.
Sixty miles of border : an American lawman battles drugs on the Mexican border / Terry Kirkpatrick.
p.   cm.
ISBN 978-0-425-24762-4
1. Kirkpatrick, Terry.   2. U.S. Customs Service. Office of Investigations.
3. Drug control—Mexican-American Border Region.   4. Drug traffic—Mexican-American
Border Region.   5. Marijuana—Mexican-American Border Region.   I. Title.
HV5831.M46K57 2012
363.45092—dc23
[B]
2012001301

PRINTED IN THE UNITED STATES OF AMERICA

10 9 8 7 6 5 4 3 2 1

Penguin is committed to publishing works of quality and integrity.
In that spirit, we are proud to offer this book to our readers;
however, the story, the experiences, and the words are the author's alone.

These are the true stories of federal narcotics investigations and operations in Arizona, Texas, and Mexico. The border of Arizona and Mexico is open and offers an opportunity for anyone to cross for any reason. This account is meant to shed some light on the life of narcotics agents, their dealings on the border, and the effect on their daily lives. It isn't intended to glorify the agents or make them out to be anything more than the crazy, dedicated characters who make up much of law enforcement.

Hundreds of special agents have passed through the border offices; some don't last six months before they beg for a transfer. The few who stay on the border proudly call themselves "Border Rats." As a diehard member of the Border Rat pack, I hope to put you in our boots and allow you to see the border through our eyes.

There is a thin line between sanity and insanity; on this job we learn to laugh at ourselves and others, just to stay on the right side of that line. No matter how awful the event, we always try to find an enlightening moment as a psychological means to keep from losing our minds. Being a true Irishman and loving a good story, I'd often teach new agents with my own version of our deeds. That's my goal here.

Every day, along the southwest border, agents face danger and unimaginable frustration. The events, characters, and antics are factual. These accounts are of the devoted U.S. Customs special agents who work the southwest border in Arizona and Texas, as well as of the notorious narcotics traffickers who have controlled and still control the *Zone Norte* of Mexico. The names of some of the special agents and the confidential informants have been changed to protect them. The names of the traffickers are real; some are still terrorizing Mexico.

AN AGE-OLD PROFESSION

SMUGGLING has occurred in Arizona since the 1800s. In one way or another, horses, cattle, people, liquor, birds, snakes, and narcotics have crossed the border going back to the time when the first railroad was built. In the days of Wyatt Earp and Doc Holliday, cowboys were smoking opium. When opium was outlawed, the Chinese began smuggling it into the United States.

During the 1940s and 1950s, the Chicago mob hid out in Nogales, Sonora, Mexico. Pictures of Pretty Boy Floyd, John Dillinger, and others were displayed on the wall of the Cavern restaurant.

Mexicans write songs of the traffickers' exploits, making them sound like a kind of modern-day Robin Hood. Today, the government of Mexico is engulfed in a losing battle with the traffickers as the government seeks to retake control of the Narco Nation. The cartel groups are ruthless, violent beyond measure, and have left a trail of death in the border cities of Mexico. It's only a matter of time until the violence spreads into the United States. Some argue that with the deaths of local ranchers and the killing of a border patrol agent, it is already here.

Most quaint border towns in Mexico have a center square called the plaza; this was the traditional meeting place for residents on the weekend to gather, socialize, and listen to bands. The plaza is the heart of the town. The *jefe de plaza*, or boss of the plaza, is a trafficker who controls the border city. The cartels distribute drugs to the plaza boss, who distributes them to the local smugglers. The *jefe de plaza* bribes the mayor, federal and local police, and business leaders for political favors and immunity from arrest. Money is no object to the cartel bosses, who are listed in the Forbes 500 as some of the richest men in the world. They buy the best equipment available: guns, armored vehicles, encrypted communications, and aircraft.

The special agents of the U.S. Customs Service, Office of Investigations, are charged with the daunting task of deterring smuggling and arresting anyone who smuggles contraband across the border. The investigations, seizures, and arrests are seldom publicized. Publicity is the last thing the office and the agents want; being discreet enables us to do our job more effectively.

HUNTED OR HUNTER

IT was a sticky, moonless summer night, darker than normal, perfect for drug smuggling. An old Vietnam veteran once told me there is a thin cloak between being the hunter and being the hunted. That thought kept going through my head as my partner, Tom, and I hugged the dirt on a border hillside. We had been creeping along when a sudden sound caused me to drag us both down to the ground.

I lay there barely breathing and analyzed our situation. There was no cover, no place to hide; we were lying on the upward slope of a hill with the border fence about thirty feet above us. Below us were a few dilapidated old adobe houses, and below them, a few parked cars, which were too far away to reach.

I raised my head, straining my eyes to focus on something, and then the night seemed to explode. A flash from a muzzle lit up the small houses in Mexico, and the gunfire was deafening. It sounded like a cannon going off. Instantly I recognized the unmistakable blast of a .45-caliber semiautomatic; hell, my service weapon was a .45 automatic. The smell of gunpowder and smoke filled the night air and my lungs. I flattened my body closer to the ground. Three more rounds, four, five rounds went flying over our heads. I could hear the bullets zinging past, hitting a brick wall below. In the distance bullets also tore into a parked car like an explosion. Tom and I were frozen flat to the dirt. We'd drawn our guns when we hit the dirt, but we didn't dare look up to find a target. I knew I had to do something, so without aiming, I squeezed off two rounds into the dark in the direction of where I'd glimpsed the first muzzle flash, and then everything went silent. The incident took only a few minutes, but it was as if time had stopped for us.

The genesis of this incident occurred two days earlier. I was sitting in the office with my feet propped up on the desk writing reports. We wrote them on legal pads and the office secretary typed them out for us. The U.S. Attorney's office was always busting our asses to have the investigative case reports for arrests and seizures on their desk within three days of each arrest. I'd already made two arrests this week on narcotics cases and still hadn't written them up. I even had one from the week before. I knew they were long overdue. In the days before computers, if an agent had to make corrections to a report that was already typed, it was the secretary who retyped it, and her wrath was as bad as the supervisors'.

My supervisor was already on my ass, but I wasn't alone. It was the end of September and the marijuana harvest season in Mexico had begun with a vengeance. The entire office was already overloaded with cases.

My name is Terry Kirkpatrick; I'm a special agent for the U.S. Customs Service, Office of Investigations, in Nogales, Arizona. The sister cities of Nogales, Arizona, and Nogales, Sonora, are located along the international border and consist of cramped shanty neighborhoods butting up to the border fence. This entire area is hemmed in by rugged hills and canyons on both sides. In these dark canyons drug smuggling and illegal-alien crossings are rampant. The drug smugglers and coyotes who cross people are ruthless and would do anything to get the drugs and people into the United States.

We often existed in the shadows. The public seldom heard about the work of Customs special agents until a major organization was dismantled, which sometimes could take years. Customs agents were seldom mentioned in the press; major undercover operations that use confidential sources are best kept secret. Good operations sometimes last years; even as of this writing, operations are being conducted in Nogales and throughout the United States and internationally that may never be made public.

So, it was the marijuana harvest season in Mexico and everyone in the office was busy working six or seven days a week. Hell, most of the time it seemed as if we slept in the office. Out of the twenty-three agents, nineteen had been through at least one divorce, and some guys two or three. This job was not really conducive to marriage. The old-timers would say, "Boy, if the government wanted you to have a wife, they would have issued you one."

The office secretary, Anna, buzzed my phone extension and said, "Patricio, someone wants to speak with you." "Patricio" was the pseudonym that I gave to all my informants. "He's on the line. Would you like me to pass it to someone else?" She knew I was buried with reports. Anna had a soft sexy voice that could be distracting. I gathered my wits and agreed to take the call.

The caller said his name was Jose in a rough, broken accent, and he needed to speak with Patricio in person. He had a deep voice that was a little creepy. Shit, I couldn't catch up now, but what the hell, it's like an addiction. I agreed. I told Jose I would meet him around four P.M. at the Sacred Heart Church parking lot.

I often used this location to meet potential informants. The church parking lot was open, yet surrounded by trees, and was located on high ground above Grand Avenue, Nogales's main street. I always parked in the southwest corner of the lot for the clear views below. There was a steep wall and no one could approach my car except from the front. Besides, I always felt safe there. The traffickers wouldn't shoot anyone on Catholic Church property; it would be bad karma, or so I hoped.

Sometimes I took someone with me if the subject couldn't speak enough English because my Spanish was limited in my early career. I could handle basic conversations, but if someone spoke really rapid Spanish, I was lost. At about four, I saw a man climbing the church stairs toward the parking lot; I figured this was Jose. During our brief conversation on the telephone earlier, Jose told me he had information on my favorite smuggling area of Short Street in Nogales. Jose told me he'd be walking and that he was wearing a blue jacket and white baseball cap.

I had arrived about ten minutes early and was going over in my head what I wanted to say and to ask Jose; I had a lot of informants providing information on a regular basis. I was a good salesman and was respected by my peers for recruiting good sources of information. I told Jose I would be driving a white Ford with a maroon top; this was my *G-ride*, government-issued vehicle, a 1978 Ford LTD. I'd seized this car in Tucson after finding a load of marijuana in it.

The guy shuffling toward my vehicle was a middle-aged Mexican male. As he approached my vehicle, I rolled down the window and motioned for him to get in. Jose was weathered, and I suspected he was either a ranch hand or laborer; his boots were scraped and rough. Jose seemed a little nervous, but he got straight to the point. He said someone had given him my name, but he wouldn't elaborate, a common stance. He said he had heard there was a stash house right on the border at the dead end of Short Street. He described the general area where the stash house— more of a storage shed or garage—was supposed to be located, and he believed the dope stored there belonged to the infamous trafficker Jose Luis Somoza, aka El Quemado, meaning "the burned one."

Quemado was a nasty young smuggler who had been burned badly on the side of his face and arm when he was about thirteen. According to stories from several sources, a smuggler who caught Quemado hanging around his stash house in Mexico decided to teach him a lesson. The smuggler, just to be a mean rotten bastard, grabbed Quemado, slapped him around, and knocked him to the ground, then doused him with lighter fluid and set him ablaze.

Quemado grew up in the Buenos Aires neighborhood of Nogales, Sonora, Mexico, just east of the main Nogales port of entry (POE) and south of Short Street. This area has a reputation for being the roughest zone of Nogales. The cops seldom patrolled there, and if they did, they were working for the traffickers. Buenos Aires began as a shantytown where squatters built cardboard houses; there was only one road leading into the area. Most of the residents walk in by means of a stairway running along the border fence on the Mexican side.

For years, there was no running water, no sewers, and no electricity, and then, slowly, the area grew from cardboard into brick construction of small homes clustered through the area. Garbage is thrown about and raw sewage still flows into the streets and into Tricky Wash on the U.S. side of the border. During the summer the smell of garbage is suffocating, like going to a city dump; during the winter the residents burn firewood and garbage along with tires in the backyard, anything to stay warm.

These are the forgotten residents of Nogales: unemployed, left to fend for themselves. The girls sold themselves on street corners; the boys lined up for jobs crossing marijuana for the traffickers or became thieves.

The place we live in often shapes us into the person we become. Quemado became a person who, at the ripe old age of sixteen, got even with the bastard who had burned him. Quemado ambushed him at the stash house one night and shot him and another guy to death. Quemado stole approximately fifteen hundred pounds of marijuana, paid off the supplier, and began his career in the drug-smuggling business.

Quemado then recruited other kids his age, and his gang grew until it finally took control of the shantytown housing area known as Buenos Aires, or "good air." Good air, my ass; the whole area smelled like raw sewage. By the estimates of various informants, Quemado was around twenty-two when I had my first encounter with him. One thing's for certain: the mention of his name scared the living shit out of everyone who lived in the area.

Quemado's reputation for terror was built on shooting workers and suspected *dedos*, the Mexican slang meaning "fingers" or snitches. Quemado burned a suspected snitch to death, leaving the charred remains of the crispy critter at the hole in the fence on Short Street, just two feet over the U.S. side. The Nogales fire department responded to a call about a brush fire in the area and quickly backed out of the area on seeing the dead, burned body. I heard the radio call for the Nogales police department to respond and headed that way. I vividly remember seeing the charcoal-black remains of a body in a fetal position with the arms at the chest level as if praying for mercy. One arm was still in the air making a fist with what should have been fingers. The body was burned beyond recognition.

On another occasion, Quemado and his crew took a suspected snitch out to the desert. Quemado ordered all of his workers to come along to witness what happened to snitches. Quemado then tied the man up by his hands and feet, with one arm and one leg tied to one pickup truck and the other arm and leg tied to another. The trucks then slowly pulled the man apart as Quemado questioned him, until his arms and legs were ripped from his torso.

Quemado was a lieutenant for a major trafficker named Jaime Figueroa-Soto who moved massive amounts of dope from Sonora, Mexico, into Arizona. Figueroa-Soto was around forty years old and known as a notorious trafficker in Magdalena, Sonora, Mexico. He was rumored to have killed three rival drug traffickers for trying to distribute marijuana in his area.

I had recruited several informants who lived in this area, and Quemado was the main target of my investigation. I knew the Drug Enforcement Administration (DEA) was investigating Figueroa-Soto, who had residences in Phoenix and Magdalena. I was just hoping to arrest Quemado.

The man who had met me in the church parking lot, Jose, had gotten my attention by mentioning Quemado. I started my recruitment of Jose in an attempt to document him as a source of information, but Jose claimed he didn't want anything for the information. He didn't want to be paid and he didn't want to be documented. Jose just wanted to let me know about the stash of dope in a garage and that he heard the smugglers say they were going to cross more dope tomorrow night around ten P.M. I studied Jose's facial expression and decided he was serious; it was hard to tell why he was providing the information. He spoke rapidly and told me what he had to say, and then, just as fast, Jose said, "I have to go." I tried asking him more questions. How did he know? Did he work for Quemado? Jose was evasive. He said he had to get back across the line, walking away briskly back south toward the Grand Avenue POE gate.

I pondered his motive. He didn't want any money; Customs paid its sources well when we made seizures based on their information, but he didn't want anything. His family didn't need a border crossing card (BCC); for a Mexican, a BCC card is better than cash. I had a gut feeling, as agents do, but I couldn't quite figure it out. I shrugged it off to hunger and grabbed some lunch. Who the hell really knows about that sixth sense feeling? I'm sure I had it several times; I just ignored it until after something happened and it was too late.

What the hell, I thought, as I drove back to the office. Back at the office the guys were hanging out, bullshitting; I discussed the information Jose had provided on the stash house and asked if anyone wanted to go lie into the area, and heard the gleeful response, "Fuck you," several times. No one liked working the area, especially lying in by the border fence. When I said, "Come on, I've got a great strategic operational plan," everyone laughed. "It's simple," I said, "we can just hike into the area on foot, find cover and wait to see if a load crosses, then follow the mules to the garage."

I regarded Short Street as my area. I knew the trail along the international border fence and had walked the area numerous times. The best way to get there undetected was on foot. I wanted to get there early and lie in before the smugglers crossed. Then if I saw them take their stash into a house or garage, l could easily obtain a search warrant and seize everything.

Again my brilliant plan was greeted with more verbal insults; the other agents hated lying in and disliked being that close to the border. Most of the agents were busy with their own investigations and sources and had reports to finish writing. Finally Tom volunteered to go in on foot with me. The man lived for camping and being in the desert or remote areas. Tom wasn't an agent; he was a Customs patrol officer. He was as capable as any person in the office and a hell of a lot better than most. I had been out with him on several occasions, and we worked well together. When Tom was a kid in California he lost his right arm in an accident, and thus he was nicknamed "Lefty"—a typical cop way to express respect.

The following night Tom came out dressed in full military camouflage clothes; I just wore a long-sleeve black shirt and Levi's. Every agent in the office had various forms of clothing in their

vehicles: ninja black pants and black shirts, full military camouflage pants and shirts, raid jackets, rain gear, bulletproof vest.
Every agent also had a complete set of extra clothes packed in
what we called a didi bag. The term came from Vietnam veterans
and was short for *didi mau*, a Vietnamese term meaning "to get
moving." We traveled a lot doing controlled deliveries of drug
loads from Arizona to California.

Tom and I parked at the bottom of the hill leading up to Short
Street. Other agents—Rene, Joe, and Ricardo—were going to
stand by in their vehicles in the general downtown area if we
needed assistance. None of us gave much thought to the operation; this was what we did every day. Tom and I both grabbed
what gear we needed and in our best stealth mode slowly started
making our way up to the steep trail in the dark.

It was a warm late-September night; the monsoons were over,
but it seemed muggy and humid out. I wore a long-sleeve shirt at
night because Arizona comes alive after dark with scorpions and
other crazy creepy crawly things. If I was going to be in the weeds,
I wanted to be prepared. There was no moon out; it was pitch
black, and the hill on the Mexican side of the border was tall and
cast a dark shadow over the United States side. This made the
climb along the border fence slow going, but I preferred the dark
shadows over walking in the moonlight.

The Short Street area was dangerous then and is still dangerous today. The traffickers on the Mexican side have the high
ground for visibility and sit on the roofs of their houses and watch
anyone driving into the area. They basically control the neighborhoods on both sides of the border. Tom and I stayed in the shadows, inching our way up to the rocky hillside. There are no trees

once you pass the few run-down houses scattered along the edge of the hill. Tom and I didn't say a word to each other; I led the way, and he followed right behind me.

My senses somehow went into a heightened state of alert after dark: every sensory nerve, hearing, sight, and smell kicked into warp drive. Many times during operations Tom and others said I had better senses than wild animals.

I seldom used the night-vision goggles; Tom joked that my night vision was better than an owl. We hiked up the hill, moving about twenty yards at a time, and then I stopped and scanned the area and listened for any signs of activity. I continued this move-and-listen tactic every twenty yards; this was my routine. Just before I reached the crest of the hill, about thirty feet from the international border fence, I froze. There it was again, that sixth sense or my guardian angel whispering in my ear to stop. Somewhere in the outer limits of my mind I'd heard something. I wasn't sure, but I thought I heard the sound of an automatic pistol's slide move; it was ever so faint, like someone had just slightly moved the slide a tiny little bit perhaps to see if a round was in the chamber.

Then, suddenly I felt every nerve in my body tense up; the hair on my neck stood up like needles sticking me. Something was wrong. I turned to Tom and softly whispered to get down. Tom hesitated. I motioned with my hand and reached back, grabbing Tom's shoulder, and said, "Get down." Instinctively, Tom and I fell into a prone position, lying flat in the dirt and rocks. There was no cover, no place to hide; we were lying on the upward slope of a hill. The border fence was only about thirty feet above us; below us was nothing but a few houses and some parked cars that were too far to run to. It was a matter of seconds from the time my senses were alerted to the threat to the time it took for Tom and me to hit the ground, although it seemed like minutes. The only thing in front of my head was a football-sized rock for cover. I felt my whole body tingling. A huge adrenaline rush had engulfed me like an explosion.

Then everything happened in an instant: a flash from a muzzle and the sound of gunshots rang out from Mexico. I knew the sound of a .45-caliber automatic; my service weapon was a Colt .45. The smell of gunpowder filled the night air. I flattened my body closer to the ground as three, four, five rounds went over our heads. I could hear the bullets zinging past, hitting a brick wall. Below us, in the distance, we heard the sound of metal on metal as the bullets tore into a parked car below like an explosion. Tom and I were frozen flat into the dirty hillside like reptiles in the sand. We'd drawn our guns, but we didn't have a target. I knew I had to do something, so I quickly squeezed off two rounds into the dark in the general direction of the area where I'd glimpsed the first muzzle flash. Then everything went silent.

The bastard had us trapped. We just lay silent, face down on open ground; I didn't dare raise my head. The sound of the bullets tearing through the metal on the car was surreal. I made sure Tom was okay.

He asked, "Did you hit him?"

"No, I don't have a clue where he is."

Tom was already on the radio, calling out, "Shots fired, shots fired." The smoke from the gunpowder was like a fog floating in the air. A million things ran through my mind, but I can only remember thinking, *This might have been a good night to wear my bulletproof vest.* I hadn't worn it because it was too hot.

I raised my head just a little and tried to focus my vision, scanning the area where the shots had originated. Then I saw him in the shadow of a two-story house about twenty yards south of the border fence in Mexico. His silhouette was suddenly outlined as he slowly struck a match and lit a cigarette. It was as if he were holding the match up to deliberately say, *Here I am.*

That son of a bitch, I said to myself, *that asshole actually took the time to light up a fucking cigarette. He wanted us to see him.* I wondered if it was Quemado standing in the shadows, or if Jose was the bastard who shot at us. The man took two drags on the cigarette, his silhouette outlined, and then he disappeared, fading into the shadows of the houses. Within seconds, we heard the cavalry responding as every law enforcement unit in the area arrived with sirens blaring. It took two minutes at most for the first agents to arrive. They took positions along Short Street, their vehicle lights aimed toward the border.

There were at least six units in the area; the fence was lit up with spotlights. Tom called out "Code four" on the radio: the situation is under control. Right then, I started thinking Jose had set me up for a hit. Did that son of a bitch work for Quemado? My body was overflowing with anger and emotions, not to mention the adrenaline rush. I was mad at the asshole who'd tried to kill us, and mad at Jose, but mainly mad at myself; I should have seen the guy before he got the drop on us.

Tom and I sat up on the ground and looked at each other for a minute as we realized how close we had come to death.

Tom asked, "What the hell made you get down?"

"I heard someone checking his gun, like the sound of a metal gun slide moving."

Tom smiled.

The anger and adrenaline rush quickly subsided, and Tom and I both started laughing the situation off; we gave each other the customary pat on the back and slowly stood up to get the hell out of the area. I looked around. The area was covered with law enforcement; at least six Customs special agents with rifles and shotguns had taken cover outside their vehicles and were aiming at the Mexican border fence. Nogales police officers were present and were trying to contact the Mexican authorities. Then one thing really caught my eye and made me take notice. It was Rene.

Standing alone, Rene had rushed twenty feet toward the border and was in the middle of a cleared area, a streetlamp above him and several vehicle headlights shining on him; the reflection made him stand out in the dark like a neon sign. In this neighborhood, that was an invitation to get killed.

Rene was the office resident technical genius. He was a master mechanic, a high-tech wizard; there was nothing Rene didn't know how to fix. He was well read, a scholar of sorts. Rene was about nine months younger than me; he was known as "Mr. Safety" and was as cautious as an agent could get. He thought every situation through and kept us out of trouble more often than not.

But in spite of his great skills, Rene obviously needed help buying clothes. Earlier that day Rene had bought some new clothes, which he wore to work. When Rene told our group about his shopping, Ricardo jumped on the opportunity to tease him. Standing in the office with one hand on his hip and another pointing at the wall, pretending to be Rene shopping, Ricardo imitated a gay man speaking to a sales clerk: "I need clothes; I want what the mannequin is wearing, so just strip him down and give me his clothes." Ricardo had us laughing our asses off. We didn't really give a shit about Rene's clothes, but Ricardo's impression of Rene as a Mexican gay male from across the line was hysterical. Hell, Ricardo was so good we started teasing Ricardo about how he knew so much about gay shoppers.

Regardless, Rene was proud of the clothes he'd worn to work tonight, and he'd pranced around the office all day asking the secretary if she liked his outfit.

Tonight was different. Rene stood out in the open, in the middle of a gun battle, with his peach-colored shirt and light tan slacks glowing under the reflection of the streetlamp. He was quite a sight; we couldn't help but start laughing as we climbed down the hill to the units. Joe arrived, saw Rene, and yelled at him, "Get the hell out of there. You're glowing in the fucking dark." Rene suddenly realized what a tempting target he made. A look of absolute fear flashed over his face as he glanced around and sprinted back to the cover of his vehicle.

The sight of Rene glowing was more fun to talk about than the shooting incident, and it helped us relax. While Rene was laughing at himself, we were laughing at Ricardo's reenactment of the shopping story. Rene tried to explain how he'd raced into the clearing, thinking he needed to rescue Tom and me, ending with, "Oh shit, I was a bull's-eye target. What was I thinking?"

As the expression goes, "No good deed goes unpunished." After every shooting incident comes tons of paperwork. I wrote reports justifying my actions: Why did I shoot? Did I have a target? Why didn't I wear a bulletproof vest? This was followed by days of questions from the older agents, who added their opinions and interpretations of the events. Agents and cops from every law enforcement agency live to give each other a hard time and bust each other's balls every chance they get. This teasing is really another form of training; with enough peer persuasion you seldom make the same mistake twice.

As a young agent, I learned daily from my mistakes. *Learn by doing* was my motto. I was told by a veteran agent that the day you take the attitude that you know everything is the day you'll get killed.

SANTA CRUZ COUNTY

SANTA Cruz County lies in south-central Arizona and shares approximately sixty miles of border with the state of Sonora, Mexico. It is the smallest county in Arizona. The two large economic bases are smuggling and agricultural trade. Nogales, Arizona, and Nogales, Sonora, Mexico, are known as sister cities because they share the same name. The sister cities are situated in a canyon with rolling hills and mountains in every direction. *Nogales* means "walnut" in Spanish; walnut trees once covered the entire canyon pass where the cities were built. The Mexicans asked the United States to build the first fence to keep out the rowdy American cowboys who came to town.

Geographically, Santa Cruz County consists of mostly wild places. People from the east tend to visualize Arizona as being flat, dry, sandy desert where tumbleweeds roll along in the barren sand, but much of the county is part of the Coronado National

Forest. The mountains and lush valleys attract painters and photographers from all over the world; the beautiful and panoramic sunsets casting romantic colors over the mountains are an artist's dream.

Eight mountain ranges in the county flow together, overlapping in a way that they appear to be one continuous range. The elevation of the sister cities is around four thousand feet; to the east lie the Patagonia Mountains, San Cayento Mountains, and Santa Rita Mountains, which stretch twenty-six miles, with the highest peak, called Mount Wrightson, standing at 9,450 feet. To the west lies a series of smaller mountains that intertwine each other, stretching out in all directions from six to twelve miles. They are the Pajarito Mountains, which connect to the La Esmeralda mountain range in Mexico; the Atascosa Mountains, with their highest peak at about 6,500 feet; and the Tumacacori Mountains.

The flora of these peaks and canyons are all different, with multiple species of pine trees and fir trees in the mountain ranges and mesquite, oak, and cottonwood trees in the lower elevation of the canyons. There are running creeks, the Santa Cruz River, which floods over during the monsoon season, and two lakes in the mountains. These mountain streams support abundant wildlife such as squirrels, raccoons, deer, javelina, black bears, and mountain lions. The mountains are full of old abandoned mines and caves from early prospectors.

This is the border terrain that also provides shelter and hiding places for the smugglers. Road vehicles can't navigate this area. Law enforcement uses all-terrain vehicles and horse units to patrol some of the areas because high-tech equipment is useless as a deterrent to drug smuggling.

Nogales, Sonora, is considered prime real estate to drug traffickers; Interstate 15 in Mexico goes from the border to Mexico
City. It passes through every major city in Sonora: Nogales, Imuris,
Magdalena, Santa Ana, Hermosillo, Guaymas, and Ciudad Obregón. Then it passes through Los Mochis, Culiacán, Mazatlán,
and Sinaloa and on to Mexico City. Travel on Interstate 15 is
controlled by the traffickers as much as it is by the Mexican police
and army.

Nogales, Arizona, has some families who have been smuggling
for three generations; they know the terrain and trails. The border corridor is valuable because it provides easy access into the
United States. Up until recently there were no fences in many
areas. Interstate 19, the U.S. highway from Nogales to Tucson, is
a sixty-mile stretch of straight driving allowing for a forty-five-
minute drive to the major east-west corridor of Interstate 10. Once
on I-10, narcotic loads have almost free passage to cities on either
U.S. coast.

Nogales, Arizona, has a population of around 40,000, while
right across the border the population of Nogales, Sonora, is in
excess of 350,000. Visitors to the border cities seldom notice the
shantytowns in the hills, where people from Mexico, Nicaragua,
Honduras, and other Latin American countries live in eight-by-
eight-foot quarters with dirt floors made from discarded boards,
plywood, and cardboard boxes. These residents burn garbage
to keep warm, have no employment prospects, and become an
endless workforce for the smugglers who hire them to backpack
the drugs into the United States.

The sister cities of Nogales were once considered quaint, quiet
border towns where tourists from the United States went on the
weekend to buy Mexican curios and eat at the great restaurants

like La Roca, El Cid, the Cavern, and others. The once over-crowded curio shops in Nogales, Sonora, are now deserted, its streets void of American tourists.

If the cartels were to envision building a city along the border for smuggling, the sister cities of Nogales would be the model. In addition to the surrounding canyons and mountains, the areas within a mile of either side of the POE are just as active for drug smuggling.

Directly below the city streets lies a complex underground catacomb of drainage systems, with the main drain twenty feet wide by twelve feet high, that runs below Grand Avenue and Morley Avenue onto the Mexican side, where it is open for anyone to access for a price. The main drain is connected to hundreds of three-foot storm drains in the downtown area. These three-foot drains provide smugglers a conduit for building tunnels to businesses and houses. To date, more than sixty-five drug-smuggling tunnels have been discovered in the city of Nogales Arizona alone. The CBP (Customs and Border Patrol) fought a constant battle to find and close these. When one was discovered, we staked it out to catch the people who were using it. Once they were arrested we sealed the end of the tunnel with concrete. Still, for each one that was closed another was opened elsewhere.

The Santa Cruz River flows north, and so does all the drainage of water from Mexico. During the heavy monsoon rains, the Santa Cruz River runs over its banks and the streets of Nogales, Sonora, are often flooded.

The manhole covers in Nogales, Arizona, have to be welded shut to prevent smugglers and illegal aliens from popping up and out onto busy streets. I saw a group of twelve illegals climb out of a manhole at the intersection of Grand Avenue and Interstate 19, where eight lanes of traffic converge in the downtown area. They pushed open the heavy steel manhole cover and started running down the street in different directions, leaving the cover off for an unsuspecting vehicle to drive into.

As with most border towns between the United States and Mexico, there is little or no employment. The two hundred thousand immigrants from Central America who make it to the border are usually broke and desperate.

Entire generations of families in Santa Cruz County have done nothing but smuggle; fathers, sons, and grandsons have made smuggling their livelihood. They have driven down every road and walked every trail. The smugglers have befriended many law enforcement officers through social networking at parties, where information is gleaned from wives, girlfriends, and relatives to learn the schedules, habits, and haunts of law enforcement officers. Numerous federal and state law enforcement officers in Santa Cruz County have taken the path of corruption and tarnished the rest of law enforcement.

So as the water from the mountains and rivers flows north, it seems only natural for the flow of drugs to follow the same path. This is the geographic wilderness in which this story takes place. I arrived as a feisty young man of Irish heritage who didn't speak the language, didn't know any local customs or history, and was an outsider in this mostly Hispanic enclave made up of Old West and border cultures.

In the West you learn to listen to old-timers who know the ranches, trails, and mountains. From the San Rafael Valley in the east to the mining town of Arivaca in the west, we responded to information from our sources. As I worked in Santa Cruz County, I explored the mountains and valleys and learned to respect the land, the people, and the culture of a place that has become my home. I knew I could never take this rugged environment for granted. I never knew where I'd be working each day, as the traffickers shifted from one location to another to cross the dope; each day became a new adventure.

THE OFFICE

THE Treasury Department was originally structured with four investigative divisions: the Secret Service; the Bureau of Alcohol, Tobacco, and Firearms (ATF); the Internal Revenue Service (IRS); and the Customs Service, Office of Investigations. Treasury agents were very competitive with the Federal Bureau of Investigation (FBI) and the DEA. As special agents in Customs, we investigated crimes similar to those investigated by the other agencies, such as narcotics, money laundering, child pornography, gun smuggling, and white-collar crimes. Our investigative jurisdiction overlapped, which caused ongoing turf wars.

The U.S. government considers Nogales a hardship post for its agents. It's a standard three-year tour of duty. If you screwed up you were gone quickly, but if you did a good job then you were trapped. We often sang the Eagles song "Hotel California": *You can check out anytime you like, but you can never leave.*

When I first came on board, the Nogales office was located in a nondescript one-story building that looked more like a poor real estate office than a federal facility. It was a small building set off from the road between Scotty's Pub and a Circle K store. There were no security cameras, no bulletproof glass, no combo lock on the front; anyone could just walk up and enter the building. This was a far cry from most federal buildings located in downtown Tucson or Phoenix.

The building was cramped, with agents crowded together two and three to an office. We were so overcrowded that one day when a new agent arrived, the poor bastard entered and asked where his office was. Someone said, "Follow the signs." We had put up several signs saying JIM'S OFFICE with arrows below pointing down the hall. He walked down the hallway and ended up out the back door, where, next to the fence, was a desk with his papers on it. Turns out he had no sense of humor; he was so pissed off that he worked out of his car for several days.

Of course, having Scotty's Irish Pub located next door was a plus. The pub became the place to solve our problems; stress was a definite factor, and at times we would be ready to kill each other in the office. Tempers flared and even the occasional punch was thrown, but quarrels were generally solved by having a few drinks at Scotty's Pub. We yelled at each other before ordering the first drink, and then by the third drink we were reflective; by the time we ordered the fifth or sixth round we were hugging and laughing. That was the nature of the beast along the border.

Working on the border is a twenty-four-hour-a-day job; the confidential sources who worked for me were out and about night and day, so when they called about a load crossing the border, I had only thirty minutes or less to respond. Many of the agents had issues at home with their spouses. Stress was a major factor; many of the wives complained the husbands were never home. At one time nineteen agents out of twenty-three were divorced, and some were on their third marriage. The border motto is *Get over it, suck it up, and move on.*

Once the local citizens knew who we were, they'd challenge us at every opportunity. In bars, on the street, it didn't matter; they had a hard-on for narcs. Little did they know that if you fight one, you fight the whole office. At the time I didn't think much about how the City of Nogales or Santa Cruz County police departments operated. In the early years the Nogales police and the county sheriff's department didn't work narcotics; they said it was a federal problem. Thankfully that changed over the years. Rumors were rampant about corruption in both departments, and through the years several officers had been arrested and charged with drug smuggling.

The Customs office secretary, Anna, was a hot-looking woman. She was leggy, around five feet nine, and slender, with ample headlights. She was always dressed to the nines and she could answer the telephone, type lightning fast, carry on a conversation, and do filing all at the same time. Before the age of computers, she typed the reports for all the agents. She worked nonstop. She smiled at everyone and spoke in a sexy voice that men love to hear. Anna was the office sweetheart and a heartthrob to a few guys in the office. She was married to a macho Mexican dude who at one time wanted to be a bullfighter.

There were three groups in the office. Mine was narcotics; Carlos was the supervisor, with Ricardo, Rene, Joe, Layne, and Tom working alongside me. As a group we worked an average of fifteen hours a day; some extended surveillances lasted three or four days straight. Each month we averaged 120 hours of over-time. The squad backed each other up; we ate together, drank together, partied together, and at times fought like brothers.

The white-collar agents in the office called us prima donnas. Working narcotics for one year in Nogales was the equivalent to ten years in any inland office such as Kansas City or Denver. Working the border makes you callous and rough around the edges. President Richard Nixon was the first person who used the term *war on drugs*, but we knew there was a war; we fought daily battles and focused on one case at a time.

Carlos, the supervisor, was a Mexican American born in Texas, fluent in Spanish. His dad was an old rancher in Texas. Carlos was easygoing and didn't hesitate coming out on operations with us. His philosophy was that you learn from your mistakes, and he enjoyed the excitement of the job as much as the rest of us. Carlos covered me on surveillance and corrected my dumb-ass rookie mistakes during my first few years on the job. I learned a lot of things from Carlos that I believe kept me alive and out of trouble many times.

Layne was a senior special agent. Years earlier he'd been a city cop in Phoenix, Arizona, before joining Customs. Layne was ten years older than me and a good agent, but he had made his share of rookie mistakes. When we screwed up, Layne related his sto-ries to us to ease the misery. He was the buffer between the old agents and the younger ones. Divorced and a single father raising two teenage daughters, Layne didn't move for promotions. He decided to raise his daughters in one place so they could finish high school. He knew the ropes and was the rock of the group; he was always able to put things in perspective, explaining why we shouldn't get frustrated and do certain things. He provided the wisdom that can be achieved only after years on the job.

Joe was from Brooklyn, New York, Italian by heritage, but defiantly not your typical New Yorker. He fit the stereotype of an Italian mobster: big, heavyset, black hair, and always well dressed. He could have easily played a mob boss on the set of *The Sopranos*. Joe was nicknamed "Joey the Arm" because of his big arms and his habit of pounding on the desk. Some Italians talk with their hands; Joe used both arms.

Joe's decision to move to Arizona came to him one day in Brooklyn while he was looking for an address. He walked in the wrong door of a warehouse, and right in front of him were five Italian goons counting money. They jumped up from the table and began yelling at him. One grabbed a pipe and the others started telling Joe how they were going to beat the shit out of him. Joe instantly took out his badge and gun. This just pissed them off more; they told Joe they were going to take his badge and gun and shove them up his ass. Joe managed to get back out the door with his gun drawn and the group still advancing.

Joe's version of the story was great; he said, "I had visions of my gun with the four-inch barrel and large night sights sliding up my ass." That was when Joe decided he had had enough and moved to Arizona, where he married a local Hispanic woman. Joe would tell the young agents that they should each be the boss of the house, like him. One evening Joe arrived home very late after working surveillance. His wife was very upset because she'd made his favorite dinner, spaghetti and meatballs, expecting him home at exactly five. In typical Hispanic female fashion, she began to yell at him. Feeling his Italian heritage, Joe grabbed the plate of spaghetti from the table and threw it into the dining room wall, smashing the plate and covering the wall with spaghetti. Then he yelled, "Now you have something to be mad about. Don't ever yell at me for working late." After listening to this, most agents decided Joe was not the go-to guy for marital advice.

Tom was from California; he'd worked as a civilian for the government during the Vietnam War. He was one of the last Americans to leave Saigon when it fell to the Communists in 1975. He married a Vietnamese woman who could field-strip a .45 automatic and put it back together faster than our best agents. Tom wasn't an agent, but should have been. Tom was a Customs patrol intelligence officer. Because he'd lost his left arm as a kid, by regulation he wasn't allowed to become an agent. Tom spent thirty years of his life fighting this decision with lawsuits against the government. Tom loved the job, however, and regardless of the operation he'd always respond. Like a few others, he was bound to the job because he truly enjoyed what he did every day. I worked with Tom in a lot of different situations, and he never let me down. He was better than most with any weapon, but at times he could be a real hardhead.

Rene was from New York and of Puerto Rican descent. His dad was a career military guy, and his stepfather was also a former military man who had joined the Customs Service. Rene followed in their footsteps. Rene was disciplined, well read, and more politically correct than most agents in the office. He joined the U.S. Air Force right out of high school, and then, after his enlistment was up, he joined the Customs Service. He was assigned to the small town of Ajo, Arizona, for about four years before he was transferred to the Nogales office.

Rene was known as "Mr. Fix-it." He was a C130 aircraft mechanic when he was in the Air Force and could work on electronics, car engines, and just about anything with moving parts. Rene
was also very careful, almost overly cautious. He had a mothering
or nurturing instinct and wanted to overthink every situation.
Rene was the only one who talked to the women in the office about
recipes and the latest clothing fashions. He was one of the few
guys who knew colors such as chartreuse or fuchsia. Men know
seven basic colors: black, red, white, green, yellow, brown, and
blue; to the rest of us, *fashion* was how much cleavage was showing.
I joked with Rene about having an extra female chromosome. Rene
was the administrative brains in the group. He read all the policies and procedures. He could recall every document the brain-
dead, useless headquarters staff in Washington wrote, telling field
agents how or how not to do our job.

Ricardo was born in Nogales, Sonora, Mexico. His father died
when he was young, and then his mom remarried an American
citizen, who adopted him; he immigrated to the United States with
his family when he was a kid. Ricardo had a Mexican maternal
name and an American paternal last name. In Mexican culture,
the mother's paternal name is used as a last name on a person's
documents, unlike the American tradition, in which the father's
surname is used.

Ricardo knew every area of Nogales, Sonora, and Nogales,
Arizona; he was street savvy. He joined the army, served in Vietnam, and earned his GED. Following his military time he joined
the Santa Cruz County sheriff's department and the Nogales police department, and then he was a Customs inspector before becoming a special agent.

Ricardo was excellent at undercover work. A player who had the talk and the walk, he used his skills to recruit some of the best confidential informants in the office.

Ricardo was selected to be a special agent and assigned to Nogales. But within two years Ricardo had to be transferred out because of death threats. His greatest strength was that he knew all the people in town who were the subjects of investigation. This was also his greatest weakness; everyone knew him as well.

As for myself, I never thought I'd end up as a special agent working narcotics. Hell, if you had taken a survey at my high school, the student body would have said I was most likely to end up in jail. My parents divorced when I was around four years old. As kids, my brother and I were shipped from one parent to another. We traveled by Greyhound bus, sometimes for three days, from California to Illinois and back. I lived in some bad-ass neighborhoods in Chicago and St. Louis. By the fifth grade I carried a spinning chain with a piece of lead on it. I wasn't looking for a fight; I simply had to fight to get home. I attended as many as four schools a year. By high school I was sent to live with my grandparents. Finally I had some guidance.

In my senior year, they moved to New Mexico and I stayed in Illinois and lived alone in an apartment above the local pool hall. I finished high school and did two years at Southern Illinois University before moving to Tucson, Arizona, at which point I was drafted. I married at twenty-five, not because I was madly in love, but because I thought it was the right thing to do because of my age. I thought I was supposed to settle down. Within a few years there were issues, but I considered divorce failure. Regardless, we got divorced. I can't blame my first wife. I lived for work, and soon the job was my mistress.

Because Rene, Ricardo, and I were the same age, the three of us formed a close bond. They taught me about Mexican culture as well as the language. The language is only a small part of being able to live on the border. Learning the Mexican culture is the real key to blending in and being accepted. Mexico is the country of *mañana*, or "tomorrow." No one is ever in a hurry. Thousands of hand signs, nods, and gestures go with the language. Obtaining this knowledge proved invaluable to me when I worked in Mexico. Our group drank together many times in what's called "choir practice," the police term for drinking your troubles away or decompressing after a shitty night at work. During these sessions I learned Spanish; the more tequila I drank, the better my Spanish became. Ricardo said, "If you want to learn Spanish, get a Mexican girlfriend."

I had street savvy, and this job provided me an opportunity to use every tactic I'd ever learned. I found myself wanting to take risks. I needed to prove to myself that as an agent, I was as good as or better than most. Respect was never given; it was earned by fire. I knew I had the calling; for the first time in my life, I felt as if I excelled at something. I became recognized by my peers and by other narcotics agents working undercover. I looked for difficult assignments, which increased my recognition, and the desire to succeed became my driving force.

I developed a large cadre of confidential informants from every walk of life: businesspeople, laborers, individuals working in telephone companies, utility company employees, waitresses, cooks, and people directly working for the trafficking organizations. Between Ricardo and me, the volume of dope we seized was about the same. In one year, Ricardo and I accounted for two thirds of all narcotics seizures and arrests for the entire Arizona district. Ricardo and I were competitive with each other, and yet we were a team as well. For three years running we were an invincible force.

Most agents are Type A personalities, competitive and relentless on the job. On my first case I asked an older agent for advice while on surveillance. He responded, "It's your damn case, boy. You figure it out." The older agents let you make minor mistakes. Hell, they wanted you to make mistakes so they had a reason to chastise you. You learned by trial and error. It didn't take long to learn with three cases a day, working six and seven days a week. The art of covert surveillance became easy.

Every agent worth his salt quickly learned some very important things on this job. First, *Not every rule can be followed to the letter. They are just guidelines.* Second, *Never tell the supervisor everything, only what he or she needs to know.* I learned quickly that it's better to leave the boss in the dark until after you accomplish your mission. Third, *Keep your mouth shut.* After twenty-eight years of service and working with more than four thousand agents, I can count on one hand the agents I trusted with dead-man tales: the stories you take to the grave with you.

I had developed a reputation as a no-nonsense agent. On several occasions, I was involved in fights with some local bad-asses at the watering holes we frequented. After beating the crap out of a big-time smuggler one night, I became known as a mean, nasty SOB who never backed down from a challenge. I had learned on the streets how to fight dirty; I didn't hesitate to hit first and use any object in reach as an equalizer. Most fistfights are over in seconds, but the rumors last forever.

* * *

ONE night, after a long evening of drinking with a couple of friends who were Customs inspectors, we pulled over to take a piss on the side of the road in front of the Preston Trailer Park. The Preston Trailer Park was at the dead end of Mariposa Road and known for drug smuggling. Several shootings had occurred in the park and it had a bad reputation as a gangbanger neighborhood.

The three of us walked to separate corners of the truck. Colin and Leo went to the rear and I went to the front; we were all pissing at once. Colin had a full-size Chevrolet truck with a camper shell; we had the music blaring and the doors open to hear it better.

Just as Colin and Leo were finishing, two cars leaving the trailer park drove up to the rear of Colin's truck and a bunch of young punks got out. The eight punks walked up to Colin and Leo and started talking trash: "What'chu doing in our barrio, gringos?" The punks saw fear on Colin's and Leo's faces. The leader said, "What the fuck are you *putos* [queers] doing pissing in our barrio?" Colin and Leo thought for sure they were all about to get their asses kicked; they had backed up to the camper shell, where the punks had them surrounded.

Meanwhile, I was still at the front of the truck pissing out at least four beers; I hadn't seen or heard a thing, because I was enjoying the blaring '70s rock-and-roll music. I finally finished, tucked my amigo away, and strolled back to the rear of the truck. Coming around the back of the truck, I saw the group and said, "What's happening?" Hell, it looked like a party. I staggered right in front of Colin and Leo and was now between them and the punks. Colin grabbed my shoulder, and Leo tried to warn me of the danger. But I was so shit-faced, I couldn't focus on the totality of the situation.

The punk who'd been the mouth of the group looked at me and yelled, "Hey, it's Patricio the narc." The group mumbled among themselves, and then the mouth stepped forward and extended his fist toward me for the barrio handshake. The barrio handshake involves touching fist to fist, knuckles to knuckles, then fingers to fingers, then knuckles again. It's a Mexican border thing; I learned it from Ricardo. Still clueless, I smirked at the leader and repeated loudly, "What the fuck's happening?"

The leader stepped back and said, "*Nada*, Patricio, *nada*, man, it's cool, take it easy, man." The group started joking and smiling, and then they said *adios*, waved good-bye, got into their cars, and left.

Colin and Leo were in total disbelief; they were scared shitless and sober at this point.

Colin asked, "Who was that guy? Did you know that guy?"

"No, why?"

They proceeded to tell me what had happened. The next day they embellished the story to the point that they were staring down a dozen guys with guns and knives and were about to be killed. Stories like this spread quickly around the law enforcement groups and the city. The stories of my exploits grew, and I loved it. I did more dangerous deeds and took risks to perpetuate them. I enjoyed the fame when I was a young agent and the notoriety as an old agent.

LUSCIOUS LOLA

LUSCIOUS Lola was a real Mexican beauty. She stood about five feet eight, with dark curly hair dangling down the middle of her back, and she had more curves than a roller coaster. Her eyes were round and so dark you could see your reflection in them. Her lips were full and ever so inviting. She was every man's dream woman.

Confidential sources come and go like the wind. Most are forgotten, but there are some that you couldn't forget if you had Alzheimer's. Luscious Lola was just such an individual.

Nogales had one all-night coffee shop: Denny's. On any given night, every law enforcement agency was represented there, having coffee and enjoying a break. After the bars closed, every drunk and smuggler also piled into the place. As with most small towns, everyone knew each other. Cops and traffickers exchanged glares and evil eyes along with a few underhanded comments.

Luscious Lola worked as a waitress at Denny's. She was

affectionately called Luscious Lola after a famous Mexican movie star who portrayed a lady of the night. She was always flipping her hair around in a suggestive manner. She was at least a nine on most men's scales. Her most alluring feature was her ample breasts. I heard more than one cop say he'd walk barefoot through a mile of broken glass just to see her tits.

Lola knew she was hot, and she used every trick to get a man's attention: twisting her hair, wearing low-cut tops, bending over at the table to expose her cleavage, and sitting with lots of leg showing. To her, pouring coffee was an art of erotic suggestion. She slowly bent over and gently rubbed her DD breasts on a man's shoulder or across his head. Her breasts were usually the main topic during our coffee breaks.

Lola was a big flirt; she would rub a cop's shoulders, run her hand through his hair, and sit on his lap to get her kicks and giggles. There was no doubt that she viewed every cop as a conquest and kept score to see how many she could sleep with. I must admit, I was as tempted as the next guy. I won't name those she notched on her order pad, but the list was long and distinguished.

There was only one thing I found disturbing; she played the traffickers the same as she played the cops. She was like an exotic dancer in a strip club; she didn't care where the dollars came from or who put them in her G-string.

Lola also had a dark side. She sold Kirby vacuum cleaners door-to-door and took the art of selling to a new level. She had a twisted yet genius idea unknown to most people in sales. Numerous law enforcement agents would teasingly ask her if she could suck like the vacuum cleaners she sold. Lola just smiled and asked if they would like to find out. As I said, Lola was a master in the art of selling them. After every new conquest and indiscretion with some unsuspecting law enforcement officer, Lola somehow managed to find out where they lived and had a unique way of showing up at their house. She'd arrive with vacuum in hand, knocking on the front door.

The poor dumb-ass cop would be at home with his wife when Lola arrived. She'd politely tell the wife how nice her husband was when he came to the coffee shop. The whole time the cop would be scared shitless, thinking she was going to mention their fling. Then Lola would start her sales pitch about how great the vacuum was. Of course the cop always said, "Yes, honey, I think we do need a new vacuum cleaner." I know a lot of Nogales police officers, sheriff's officers, and border patrol and Customs officers who were more than glad to purchase a new Kirby vacuum for their spouses.

EARLY one morning, I was out driving around checking a neighborhood for load cars before going into the office. I was just driving along Morley Avenue by the post office when I noticed a young kid in a fairly new car turn from a side street, so I followed him. He didn't fit the car, and the car didn't fit the neighborhood. At this time it wasn't called *profiling*, it was called intuition. When I finally pulled the kid over, he was scared shitless and he started to spill his guts. The little bastard said he was paid five hundred dollars to drive the car north to Valencia Road on the south side of Tucson. It was his first time (this is drug smuggling 101: it's always the first time). Hookers say the same thing: *I've never done this before for money.* However, the kid provided some great information. He'd picked up the car on Perkins Street in Nogales from the residence of a waitress who worked at Denny's. I asked him to describe the waitress. There was no doubt in my mind it was Lola. The kid said she allowed the smugglers to park load cars in her carport.

Sometimes things just have a way of falling into your lap. The kid was seventeen years old. I hated dealing with juveniles because they're a pain in the ass administratively. The federal court system usually releases them to the custody of the parent and seldom takes action, so I interviewed him on the street, and with the concurrence of the U.S. Attorney, I let him loose on the spot. I made him promise never to tell anyone what he'd told me. I also told him that he was now my source and was supposed to work off his release by calling the office with drug information. The kid thanked me. I had him run all the way to the border and tell the traffickers he bailed out of the load vehicle when I stopped it.

I returned to the office and discussed the situation with Ricardo, and we decided we would have some fun and lure Luscious Lola to the Americana Hotel.

Ricardo said, "You sure you haven't done her?"

"No," I said. "Have you?"

Ricardo laughed and said, "Shit, maybe we should just do her and forget about her being a source." I'm sure the thought crossed both our minds more than once.

Lola had flirted with me on several occasions, but I was evasive and hadn't succumbed to her charms. Now I would flirt with her and go along with the trap. I approached her at the restaurant just before the end of her day shift. I sat at the counter and smiled as she poured my coffee and flirted.

I flirted and suggested we hook up. This surprised her; I hadn't really flirted before, and she thought I was shy. I told her that I had a room at the Americana Hotel and asked her to meet me later.

She seemed eager and didn't hesitate at all before saying okay to an afternoon fling.

I went back to the room and told Ricardo.

He chuckled and said, "You stud, are you sure you're not ninety-eight?" That was a ten-code we used when we hooked up with a woman. A lot of times when we were cruising and saw a hot chick, I'd say, "I'd sure like to do her," and Ricardo would say, "Ninety-eight," his bullshit response most of the time.

Lola was right on time. I had given her my room number, and when I opened the door she was posing with her hand on her hip, smiling, with bright red lipstick on. Her low-cut dress revealed her black lace bra, barely holding her breasts, which were exploding out of the outfit. High heels made her look taller. Wow, she was looking smoking hot. *Christ, what the hell was I thinking?* I'd never seen her dress to the hilt before. I could see why the boys in blue were lined up waiting to have sex with her. Her expression said it all. I must have shown my total satisfaction; to paraphrase the words of President Jimmy Carter: I lusted with my eyes. Boy, did I ever.

I just stood staring at her, and then my brain snapped back into reality, after my initial thought of just screwing her. I led her into the room, where Ricardo was sitting at the desk in the corner. Upon seeing Ricardo, Lola froze. I think her initial reaction was that we were kinky and she was going to be in a threesome. She knew Ricardo and I were a team and figured we had done this before. Ricardo took out his badge and told her this wasn't a social call. Lola's face lost all expression and turned white behind the red lipstick and black eye shadow. Ricardo read her Miranda rights in Spanish. First we asked Lola if she understood, and then Ricardo asked if she wanted to cooperate.

Lola began crying hysterically and pleading her innocence, makeup running down her cheeks. Ricardo and I just watched her dramatic performance and let her cry. We'd seen more than our share of female violators cry before; little did she know her tears were wasted on us. Finally she realized the innocent act wasn't going to work. She asked to use the bathroom and reapplied her makeup; when she came out, she opened up and confessed every detail.

Luscious Lola had gotten caught up by her own games; one night she lured a trafficker home, hoping for extra money after sex. The trafficker paid her but was more interested in the location of her house. He promised her money for simply allowing cars to be parked in her carport at night. It sounded like easy money, and she didn't have to do anything. He just started bringing over a car and parking it in her carport. Sometimes she heard noises outside in the middle of the night, but she didn't look out; she knew the smugglers were loading the car. Then she was told to drive the car to work in the morning. She was paid five hundred dollars a week. It happened on a regular basis, and she couldn't stop it if she wanted to. She was in too deep; if she tried to quit, they would beat her or kill her.

She gave up the names of the traffickers using her carport and admitted to driving some of the load cars herself. Lola would drive as far as the Denny's parking lot, and then another driver would pick up the car and take it to Tucson. Lola said the main supplier was, of course, my favorite person: Quemado.

I had already decided that I wanted Lola to become a confidential source. Sending her to jail wouldn't solve anything, but knowing that the loads were coming to her house was perfect.

Ricardo and I gave her the same lecture we gave all sources about how we would keep her identity confidential and never tell anyone she was helping. She had only two choices: go to jail or work for us. She chose to work. All of the agents in the office were busy with their own cases, and at times it was hard to garner support among them for someone else's case. Lola's was different; a plethora of agents volunteered to help out on her case.

Lola started calling with information the following week. This was the kind of operation we loved. The load cars were like sitting ducks. Lola called me and provided the make, model, color, and license plate number. For the first couple of weeks, the loads were rolling in. The cars would leave Lola's residence about six in the morning. Ricardo and I would follow them, usually to Tucson, where the second driver would take over. Often the load vehicles were parked at the Kmart on Valencia Road in Tucson. (It was a standing joke among cops that there should be parking spots marked LOAD VEHICLES ONLY.) We would then follow the second driver to the receiving stash house, where we would watch them off-load.

Customs and the DEA strived to take a narcotics load as far as they could in order to maximize the number of defendants arrested and assets seized. The border patrol was not an investigative agency and was not tasked with this role. Instead we turned the narcotics over to the DEA or Customs and returned to the field to patrol. When the second driver took over, our stationary surveillance units would follow it, hoping to take it to a stash house. Sometimes the vehicle continued north toward Phoenix. In these cases, we would have the highway patrol take it down as a traffic stop in order not to burn our real probable cause for the stop. In this way we earned ourselves a little more time before the cartel learned our real reason for stopping the vehicle.

Sometimes we lost a load during the surveillance, which created a hell of a lot of memos. The traffickers used multiple countersurveillance vehicles to run heat for the load vehicles. When a load car traveled north on the interstate, it was usually followed by one vehicle and led by another. If it looked like a law enforcement vehicle was about to stop the load car, the car in front would speed up and travel at an excessive speed to draw the cops. Paying a speeding fine was better than losing the load. Nowadays, with cell phones in abundance, it's a lot easier for countersurveillance to warn the load car driver that he is being followed.

In town, these same heat vehicles would deliberately not move through a green light to let the load car get away and see if cops sped through traffic to catch it. They'd block traffic at intersections and stop in neighborhoods to see if any unknown vehicles went into the area. Some of these heat drivers were better at countersurveillance than a few of our agents.

But losing a load required notification of Internal Affairs, and then a memo from every agent on the surveillance, and then personal interviews with some dick in IA, and then all the *what-ifs*. I couldn't tolerate it when assholes who'd never worked the streets or narcotics investigations second-guessed my actions after I'd worked night and day on an operation. The human element can never be taken for granted. People just tend to do the unexpected, and we have to react. Sometimes agents try to guess the next move, and it's the wrong move. I've lost a few myself and know that shit happens.

I wanted to get pictures of the smugglers to see if Quemado was by chance crossing over with the load. I figured he was too big to go with the mules, but I thought since the house was only about a hundred yards from the border, anything was possible.

I asked Lola if we could conduct the surveillance from inside her residence to take photos of the smugglers. She was scared and hesitant at first, then seemed to warm up to the idea. So I had a couple of agents dropped off at her house to set up surveillance cameras on the load vehicle before the mules loaded them. We set up cameras with night-vision lenses in order to capture images of the smugglers who crossed through the hole in the border fence. The first couple of times I viewed the photos, none of the faces were recognizable. The smugglers looked like poor peasants who were probably paid fifty dollars each to cross the dope.

The next time Lola called with information about a load, I told the agents I'd decided to end the nighttime photo taking of the mules. I almost got my ass kicked in the office, and then a couple of older agents advised me in a serious tone that taking photos of the mules was a smart thing to do.

That night, after the mutiny at the office, I had the guys try again to take photos. But during the surveillance I began to think about the boys' sudden interest in photography; after reviewing some of the photos, I soon discovered the real reason for the change.

Lola took great pleasure in having the agents inside her residence. At first she stayed in the bedroom, and the agents set up the cameras in the small kitchen. They waited inside with all the lights off for the mules to arrive. The cameras were set up on tripods. However, Lola's little devil inside her couldn't resist the overwhelming temptations. She took it real slow; at first she wore a robe, and then she exited the bedroom wearing skimpy lace negligees. Then she appeared with the robe again but without a bra. She would let the robe fall off her shoulder, revealing her overflowing breast. Lola was performing a striptease act each night and loving it; she had a captive audience, for sure.

Lola soon asked the agents to photograph her in various stages of dress, which showed her more-than-ample breasts and firm, rounded bottom. Obviously the agents couldn't care less about concentrating on the smugglers. Thankfully, we had the common sense to make sure all the photographs were destroyed.

Some agents in the office could be complete assholes and would make a big issue out of the photos, so in memory of Colonel Oliver North, we said, "Shred, shred, shred. Leave no evidence behind."

Lola continued to call on a regular basis, and I developed a good relationship with her while she worked as a source for several years. After an incident with Quemado, the neighborhood quieted down and Luscious Lola moved to another part of town, but she still called to report any information she gleaned through her work or relationships.

SOURCES

IT was a nice afternoon in October; the sun was shining and it seemed like a perfect day to relax. It was quiet in the office, so Carlos asked Layne and me if we wanted to go across the line, meaning the border, for lunch. We ate about once or twice a month at our favorite taco joint in Nogales, Sonora, next to the famous La Roca restaurant, about a hundred yards south of the Morley Avenue POE.

Having lunch in Nogales, Sonora, was common for us; we seldom thought of the consequences. In fact, it was not uncommon for an agent to leave his M16 rifle in the trunk of his G-ride when he drove into Mexico. This day we decided to walk into Mexico. We all jumped in one vehicle, drove to the POE and parked next to the small Customs building at the pedestrian gate, and walked across the border to the quaint little restaurant.

We were totally relaxed, talking sports and laughing, just

chilling out. A rare day for us. We sat down and ordered three tacos each and a bucket of mini eight-ounce Pacifico beers. Nine beers fit in the ice-cold bucket. We were sipping the beers, eating the carne asada tacos with salsa, and just enjoying life. We finished eating our first order of tacos and called the waiter over to order some more when Carlos's pager went off. Layne and I both told Carlos not to answer the page; it might be the office. Carlos, always diligent, looked at the incoming number and stepped to the back of the restaurant to make a call.

As I watched Carlos, he started looking around, then immediately came over and said in a soft voice, "We need to leave now." Layne and I looked up at Carlos, saying, "Bullshit, the office can wait. We just ordered more tacos and beer." Carlos changed his tone dramatically. "I said let's go, right now." He pulled out a twenty-dollar bill and threw it on the table. We were leaving and there wasn't any more argument.

Outside, Layne asked, "What the fuck is going on?"

Carlos glanced back and said, "I'll tell you later; just keep moving." Layne and I glanced at each other, then at Carlos, and almost simultaneously the sixth sense kicked in and we started looking around the area as we continued walking, picking up the pace as we moved.

We didn't need an explanation; Carlos's actions and manner said it all. The Morley Avenue POE was about seventy-five yards from the restaurant. As usual, a line of people were waiting to cross into the United States. Carlos led the way, walking straight around everyone waiting in line. We flashed our badges to the inspector and entered the United States.

Carlos walked around to the north side of the Customs building for cover so we couldn't be seen from Mexico. He caught his breath and explained the telephone call. A source was hanging out with a major trafficker when a flunky walked in and told the group there were three narcs in Mexico eating lunch. Someone had recognized all three of us as we crossed the border, then followed us to the restaurant.

The traffickers immediately ordered a hit on us and a group rushed out to kill us. Thankfully, the source still had some loyalty to Carlos and gave him the warning, telling Carlos the group was en route to the restaurant armed with AK-47 assault rifles. Carlos wasted no time in getting us the hell out of Mexico. We never knew for sure, but we thought the person who made the initial telephone call to the traffickers was a U.S. immigration inspector we were investigating for corruption.

More than eighty percent of the criminal investigations we conducted were initiated because of information provided by a confidential informant, or CI. Regardless of what you call them— sources, snitches, *dedos*, or cooperating individuals—they are invaluable resources in narcotics investigations. I've dealt with informants who were so vicious and sleazy that they would cut your throat given the opportunity. Others want to be your best friend and personal bodyguard. Regardless of how you feel about them, sources are the quickest and most effective way to infiltrate trafficking organizations.

They are used to make introductions to traffickers and are the agent's eyes and ears in the daily activity of the trafficking groups. Sources live in constant danger and fear of being discovered. The use of the term *snitch, informant,* or *dedo* by a trafficker to describe a person guaranteed torture and ultimately death at the hands of the cartel.

Agents try to develop a good working relationship and rapport with their sources; you just never know when they will save your life. It paid off for the three of us, or we all would have been gunned down inside the restaurant with a cold Pacifico in one hand and a half-eaten taco in the other.

When a confidential source is registered or documented, only the controlling agent and his or her partner know the true identity. The documentation card with the real identity is locked in a safe and sealed in an envelope, taped over, and then dated and initialed on the outside envelope. Only one person is assigned access to the safe, and not even he or she can open the cards. The source card is viewed only if an agent is accused of corruption, gets killed, or transfers the source to a new agent.

Sometimes agents get too close to an informant. They need to be reminded that sources work for the agency, not the agent, and a good supervisor will recognize the signs and reassign the source to someone else before the agent gets in trouble.

ON another afternoon I drove over to Mexico to meet a confidential informant. I went by myself to a restaurant at the south end of the *periférico*, or loop road, that runs around the city down by the Sonora state prison. I had met the source here before, and driving in Mexico was something I did on a regular basis. I bought his lunch and we talked over a couple of beers. It was a casual meeting. As we were about to leave, three cars pulled up and parked in front of the restaurant. A whole shitload of local traffickers got out of the vehicle and were headed inside the restaurant. The source freaked out, rapidly rattling off their names and sprinting to the kitchen and out the back.

What now? The right side of my brain said, *Leave now.* The left side said, *Order another beer*. Most agents would have been smart and followed the source out the back door. But what the hell, I thought, I wanted to see who these fucking guys were. I recognized two local asshole dopers from Nogales, Arizona; I had arrested one, but I didn't know the others. The source said they were heavy players, but he said their names so fast in Spanish I didn't understand him.

The eight guys entered and took a large round table in the middle of the restaurant; three of these guys were almost three hundred pounds. I was seated in the back of the restaurant with my back to a wall, my normal routine, as I'm sure it is for most agents and police. I never sit in a bar or restaurant unless I have my back to a wall. I dread someone sneaking up from behind. I want to see trouble coming, not get shot from behind like Wild Bill Hickok.

I slowly sipped my beer and studied the eight shitheads when the guy known as "Chewy" turned and noticed me. He quickly told the group, and then one by one they all turned around in their chairs and began looking me over. I couldn't hear the conversation, and I didn't need to. Mexicans, like Italians, talk with their hands, and the hands were pointing at me. I decided now was as good a time as any to get the hell out of there.

The situation had taken a turn for the worse; I went from being unnoticed to the subject of everyone's attention. I sure as hell didn't want a confrontation. All I was packing was a Smith and Wesson Model 60 five-shot .38 revolver on my ankle. There were eight guys and I had no idea how many were packing heat. I also had no clue who these guys were; my brain was in warp drive, like a computer trying to solve a puzzle. I had to figure out how the hell to leave the restaurant without a confrontation. I envisioned being tied up in a shed with a battery charger connected to my balls and confessing all my sins.

Being able to react on instinct seems to come natural to me; the gift of bullshit was my specialty. An idea popped into my head. I calmly got up and walked directly to their table. This took the group by surprise. They stopped talking and stared at me. Two guys sitting on the opposite side of the table pushed their chairs back and stood up, ready for a fight. I walked directly up to Chewy, the lowlife from Nogales, and slapped him on the back as acknowledgment. Then, in a voice loud enough for everyone in the entire restaurant to hear, I said, "Hey, man, thanks for the information about the dope; call me later." The expressions on the faces of the other dopers were priceless; the rest of the goons at the table began staring at the two guys from Nogales. Chewy, in a panic, yelled, "What the fuck are you talking about? I never called you."

Without saying another word, I turned and walked away. I could hear the group of guys arguing. Chewy yelled out again, "Fuck you, Patricio."

I had a bad feeling when the group walked in, and I believe in listening to my sixth sense. I had created a nice diversion and knew it would give me a chance to get the hell out of Mexico.

I figured the two guys from Nogales, Arizona, were having one hell of a time at the restaurant trying to defend themselves. I was convincing; I had ruined their day. I envisioned them being taken to a shed and beaten, or having *their* nuts hooked up to the battery charger.

CUSTOMS special agents who recruit and document someone to be a confidential informant used to be called the *controlling agent*.

Because of FBI fuckups, this was changed to *contact agent.* An FBI agent in Boston was the controlling agent for James "Whitey" Bulger, who was a big Irish gangster. Whitey was working both sides, giving up the mob and killing people and setting up his own organization. The controlling agent knew what was happening and was eventually arrested. The FBI, in their rationale, as most are attorneys and not field agents, decided that if they used the term *contact agent* instead of *controlling agent,* they would avoid any further embarrassing publicity or lawsuits.

Revenge is the number one reason why people become sources. Although they know that being detected as a source means certain death, their need for revenge against traffickers because of the loss of money or a family member outweighs their fear.

Violence committed by traffickers in Mexico was growing. Entire families were getting killed by traffickers trying to instill fear in small towns. Throughout Mexico, smugglers beat and torture thousands of men and women daily; these days, large-scale deaths get international media attention, but in the past it was covered up. Thus these individuals' last hope for revenge is to assist U.S. law enforcement, in hopes that the traffickers will go to jail or be killed in return.

Money and greed is the second motivator that lures a lot of people into providing information. Informants are highly paid for information that turns into seizures and arrests. Sources can be paid up to $250,000 for a single case. I have paid several sources in excess of a million dollars in a single year for information. Although the cartels make billions of dollars a year, they cheat their workers. Time and time again, mules aren't paid, load drivers aren't paid, and stash house operators aren't paid.

The third reason why people become sources is that just like

Luscious Lola, they don't have a choice. They're screwed. Smugglers caught with a load are interviewed, and, depending on what they say, we often let them work off the jail time in exchange for information. The violators work off their charges; for each pound they are caught with, they have to give us double poundage in return. After their commitment is complete, they often continue working for us, and then we start paying them for future investigations. With thousands of load drivers arrested each year, there's an abundance of these sources.

The relationship between agents and sources is a fine line. It's sort of like a blind date; you're cordial and pretend you like each other, so while you're together it's all nice and friendly. The agent gets the information he or she needs, the source gets paid, and you say good night and then bad-mouth each other, tear each other apart about what just happened. These relationships are unique; if either gets too close or too trusting it becomes dangerous. The handling and use of informants is the number one reason agents get fired. Any agent who becomes too involved or friendly with a source is doomed.

Female sources are especially difficult to handle. No agent should ever meet one alone; there is always the threat of alleged sexual misconduct or the jealous boyfriend to deal with.

Some informants are *lifers*, or career informants who have worked their entire life providing information to every agency in existence: FBI, DEA, Customs, ATF, IRS, and state and local police departments. They show up at the door and don't always tell the agents they work for three other agencies. These are the worst sources because they know the system and how to play it. I've watched agents conduct interviews with these sources and observed the informant do a better job of retrieving information from the agent than vice versa.

Good informants are paid well. On the average they get five dollars a pound for marijuana and ten to fifteen dollars a pound for cocaine. The more a source works, the larger the payment. The source signs the paperwork with a fictitious name and the money is paid in cash.

Sources also know the penalty if the traffickers discover they are working for law enforcement. The penalty is usually death. I have recruited hundreds of informants over the years and lost a few. One source who worked for me was a heroin addict and not very discreet in his snooping. He was picked up by the traffickers and promised some heroin for his cooperation. He quickly talked and was given a "hot shot" of heroin—a pure amount that causes instant death.

Another source, called El Toro, or *The Bull*, was a big cowboy type, well over six feet four and 280 pounds, a massive man. El Toro wasn't the sharpest knife in the drawer. He had to write everything down on a little notepad he carried in his shirt pocket. I told him constantly to get rid of the notepad, but he just laughed and chuckled. He thought he was invincible.

El Toro worked odd jobs doing masonry, laying block, and building walls or houses; if it paid a little cash, he did it. He noticed a lot of things as he worked on people's houses and would write down the license plate numbers and addresses in his little notepad in kind of a code, as if he were noting measurements for concrete or lumber, but it was his way to keep track of what he saw. He provided information on several stash houses and load vehicles and made fairly good money as a confidential source.

He was a likable guy. I trusted him, and at times I would cross into Mexico with him through the hole in the fence to check out a stash house in Buenos Aires. We acted just like all the other illegals. We jumped through the fence on Escalada Drive and walked around the area as he pointed out the stash house. Then we dashed back to the border and crossed back into the United States before being noticed by traffickers or the border patrol. Rene said I was completely insane for crossing into the neighborhood at night. I had to agree with him, but things were different then; if someone did that today they'd probably be fired on the spot.

Then, for no reason, I didn't hear a word from El Toro for three months. I just figured he'd left the area or was on a drunken binge or, in a worst-case scenario, dead. I checked the newspapers and saw nothing about any deaths, so I just assumed he had moved away. I tried to call him several times, without results. I always called my sources every week or two, especially if they had not contacted me in that time. It was a subtle reminder to keep them motivated. Surprisingly, El Toro called about three months later and said he needed to see me; he had lost his BCC and would wait at the POE.

I drove to the POE and asked the supervisor what room my visitor was waiting in. I entered and didn't recognize the guy. The man sitting in the room was tall and thin, about 150 pounds; his skin was multicolored, a mixture of black, yellow, blue, and red rolled into one, and his right arm was in a cast. Whoever this guy was, he looked like shit, but this wasn't El Toro; I had no idea who the hell he was. I'd started to leave the room when the guy stood up and said, "Patricio, it's me, Bull."

I was in total shock. Here were the skeletal remains of what had been a giant of a man. Bull proceeded to tell me what had happened. Three months earlier he'd been in Buenos Aires working and saw what appeared to be a main storage house for cocaine. He was building a wall and pretended to take a break and walk by the house to get some shade, but in his attempt to get a license plate number he was spotted. As he was leaving for the night, several men with guns grabbed him and drove him to an abandoned building, where he was chained to a wall with his arms cuffed behind him.

What followed was a nightmare. Bull was interrogated for days by the traffickers. They beat him repeatedly, breaking his ribs, fingers, and arms as he became a human punching bag for everyone who came to the building. On the third day, a head henchman for the traffickers started really beating on him with a vengeance, breaking his hand with a hammer, then his leg. Bull's face was now just bloody tissue. Bull remembered drifting in and out of consciousness. He did not eat or drink the entire time. By the end of this cycle of beatings he confessed everything: working for Customs, my name and those of other agents in the office, everything. Bull just wanted to die and get the pain over with.

By the time the trafficker finished, Bull was only a shell of a man. The traffickers decided to dispose of him; they placed him in a van, then took him to the edge of Nogales, Sonora, where they threw him out of the van by the side of the road. The traffickers were drinking beer and having a party to celebrate his execution as they took a gallon of gasoline from the van and poured it over him. Then just before they lit the fatal match that would have incinerated him, a Mexican patrol car came down the road. The traffickers jumped in the van and drove off. Had the Mexican cops appeared five minutes later, Bull would have been burned to death.

Bull had been in a Mexican hospital for months when he appeared at the POE to meet me. All he wanted to do was let me know he was alive, but he was never going to work as a source again. He also wanted to warn me and apologize for giving up my name. He moved south to another state in Mexico, and I never heard from him again.

IT was the fall of 1984 and the violence was increasing in Nogales, Sonora. A U.S. immigration inspector's brother was gunned down coming out of a bar. The inspector was thought to be dirty but he resigned before any investigation was done. Two other men racing into the POE late one night had been shot in the back and head. The traffickers were having a battle for the plaza in Nogales, Sonora, and shootouts were occurring on a regular basis. This didn't attract international attention as it does now; it was considered routine and not given much thought.

Sometimes sources were our worst enemy—one in particular. Oscar called constantly and was known as "Mr. Hummer" because nine out of ten times nothing ever happened on a case he was involved with. A hummer was a waste of time where no arrests were made. Time after time the little rat bastard called and we set up surveillance and wasted many hours for nothing. Rene hated the guy and was certain Oscar was working directly for the smugglers, providing us with misinformation to move us to the opposite area of town from where the load was really crossing.

Finally, we called Oscar in and sat him down in an office and decided to screw with him. I took an old piece of electronic equipment that had different wires and cables on it like an oscillating machine and taped the wires to his arms and hands and clipped a cable to his ear. He looked like a bad experiment with all the wires hanging on him. I turned on the scope and it made a slight noise as it ran, but when I pushed a button on the front it made a higher-pitched sound. We told Oscar it was a lie detector, and then we hammered him and every time we didn't like his answer I pushed the button and made the sound change. After about thirty minutes of this, he finally admitted he wasn't working for any group. He simply called and told us to watch a certain area, hoping we would get lucky and catch a load so he could get paid. The little bastard was blackballed on the spot and told never to call the office again.

THE POWER OF PERFUME

ONE night I just didn't feel like going home, which wasn't unusual considering my failure at marriage. I was driving around checking a suspected stash house, writing down license plate numbers, and looking for activity. I loved working late at night. The traffickers cross most of their merchandise from ten P.M. to two A.M. As I drove north on Morley Avenue, I observed a van in the parking lot of the U.S. Post Office about eleven P.M. On a normal night, I would've stopped and checked the van because traffickers often used the post office parking lot to park load cars. Tonight, however, I smiled as I drove slowly by the parking lot, and I didn't give the van a second thought because parked next to it was senior special agent Layne's new sports car. It was fall and the temperature was cold at night. I could see that the windows were fogged over and the car was a-rocking. For one brief second I thought I'd screw with Layne by parking behind his vehicle and turning on the siren or walking up and shining a light into the window like the cops do. I quickly dismissed the idea, though; Layne was a big guy, six feet three inches, and tough. I doubted Layne would find the situation as funny as I would, and if he pounded the shit out of me I wouldn't think that would be funny, so I just kept cruising.

The following morning Carlos said, "What the hell were you guys doing last night? DPS [the Arizona Department of Public Safety] took down another van. Why didn't anyone in this office find the damn thing?" Carlos said he heard on the news that the van was loaded with two thousand pounds of marijuana and was taken off around five A.M. by the Arizona highway patrol.

Rene said he would call over to DPS and get some details; he quickly grabbed the phone and called Arizona DPS, hoping to appease Carlos. The rest of us followed Carlos to his office to await the results. In a few minutes Rene entered Carlos's office and proceeded to tell everyone the details of the arrest and seizure and the description of the van. Just about the time Rene was describing the van, Layne entered the office he shared with Carlos. Rene continued with the description of the van.

"Christ," I said, "I saw that van last night." I couldn't recall where. I was tracing my path from the night before in my mind, trying to recall. Where the hell had I seen it?

Layne, who had walked in late, was still standing in the doorway listening to all this, and then he just started laughing. Carlos and the rest of us stopped, all staring at Layne.

Carlos asked, "What the hell is so funny?"

Layne closed the office door and said, "Well, boys, I know where the van was parked last night. Hell, I even pissed on the tires. I was parked next to that van last night."

Suddenly I remembered seeing Layne's vehicle. "You asshole,"

I said, "I drove by your fucking car last night and didn't stop to check the van because you were parked next to it at the post office."

Layne laughed some more, then proceeded to outline his evening. He described how he had the best sex of his life and that his date had given him the absolute best blowjob in the world. Between his few beers too many, her perfume, and his numbness of body and mind, he didn't have a clue that the van had two thousand pounds of marijuana in it. Layne couldn't smell a damn thing.

Carlos and Layne went way back and were best friends. Carlos was happy that Layne was back in the saddle again. Layne's divorce had been hard on him, especially since he was raising two teenage girls. The rest of us took great pride in finally being able to bust his balls; Layne was a serious agent and seldom made mistakes. I said, "How in the hell can you not smell a ton of weed in a van?"

NOGALES, Arizona, and Nogales, Sonora, are typical border cities. The engineers laid out streets paralleling the international border fence. This is all right except when young Mexican teenagers throw rocks from the Mexican side of the fence at any vehicle they think belongs to a narc, border patrol, or police. In the spirit of sportsmanship, if they threw rocks at my vehicle, I would simply stop my car and throw rocks back. I was quite adept at hitting the little bastards and sometimes nailed them or parked cars in Mexico. The kids hid behind the cars, thinking I wouldn't throw rocks at the vehicles. Wrong. I deliberately hit the cars. I knew if one of those vehicles belonged to some tough hombre he'd kick the kids' asses for hiding behind it. That was just one of the many border games we played on a daily basis.

One night, however, this game became deadly. We received information about another large van load. We began our surveillance. The trafficker loaded it, then parked it at the Auto Zone parking lot; a second driver picked it up and began driving around looking for surveillance until he finally observed one of the agents either following too close or being an idiot in some fashion. Then, as always, the chase for the border was on. We blocked the POE so the driver couldn't enter Mexico. Instead he drove to West International Street, hoping to escape. The sirens were blaring and red and blue lights were flashing all around town, and I'm sure all the asshole smugglers in Nogales, Sonora, were listening to the sirens, wondering about their own loads.

The driver raced straight to the dead end of West International. The road there ends in a flat clearing and a forty-foot circle for turnarounds. The driver slid to a stop at the edge of a small slope and bailed out of the van, running the ten feet to the border fence, where he jumped through a hole into Mexico. He left the load car running with the keys in the ignition. Our police cars stacked up on the narrow dirt road, one car behind the other, with the load car blocking anyone from turning around.

Before we even approached the van, a group of twenty kids started yelling insults and jeered at us and simultaneously lobbed a barrage of rocks, bricks, pipes, bottles, everything they could find on the ground in Mexico by the border fence. We were pinned down. I was on the passenger side of the two lead pursuit vehicles. We radioed for the Nogales police department to contact the Nogales, Sonora, police to disperse the kids. Someone called out that the Nogales, Sonora, cops were responding, so we just thought we could wait out the insane barrage of missiles.

Our cars were getting battered. It sounded like someone was hitting them with a sledgehammer. The sound of our windows getting smashed and rocks and bricks hitting the vehicles was pissing all of us off. Then, just when we thought the fucking situation couldn't get any worse, Tom decided he was going to make a dash for the van. He thought if he turned the van around, the rest of us could depart the area. He made it about ten feet and got slammed in the side of the head with a brick. Son of a bitch, the sound of the brick hitting him in the head was like someone taking a bat to a softball. We thought he was dead. The assholes on the Mexican side went nuts seeing Tom go down and became even more crazy, increasing their barrage of rocks and bricks. We could see the gash on the side of Tom's head and couldn't tell if he was out cold or dead. We radioed for an ambulance. We could hear the sirens on the Mexican side; their cars have the old wailing sirens.

Rene and another agent raced to Tom to drag him to safety as someone yelled, "Shoot the fence, fire a shotgun blast into the fucking fence." Either no one had a shotgun or no one heard the order to shoot. Rene dragged Tom to safety. Within minutes the Mexican police arrived and the crowd dispersed. Tom was shaken and needed quite a few stitches in his head, but he was all right otherwise. Tom, who was already a hard case at times, now became known as "Hard Head Tom."

To be an agent on the southwest border is considered insane to most people. Every day on the border is a learning experience, and as Nietzsche said, "That which does not kill you makes you stronger."

THE Arizona Department of Public Safety (DPS), or highway patrol, as most people refer to the state police, had three special narcotics officers working in Nogales: Louie, Charlie, and Harold. Customs and DPS had an outstanding working relationship; they supported us on most operations, and we supported them. When the U.S. Attorney's office declined a case, DPS was there to prosecute the case in state court.

Louie was Hispanic, a major in the Arizona National Guard, and he enjoyed working. After Ricardo transferred to Tucson, I started working with Louie rather than the agents in my own office. Louie was always upbeat and cheerful; his energy and attitude on life provided some positive influence to most of us. Louie was always saying, "Cheer up, don't worry about it."

When Quemado was about seventeen years old, Louie caught him with a couple of hundred pounds of marijuana in a stolen vehicle. Quemado claimed that it was his first time and that he was simply paid to drive the vehicle; he had no parents to contact and no papers to be in the United States, so the county attorney declined prosecution. Louie interviewed him and talked to him about providing information. I went to the DPS office that night to talk with Louie and saw a skinny kid handcuffed to a chair; I couldn't help but feel sorry for him. He looked pitiful with the side of his face scarred from the burn. Louie interviewed him, documented his real name, and took his fingerprints. He said he was called Quemado, "the burned one." Louie and I often reflected that it would have been nice to have a crystal ball to see the future. Who would have guessed that the kid in front of us then would become a psychopathic killer and head of his own narcotics trafficking and distribution group three years later?

Louie's partner, Charlie, was a large guy, around six feet three inches, and weighed well over 240 pounds. He was wide in the shoulders and spoke loud and rough. Fluent in Spanish, he intimidated people with his size. Charlie was great at interviewing suspects. He'd attended one of the first formal interview schools, where he learned that if you got up close and personal with the violator, you could break down barriers. Charlie would sit in a chair in front of the person being interviewed, ask a few questions, then casually move his chair closer until his knees were just inside the knees of the other person. This looked very odd, since Charlie towered above most violators. Unless you were a big person, you were looking up at him. The concept worked, and he generally got a confession nine out of ten times.

Whereas Louie had grace and charm, Charlie was all muscle and brawn; they made great "good cop, bad cop" partners. Charlie was the guy you wanted with you to enter houses or when some asshole smuggler decided to resist and fight you.

One night after a surveillance and vehicle stop, I followed a suspect to an apartment complex and stopped the load driver. I was assisted by the Nogales police department and Charlie. The driver was a real asshole, and we had to fight to place handcuffs on him. One of the city cops was trying to get him in the backseat of the patrol vehicle, but the guy was being a prick and wouldn't put his feet inside the patrol car. The poor cop would lift the guy's feet to place them inside but the bastard kept putting them back on the pavement. Charlie walked over and told the guy one time, "Put your damn feet inside."

The guy told Charlie, "Fuck you."

Charlie stepped back and kicked the guy square in the chest with his size thirteen boot, knocking the jerk clear to the other side of the car. Charlie usually didn't tell people to do anything twice.

The following day the jerk Charlie had kicked was taken before the judge for his initial appearance. As the judge read the charges for drug smuggling, the defendant took off his shirt and claimed that he had suffered police brutality. Imprinted on his chest was a perfect boot pattern; every groove of the sole could be clearly seen. The old judge turned to Charlie and asked if there was an explanation. Charlie answered, "Yes, sir, he resisted."

The judge then turned back to the defendant and chastised him for resisting arrest.

HAROLD was an older gentleman who was always happy and reminded me of the cartoon character Yosemite Sam. Harold had been in the Bureau of Dangerous Drugs, an obsolete Arizona agency disbanded around the time the Arizona highway patrol organized its own narcotics squad. Harold was transferred to the highway patrol narcotics division.

The highway patrol had also stopped several van loads, and most of the drivers invoked the right to remain silent, but a few did say they picked up the vans along Morley Avenue in the shopping centers in the downtown area. By now at least six vans had been seized. Every agency patrolling the Interstate 19 corridor was looking for large vans with single Mexican male drivers. We didn't think it was profiling, just good Las Vegas odds; if you stopped a van, chances were it would be loaded. All agencies profile; that's reality, it's all about how the officer approaches the car and explains the reason for the stop.

Louie and I teamed up as much as agents from my own office did. I liked his sense of humor. One night, coming back from a long surveillance in Tucson, I fell asleep in the passenger side of his vehicle, and just for kicks he pulled up on the back end of a semi going down the freeway and then suddenly woke me up screaming as he slammed on the brakes full force yelling, "Look out, we're going to hit it!"

I awoke from a dead sleep to see the rear end of the semi ten feet in front of us as he yelled and screamed at the top of his lungs while honking the fucking horn. I damn near crapped my pants. I threw my hands out, grabbing the dash so hard my fingers dug into it. I twisted up into a pretzel in the seat, expecting a total collision with a semi. Louie started laughing hysterically and said, "It's not polite to fall asleep while I'm talking to you."

"Yeah, funny," I said. "I just about had a fucking heart attack."

His tires were still smoldering from the brakes being applied so hard.

I said, "I hope your tires go flat, you asshole."

Louie, of course, just laughed. The following day Louie told the whole world how funny it was and how I freaked out in the front seat. This is called a sick sense of humor.

ON another occasion while I was riding with Louie, he stopped a car suspected of being loaded. The driver pulled over and, before we'd even stopped behind him, bolted from the vehicle, jumped the barbed-wire fence, and ran into a field to the east of Interstate 19. We sort of ambled to the fence and as we started to climb over, the bastard turned and fired off several rounds over his shoulder from a small-caliber pistol. Louie and I immediately took cover. The kid was fifty yards away at this time, running full speed. Hell, from that distance I couldn't have shot back effectively with a rifle.

Louie looked at me smiling and said, "You go after him; I'll wait here by the load vehicle."

I said, "*You* go after him and *I'll* wait by the load car."

We both laughed. We knew we couldn't catch the little bastard; as fast as that kid was running he was a mile away by now. At least the kid was nice enough to leave the keys in the load car.

A week later another source named Nacho contacted me and said a guy in Tucson wanted him to drive a large load of marijuana from Tumacacori, Arizona, to Tucson. He was a nervous sort of guy and was afraid of everything. He said the smuggling group was very mean. Nacho was a real chicken; he didn't want to take any chances with getting caught by us again or risk losing the load and getting beat up by the traffickers. So he determined that his best option was to tell me about the load so he could get some cash and stay out of the whole mess.

According to Nacho, the load was going to cross on the west side of the Tumacacori Mountains, go through the Rock Canyon Ranch, and, once on the east side of Interstate 19, go north along the Santa Cruz River by Santa Gertrudis Lane to the stash house. He knew when the load was leaving Mexico and when it was expected to arrive at the stash house the following night.

Once again Tom heard of the operation and volunteered to go

in on foot with me. I scouted the area and located the stash house. There was no way to get behind the house to watch the rear of the residence. My next idea was to watch the load cross Santa Gertrudis Lane and follow behind the smugglers to the house.

I had done this before. I liked to be positioned on a trail, and as the last mule passed I got up and followed right behind the group using night-vision goggles. I figured we'd do the same thing on this operation: stay about thirty yards behind the group in the dark and simply follow them.

The next night I had a group of agents ready to sit around in their vehicles all night. We'd have to wait until first light before we hit the residence anyway for safety reasons. Tom and I scouted the little dirt road around the river at Santa Gertrudis Lane and found a bunch of dead trees piled up by the road, a perfect spot to observe the group and stay out of sight. A little after dark a unit dropped us off on foot, and Tom and I moved the dead tree limbs around us for more cover and waited. Sometime around midnight we heard the group. They sounded like a herd of cattle coming. They were not concerned about the noise as they tromped through the small dead cottonwood branches and could be heard a half mile off.

We radioed the surveillance units that we had company and would be off the radio for a while until the coast was clear. The group got closer and closer until they were right on top of us. Shit, they were crossing ten feet in front of us. Tom and I didn't move a muscle. We could see their faces clearly. The moon was out more than we expected, and now we were afraid we might be seen. I was pissed that the source had forgotten to mention that the smugglers would be armed. I intended to chew his ass out for this and maybe not pay him as much. The first person we saw was a lead scout carrying an AK-47.

Mules sometimes walked three to six days straight, depending on how far the pickup point was, and then had to walk back. Most mules are paid one to three hundred dollars.

Once the mules were across, another guy with an AK-47 rifle appeared. Tom and I had counted twelve mules when a third subject with a rifle appeared. This was one bad-ass smuggling group.

They were serious and were not going to get ripped off. The west side of Tumacacori is notorious for bandits, *bajadores* in Spanish. Most people only think about Mexican bandits on the Mexican side ripping off poor illegals trying to cross into the United States. Tumacacori, Arizona, is twenty-five miles north of the border, way north of Nogales, and north of Rio Rico, Arizona, as well. Violence in Arizona knows no boundaries. In Phoenix, the coyotes who smuggle illegal aliens hold them for ransom even after they pay to be transported there. Armed groups come up from Mexico to kidnap individuals who worked for them and ripped them off.

There were constant reports of *bajadores* confronting smugglers and taking their loads at gunpoint. I often wondered if the *bajadores* were rival smuggling groups or dirty law enforcement, ripping off the loads. There was no way we would risk following this group with the amount of firepower they had. The moonlight was against us tonight; it was too light out and too risky. Tom and I had both brought shotguns, so we were no match against AK-47 rifles.

When the last of the group crossed and had moved down the trail, we radioed the information and asked if someone had an eye on the property, but the units were too far away and believed we were going to follow the load. We knew the house and told someone to pick us up so we could get back into our units and figure out what to do next.

At daylight we walked the path to make sure the dope wasn't stashed along the trail. We found the footprints crossing the pasture, so we figured the stash was inside the house. At least ten units converged on the house, fully loaded with automatic rifles, prepared for a war. We contacted the sheriff's department for uniformed officers to be present when we knocked on the door, to prevent some asshole from shooting at us and claiming he thought we were criminals ripping him off. The agents converged on the residence from all sides, taking cover. We heard movement inside and, after repeated knocking, no one answered the door. We knew the owners weren't there, only the heavily armed smugglers. Tom peeked in the rear window, which was partially covered by a curtain, and saw the marijuana bundles stacked up and someone running from the room.

Tom called out that people were running around inside the house. We didn't want to write a search warrant and stay out there for another five hours; besides, we'd have to give up too much information and reveal that we were acting on information from a source, so we persuaded the DPS to write the warrant and take down the load. To our surprise, half the backpackers had departed in the night and returned to Mexico after walking for two days.

The final result was the seizure of one AK-47 rifle, eight hundred pounds of marijuana, and eight backpackers. The other part of the group dropped off the load, rested for an hour, and then returned to Mexico with the guides. A lot of times, after the mules have delivered their dope they walk out of the area to the nearest road and walk south, knowing that the border patrol will come by and give them a ride to Mexico. At times I would stop a group on the interstate and look at their shoulders to see if they had marks left from the rope straps of the bundles they carried.

The mules who backpack are desperate people. They carry forty- to sixty-pound bales on their backs at night on steep mountain trails. They take a gallon of water and a little food, they don't take breaks every hour, and they are forced to hike three hours at a time; some wear street shoes or tennis shoes, depending on how many days they hike.

ABOUT ninety percent of everything we did was based on information derived from confidential sources. However, we had some slow times when no one called. During these periods I would just cruise to a known smuggling area, park, and wait. I placed a cardboard sunshade in the front window. The sunshade had small slits in it for visibility. My G-ride was perfect for this. It had chrome, mag wheels, and air shocks in the rear, making it ride higher in the back end; the maroon vinyl top was ratty and ripped up in a hundred places, and the windows were all tinted dark, beyond the legal limit. Only dopers and narcs drove vehicles with blacked-out windows. Hell, the vehicle's trunk still smelled like marijuana.

There was so much dope being smuggled, the guys laughed and said they could drive to a hot area and, if the timing was right, just honk the horn twice and smugglers would run out to load the vehicle until they realized it was the wrong car.

My favorite place to just park and sit was the corner of East

Street and Short Street. This was the most active area in the city for smuggling, and I was determined to screw over Quemado by ripping off every load he sent through.

Ricardo and I were parked on Short Street right below the area where I had been shot at a week earlier. My vehicle was the last in a row on the street. It paid to have a seized car for a G-ride. The neighbors never gave us a second glance as we came up the hill and parked.

It was around three in the afternoon. Ricardo and I were talking about going drinking later that night. I peeked through the shield and saw some kids who had ridden by on a bicycle a couple of times.

Realizing these kids were lookouts, we knew something was about to happen. One of the boys raced his bicycle right up the border fence to a huge hole. He jumped off his bicycle and started waving and whistling. Suddenly the area was alive. Five guys with burlap bags on their shoulders jumped through the hole in the border fence and followed the kid straight down the street toward us.

Ricardo and I laughed. All I could say was, "Only in Nogales, Arizona."

The kid led them directly to the vehicle parked in front of us. I had parked so close to the bumper of the other vehicle that they had trouble squeezing between the two bumpers to open the trunk of the vehicle. They quickly packed the marijuana in the trunk and raced back to Mexico through the same hole in the fence. We hadn't even been parked there for fifteen minutes.

The kid jumped back on his bicycle and pedaled off down the hill. Obviously this kid was the lookout for some smuggling group because he even had the keys to the load car. Ricardo called out the information on the radio. We were sitting on a loaded vehicle and requested that someone from the office take a position on Morley Avenue at the bottom of the hill.

Within minutes an agent from the office radioed us that he was in the area standing by as other units were responding. Then, as quickly as before, the kid returned on his bicycle, dismounted at the edge of the road, ran to the hole in the fence, and whistled out. The same group of guys once again started running in our direction, but this time they didn't have any burlap bundles. The kid opened the vehicle's trunk again.

What the hell, I thought, *they're going to remove the dope and take it back to Mexico. No way.*

Ricardo and I both bolted from the vehicle, guns drawn.

Ricardo yelled, "Police, don't move."

Yeah, right; if you've ever hunted quail and seen them flushed from hiding, that's about the best description I can give. It was nothing but assholes and elbows scrambling to get to Mexico. Two guys had grabbed a bundle of marijuana and tried to hang on but dropped it after several yards as the kid and smugglers sprinted toward the hole in the fence. Ricardo and I were right on their ass.

The teenager grabbed his bicycle and began pushing it toward Mexico. He was trying to lift the bicycle through the hole in the fence as I grabbed the rear tire, and a tug-of-war started. Ricardo was yelling for me to stop and take cover, as we were now at the hole in the fence with the bicycle half in Mexico and half in the United States. With one final jerk, I pulled the bike from the little bastard's hands. I raced back with the bike to the parked cars for safety. Ricardo had taken a position and was aimed in at the group, ready for a firefight. Ricardo said, "You're nuts; they could've dragged your ass across or shot you."

I never gave it a thought. I just wasn't going to let the bastard take his new bike.

A barrage of insults in Spanish was directed toward us. The kid was pissed that he'd lost his bike. The gutsy little bastard called out every four-letter word and phrase he knew. The other agents arrived and covered us as we picked up the bundles, checked the vehicle, and discovered that the little bastard had taken the car keys. We took cover positions and called for a tow truck. Everyone was still very alert after the shooting incident there a few weeks earlier. Finally, a tow truck arrived to haul off the load vehicle with a new bicycle tied on top.

Ricardo and I were the youngest agents in the office. Needless to say, the old farts took some pleasure in chiding the two of us for our inability to catch at least one of the six guys smuggling the dope. I guess *chiding* is the wrong choice of word; *a real ration of bullshit* seems more fitting. If you made the slightest mistake, you became open game for all to take a jab at. This kind of behavior kept you in line and usually kept someone from making the same silly-ass mistake twice. The supervisors just glared at me and said, "Next time, grab the kid, not the bike, and stay the hell away from the fence."

ON one occasion, we did an operation in Tres Bellotas, a mountainous canyon area south of Arivaca, Arizona, which borders Mexico. This area consisted mainly of the Tres Bellotas Ranch and a few other smaller ranches. Large trucks called *tortas*, which were actually five-ton gravel trucks, were crossing in this area on a regular basis. Two agents were friends with the ranch owners, who were upset that the smugglers cut their fences and never put gates back in place, and their cattle were wandering south into Mexico and being made into carne asada tacos by Mexican rustlers. The supervisor on the scene was Billy, and catching these trucks was his group's operation. Ricardo and I would be placed down by the international fence to call out the trucks as they crossed so the other agents could stop them and make the arrest and seizure further inland.

Ricardo and I were dropped off at the fence in full camouflage outfits and told to remain hidden and use the portable radios to call out vehicles when they crossed but not to try and stop the vehicles. Around six A.M. a large *torta* crossed, and we obeyed our orders and called it out. The radios worked only on the repeater channel, which was relayed through our sector communications in Houston back to the surveillance units. The channel two repeater can be heard by every office in the region, as opposed to the local channel, which is office to office.

Billy and the group attempted to stop the truck, but the driver managed to turn around and headed back to Mexico at full speed. Billy was obviously pissed and in his anger shouted over the radio on the channel two repeater, "The truck is headed south. Stop the damn truck."

Ricardo asked him to repeat his transmission.

Billy called out again, "I said stop that damn truck even if you have to shoot out the tires."

"Shit," I told Ricardo, "did he just say to shoot the fucking tires?"

Ricardo said, "Shoot the fucking truck if we have to."

We jumped to all sorts of conclusions. We never shot fucking tires. So this must be something very serious. We speculated that the driver must have rammed one of the surveillance units and hurt someone. The supervisor never would have said to shoot the truck otherwise.

We were concealed right at the border fence and ran about a quarter mile north so that when we shot the truck, it would stop in the United States instead of rolling into Mexico. Before long we heard the truck racing down the rocky gravel road. I had loaded slugs into my shotgun, and Ricardo had his M16. We knew that at close range we could blow the tires up and stop the truck. We staged ourselves at a curve in the road next to a group of large boulders for protection. The driver would have to slow down to navigate the curve. We were ready.

The truck came roaring down the dirt road; at best his speed was thirty miles an hour, but it sure as hell seemed like eighty. As the driver approached our position, we stood up. The driver saw us and panicked. We started shooting at the giant tires. The driver must have thought we were shooting at him, as the sound of two guns erupting at the same time must have been terrifying. He jumped from the still-moving truck and hit the ground running. We looked at the driver, and then at the truck, which was still rolling.

The driver was in a full sprint for his life. He looked back over his shoulder once and saw us with the guns still ready at the shoulder, then took off faster at a dead run toward the border. The truck had rolled forward and run right into a tree. Ricardo and I approached the truck and saw that it was loaded with more than five thousand pounds of pot. Jackpot.

Ricardo and I were feeling like heroes when over the radio the voice of the RAC (resident agent in charge) was heard saying, "Disregard that last order. Do not shoot the truck, I repeat, do not shoot the truck." Oh shit. *What now?* we wondered. Billy must've realized his mistake, and now he came on the radio, calling out our call signs. "Alpha twenty-one oh eight, alpha twenty-one twelve, hold off on that last, do not engage the truck."

Ricardo and I looked at each other. I said, "Oh shit, too fucking late. Now what?"

Billy rolled up to our location and saw the truck crashed into the tree. He jumped out of his vehicle and didn't say a word to us, going straight to the truck in a panic. He examined the truck for signs of bullet holes. There were none, other than the large rear tires blown apart. Ricardo and I stood back, not saying a word.

Finally Billy walked up to us and said, "You didn't shoot, right?"

We started to say yes, but Billy said, "Shut the fuck up and listen to me." He took a gulp of air. "You didn't discharge your weapons, did you?"

"No," we answered in unison.

"Good."

We quickly reloaded our shotguns, picked up our empty shell casings and threw them as far into the brush as we could, then wiped our shotguns down so they wouldn't smell like they had been fired.

Ricardo and I were placed in a dilemma: Do we lie about shooting our guns? Cover the supervisor's ass or tell the truth? No one was hurt, there were no signs of bullet holes, and the suspect had returned to Mexico. Would this little lie hurt anyone?

The entire squad was called back to the office because a complete shitstorm was taking shape. Billy was getting his ass chewed out by the RAC.

Then Ricardo and I were called into the office. The big question was, "Did you two fire a shot or not?"

We held to our story.

"Fine," the RAC said. He was relieved. He knew the truth but wanted to hear us say no.

The old-timers were smiling. They wanted to laugh out loud but feared the wrath of the boss. A dose of humility goes a long way, but so does a good ass-chewing.

Billy resigned for other reasons about six months later, and the incident was never discussed again.

SOMEONE in the office was involved in a seizure of dope on a daily basis. The marijuana season began in September and lasted until the end of April. The narcotics growing season and the winter produce season ran parallel to each other. This was great for the traffickers, as they used the semis to transport the dope from other states such as Sinaloa and Michoacán, Mexico, to the border in very large amounts.

One night I pulled over a vehicle by the border and four guys jumped out. One of them was a huge guy called Bear. He was big, with a full beard, and talked funny. Bear supposedly threw another doper friend of his over a second-story railing and killed the guy. They had been drinking and were ready to fight. Now Bear and the three idiots approached me, and Bear said, "So you're the narc Patricio, huh? You want to fight me?"

Thankfully I had enough good sense to know that fighting this animal was pointless. I took a step toward him, placed my hand on my gun so they could see I was packing, and then glared at him, using my Patricio stare, with my eyes fixed. I said, "There isn't going to be a fight, but there will be a killing. I'm going to shoot you and your asshole friends."

The Kirkpatrick stare, as the guys in the office called it, is my serious, nonblinking, expressionless look, intended to intimidate people. It happens naturally right before I go into fight mode. The stare had started during my teenage years in Chicago. I learned to stare down guys who wanted to fight; never showing fear and standing directly in the face of danger sometimes works better than words.

The Patricio stare must have made Bear believe I was serious. He stared back at me for a few seconds, then backed up a couple of feet and said, "Take it easy, Patricio. I was just kidding."

The confrontation ended quickly, but word of the incident was passed along the streets from doper to doper: *Patricio the narc is a serious guy. Don't fool with him.* My reputation grew, and I liked it.

I had informants calling night and day. Some agents simply don't answer the phone. If I'd had a home life, I might have ignored my phone as well, but the reality was I looked forward to the escape. Once again an informant called and reported that a car was going to be loaded at my favorite spot, Short Street. The informant, Chico, was working directly for Quemado's group.

Over the next twenty-four years Chico worked consistently for me or someone else in the Office of Investigations in Nogales, Arizona. I arrested him twice over the years, as he sometimes forgot to tell me he had been hired to drive a load. The guy was likable, and every time I caught him he promised to call the next time and usually did.

Chico had heard that this group planned to load a big red Pontiac Bonneville that was going to be parked later near his house on Short Street.

It was a dark, overcast, drizzling winter afternoon, and the drizzle turned into a sheet of solid rain in the evening. The visibility was zilch. I did several drive-bys until I finally caught a glimpse of the big red Pontiac, parked. I watched the vehicle but wasn't able to determine whether the smugglers had loaded it. As the night progressed, the rain became a downpour and I decided there was only one way to find out: I would run up on foot and sniff the trunk.

The guys in the office took great pleasure in busting my balls because they found nose marks on just about every car in town. They would drive through the Walmart parking lot and then call each other car-to-car on the radio and say, "Patricio's been here; there's a nose mark." It took great skill. First I pulled up on one side of the locked trunk several times to allow the air to be sucked into the trunk; as the trunk closed, it released the air, causing a vacuum effect. If the truck was loaded, the odor of marijuana rushed out and then, in rapid breaths, I sniffed the air as it came from the trunk. By doing this I was able to smell marijuana inside. The other agents laughed at first, but before long I caught them in parking lots sniffing car trunks as well.

I radioed Rene and Ricardo and said I was going in on foot to check the Pontiac. Rene had taken a surveillance position on the adjoining street, which was on a hill just north of Short Street. Rene quickly radioed back, saying, "Keep your radio on." He was always the safety guy; his last words to me ninety percent of the time were, "Keep your radio on for communication."

The rain was still falling steadily and wasn't showing any signs of subsiding, so I decided the time was as good as any to check things out. I grabbed my portable radio, threw on a black rain poncho, and slowly walked up the street. I just acted like I lived in the neighborhood and casually strolled down the edge of the street. Every so often a lightning bolt would light up the entire sky, but the darkness suited me and gave me cover. I had just reached the Pontiac and was bent down at the trunk lifting a corner, sniffing, when I heard a commotion coming from the border fence. I looked around and spotted a half dozen men with bundles on their backs running down the hill from Mexico. They were coming right for me. Was this the luck of the Irish or what?

I quickly grabbed my radio and called out, "Rene, I got a group headed right for me."

Rene said, "Repeat," but I'd turned off the radio.

The old Motorola radios made a little squelch sound, like a mouse screeching, every time someone spoke. The last thing I wanted was to have these guys alerted to my presence because someone was talking on the radio.

Rene was instantly on the radio calling Ricardo and asking, "Did you hear him?"

Ricardo laughed and said, "He's off the air."

What now? I was kneeling at the back end of the vehicle and had no place to go. The smugglers were coming fast; they were about thirty feet away. I had no options, so I crawled headfirst right under the Pontiac and positioned myself dead center, with my head toward the trunk. There I was, lying on the wet ground; the Pontiac had been parked on an incline, so my legs were facing uphill. I propped myself up on my elbow. I could feel the water running up my pants leg. I couldn't move as the water soaked my pants, slowly reaching my crotch. I knew the smugglers were coming, and I knew the water was coming too. I don't know which was worse.

I drew my automatic pistol and pointed it toward the rear of the vehicle. Seconds later all I could see were feet. Lots of feet. Twelve legs at the rear of a vehicle scurrying around is one hell of a sight. The guys were all chattering but I couldn't hear what was being said; the blood was pounding too hard in my ears. I heard the trunk open and felt the weight of the marijuana as each forty-pound bag was loaded inside. The shocks dropped as the weight of the marijuana bundles lowered the car right on top of me. I felt it hard on my back as I tried to stay up on my elbows. The back end of the Pontiac dropped about three inches.

I thought, *You idiot, you had to find out if the car was loaded. Well, it's loaded now.* Was I the only agent this had happened to? It was a crazy situation, but at the same time I loved the thrill of it.

I loved the adrenaline rush of being under the car as the smugglers were loading the dope. Then reality struck: What if they decide to drive off? I thought, *I'll be fucked for sure. If I don't get run over, one of these idiots is most likely armed and the shit will hit the fan.* Thankfully the whole process took less than five minutes. They finished loading the car, and I watched the feet disappear as they ran back to Mexico.

Rene was on the opposite hill the whole time, straining to see through his binoculars. He lost it after I radioed him that the group was coming in my direction, and then when he saw the smugglers arrive at the vehicle, he was screaming into his radio, calling me, telling me to get out of the area. He watched as I crawled under the Pontiac and became surrounded by the smugglers. He told Ricardo I was going to cause him to have a massive coronary and said, "If those bastards don't kill him, I will."

When they had left, I turned on my radio again and called out, "I'm clear." I walked out of the area slowly, not wanting to draw attention.

As I arrived back at my vehicle where Rene was parked, he started screaming.

"Why do you always turn off your radio?"

I looked at Rene and answered calmly. "I knew if you saw the backpackers, you would start yelling on the damn radio and get me killed."

Ricardo and Tom were laughing. For once Rene had to admit I was right.

As the guys were laughing about the situation, an enormous bolt of lightning flashed close by and lit up the entire area. If things weren't bad enough, everyone saw my soaking wet pants. Immediately the conversation shifted to my clothes. "Holy shit," Ricardo said, "you pissed all over yourself."

Needless to say I spent another two hours sitting in my G-ride waiting for the Pontiac to move. I was more than ready to take it down fast when it left. I was starting to get a real case of crotch rot, and this was one night I wanted to end. The Pontiac was finally lit up (red lights and siren on to stop the vehicle). Usually one unit pulls to the front and acts as a block to prevent the driver from going forward as another unit pulls up close to the driver's-side door, and the third unit with the lights pulls up to the trunk. This prevents a lot of high-speed races through town. We were always involved in these high-speed pursuits, and someone always wrecked. But tonight, surprisingly, the driver just stopped. We seized another six hundred pounds of marijuana.

By the end of the harvest season around June, the agents stop counting the individual seizures after seizing thousands of pounds and making hundreds of arrests. Most of us struggled to work through the season in a constant state of sleep deprivation. We were greeted by angry wives at home and angry supervisors, attorneys, and property custodians who wanted reports in a timely fashion. Most of the time the defendants were out of jail before we wrote the reports. Then, by September, sources begin calling. Life in general begins to take its toll. Year after year, agents become callous toward life and people in general. Soon you believe that everyone lies and no one can be trusted.

THE Nogales agents took turns handling calls from the POE. This was called a duty roster, and each agent was given a twenty-four-hour shift that required them to respond to all calls from the POE. Once the inspectors discovered narcotics or other violations, they called the Office of Investigations. A duty agent responds to the POE, interviews the violators, determines the facts, and contacts the U.S. Attorney's office for prosecution.

Once during my duty day, I responded to the POE nineteen times in a twenty-four-hour period. After someone is arrested, we usually book them into the county jail on federal charges until the next day, when we take the prisoner to his or her initial appearance before a federal magistrate. There are times when the Santa Cruz County jail is full and the agents have to drive arrestees to the federal prison in Tucson for the night. There have been times when an agent made three trips in one day to the federal facility. Talk about exhausted.

HOT PURSUITS

ONE night I heard that a load of marijuana was going to be crossed through the hole at the end of Escalada Drive near Tricky Wash. This load was organized by a local family known as the Cruceros, a third-generation group of smugglers who lived in several houses adjacent to the border. The father was a smuggler, the son was a smuggler, and now the teenage grandsons were smugglers.

I wanted to catch the father in the act, so I needed to get in close to see him directing the load or touching the dope. The plan was simple: just walk into the area and hide close enough to see him participate in the smuggling operation. I had Rene, Ricardo, Tom, and others on Morley Avenue to follow the load vehicle when it departed the area. All I had to do was call out the loaded vehicle for them to intercept it.

Tom and I drove into the area so we could check things out. It was crawling with people. There were at least six kids on the street, and they were setting up their countersurveillance. The kids were on bicycles riding up and down the street looking for law enforcement. The father was sitting on the front porch of his house drinking beer and overseeing the operation. I knew there was no way I could walk into the area without being seen.

I met with the group down below and revised my game plan. I decided to do a rolling bailout from Tom's car as he drove through the area. Tom would simply drive through the area real slow, and I would do a tuck-and-roll exit from the passenger side as he turned the corner without stopping. Tom and I had done this before several times, and it always worked.

The dead end of Escalada connected to a dirt road that paralleled the border fence about a hundred yards east of Short Street. The Buenos Aires neighborhood in Mexico was right there. Just off of Escalada Drive was Tricky Wash, and fifty yards east along the dirt road was Smuggler's Gulch. This area belongs to the traffickers. There was a mountain of trash all along the border fence for the smugglers to hide in, and I was going to use that trash to my advantage tonight.

Tom began to cough and choke a little as we drove into the area; he said the place always reminded him of Vietnam. Tom had spent a lot of years in Vietnam, and the smell of the burning tires and garbage that filled the night air brought back memories of the war. You could see the layer of thick smoke lingering and forming a cloud over the neighborhood.

Rene always said I was nuts for getting up close and personal with the traffickers. As always, Rene said his famous last words, "Keep your radio on."

Everyone laughed.

Tom and I had taken out all the interior lightbulbs in his

vehicle. I didn't want the interior lights to come on when I opened the door. We drove slowly back up the street, and as we approached the fence, Tom slowed to about five miles per hour as he turned onto the dirt road along the border fence. I opened the door and jumped out. Tom kept driving slowly, going about another fifty yards, and then turned around.

When I bailed out of the car I hit the ground and rolled over a couple of times until I was up against the border fence. I quickly grabbed some pieces of cardboard, paper, wooden boards, and handfuls of debris and covered most of my body with the foul-smelling garbage. I hoped that anyone who was watching would be concentrating on Tom's car headlights and not notice me. Tom drove slowly past my location. I radioed that I was code four, meaning "okay," and asked if he could see me when he drove by.

He couldn't see me at all.

I did a quick radio check with the other units and then turned off my radio. As soon as the initial excitement of bailing out of the vehicle and scrambling for cover was over, I began to realize this wasn't my best idea. The smell of the garbage next to the fence was unbearable. I might as well have hidden in a Dumpster. The smell was overwhelming: rotten food, dead animals, and sewage from the houses in Mexico. Luckily the border fence is made of landing mat and has one-inch holes all through it, so I could see into the Mexican side really well.

I wanted to move, but I could see the Crucero family still in the street and the kids on their bicycles riding up and down, so I had to stay right there. After about thirty minutes I saw the smugglers heading for the fence. They had been staged in the carport of a house less than thirty yards away. I had not seen them until they started running toward me. I didn't realize how close to the actual hole in the fence I was. The hole was about waist high and about fifteen feet away.

The smugglers dashed the fifty yards to the fence and then hid beside the hole on the Mexican side. One by one they quickly jumped through the hole with a bundle of weed, then dashed down the street toward the Crucero residence. The kids on the bikes raced down the hill to check for cops, and my target, the father, who had been hanging out in the street, quickly opened the trunk of a parked vehicle so the smugglers could load the marijuana. I checked around to see if anyone was near me so I could radio the vehicle information and that it was loaded. I noticed someone still waiting by the fence. I would have to wait until the coast was clear.

Finally, after chatting with each other for about three minutes, the mules returned to Mexico. Someone started the load vehicle and drove down the hill to Morley Avenue, the main street. I quickly radioed the surveillance units below and told them the car was moving.

As soon as the mules were walking south to the staging house, I rolled away from the fence and right across the road till I hit the other side, then crawled another fifteen feet and ran for cover by a shack across the street from the Cruceros'.

After I heard that the team had stopped the car, I started walking down the smuggler's trail in Tricky Wash, which would lead me to the main street. It was a stroll of satisfaction for another night's good work.

The driver of the load vehicle quickly realized he was being followed and made several U-turns in an attempt to lose his surveillance. He ran through several red lights, so Rene and Ricardo decided to stop him. Rene waited for the load car driver to get to the next stoplight, and when the light turned red, Rene turned on his flashing red and blue lights. Ricardo pulled up in the lane next to the car and yelled out the passenger-side window for the driver to pull over. The driver looked over at Ricardo, gave him the international middle-finger sign, and floored it. The race was on.

Ricardo hit the gas pedal of his brand-new six-cylinder vehicle, which he had just gotten a day earlier, and nothing; a bicycle had more speed than a piece-of-shit six-cylinder Chevrolet. Ricardo could only watch as the load car raced away. Before Ricardo cleared the intersection, the kid was a block ahead, with Rene right on his tail. Rene was driving an older Ford LTD with a police package. It hauled ass. The initial point of contact was about a half mile from the POE. Rene and the driver were now reaching speeds of more than ninety miles an hour, and Rene was trying to cut him off from driving south through the POE.

I was now far enough away from the Crucero residence to turn on my radio and couldn't believe what I was hearing.

Rene was excited, saying his speed was more than a hundred miles per hour. He yelled for the port to clear traffic, trying to make sure no other vehicles were in the way because the driver wasn't stopping.

The driver looked over at Rene and smiled. He then stared straight ahead at the port. Rene knew he wasn't going to stop. With less than a hundred yards to go, Rene noticed that only one lane was open at the POE. Rene and the driver were neck and neck, straddling one lane. Directly ahead was a large, concrete pillar on one side and a concrete building on the other. Crashing into either meant death at these speeds. Rene slammed on the brakes, locking up his car and sliding the final fifty yards to the POE.

92

The driver made it back to Mexico, but he crashed into a car on the other side. The Mexican customs officials had been notified of the vehicle headed their way. As the vehicle entered Mexico, they opened fire on the vehicle, hitting it and the driver. The driver continued on for several miles before he was fired on again by Mexican police in pursuit. The chase ended when the driver was killed by the Mexican cops.

On average someone in our office wrecked a vehicle monthly. This was actually considered good. In the Douglas, Arizona, office, the agents wrecked about three cars a week. In Nogales we did some crazy things, but we considered ourselves highly professional. The agents in Nogales viewed the Douglas agents as a bunch of cowboys running amok in the desert.

Three nights later I was on foot at the end of West International Street, waiting for yet another load to get picked up. I was concealed in some bushes on the side of a house. I could see a corral area and the border fence from my location. Late at night I was always amazed at how every sound is amplified. I heard the smugglers start whistling the signal that the coast was clear. Before long they came running along the driveway of the Holler and Saunders store at the dead end of West International and hid in the bushes about fifty feet from me.

The smugglers were like a bunch of gophers; they popped their heads up just high enough to see, then ducked back down into the bushes. I had watched them come though their private hole in the fence. The traffickers had used a welding torch on the Mexican side to cut a four-foot-square opening in the border fence. From the U.S. side it appeared normal, but on the Mexican side they had added hinges and a padlock so no one could use it unless they paid a fee. I had been working this group for a while and had taken off several loads already.

Tonight's operational plan was the same as the others; I took the position out on foot to watch. I could have asked someone else to get out on foot, but I loved the feeling of stalking the traffickers and getting as close to them as possible. I knew every hiding spot in just about every neighborhood in town. I loved the nighttime cover and concealment. Since the first shooting with Tom, I went alone. I didn't like the thought of someone else getting hurt. Tonight was no different. I'd watch the mules cross the dope, and then I would call out the vehicle description and the other units would stop it on I-19 as the car went north on the interstate. Rene, Tom, and Clark had already stopped five previous loads, and everything had gone smoothly.

I didn't have to wait long tonight. I saw a Nissan 280z come around the corner of West International Street, driven by a young Hispanic male about twenty years old, and pull into the load site. The load car driver had come around the corner on two wheels, and the whole time the car was loaded he revved the engine like a driver at the drag strip waiting for the lights to turn green. The car sounded great. I began to laugh as I called out the vehicle's description to the mobile units. Rene answered back, "Ten-nine, repeat, what's the description?"

"It's a silver Nissan 280z. Be ready for a chase."

This kid must have thought he was in the Indianapolis 500 and was in for a pit stop. When the last bundle was squeezed into the Nissan, it took the mules several tries to close the hatchback, but once they did, they were off and running. The driver laid rubber in every gear as he left the area.

I radioed Rene and said the load car was headed in his direction. The kid set a new record getting from West International Street to Interstate 19 and was northbound before anyone could react. All the agents saw was a silver blur racing north. As the agents tried to catch up, the driver noticed the surveillance units and did a U-turn on the interstate.

Rene and Clark were the last two units to block him from heading into Mexico. The kid made another erratic turn, which threw rocks onto Clark's vehicle, shattering his window. Clark was an easygoing, older, cowboy kind of guy, but when he was drunk or mad, look out.

Clark and Rene cut the kid off and forced him to come back down West International Street; the kid took the exit on two wheels again, but with the loose gravel on the road, he slid sideways and hit a curb, tearing out his rear axle. Still determined to get away, the kid leaped from the load car and tried to scale the border fence, with Clark right behind him. Clark pulled the kid down by one leg and had his gun in the kid's mouth by the time Rene rolled up on the scene. Rene managed to calm Clark down; his ego was shattered, and so were the windows on his G-ride.

I was listening to the pursuit on my portable radio as I walked out of the area and back to my vehicle. I knew this kid was hell-bent on getting away. I was laughing at the mess and listening to the agents' comments when one said, "Why didn't you tell us he was going to drive like a madman?"

I said, "I did. I held the radio up so you could hear him revving up his engine."

Rene said, "I heard the loud, revving sounds but thought it was your radio acting up."

UNDERCOVER

WHEN most people hear the words *undercover agent*, they envision a life like *Miami Vice*, where the agents drive custom sports cars, drink champagne, and sit in fancy nightclubs with beautiful women ready to fulfill their dreams while they smoke Cuban cigars. Unfortunately, this image isn't reality. Deep undercover work in an agency is rare and extreme. If you ask anyone who's assigned to a narcotics task force about undercover assignments, you'll be astounded how quickly they admit it's a real headache.

Early in my career I spent three years working in the DEA office, where a senior DEA agent and friend told me, "Never rush a dope deal. Play it cool. Never become needy, and know when to walk away. If you try to rush a deal and become desperate to buy dope, the dealers will know you're a narc."

This is the hardest thing for bosses to understand, especially since very few have worked undercover. I honestly don't know the true numbers, but I would guess that perhaps one in five hundred special agents have actually worked undercover.

Most agents who have worked a lot of undercover deals vaguely remember them. The deal becomes another routine assignment. You find out who the crook is, what the merchandise is, and wing it. However, just about every agent remembers that first undercover assignment. Your adrenaline is flowing, you're excited beyond belief, you rehearse your words like trying out for a play, and this is your chance to prove yourself.

On my very first undercover assignment, I was supposed to meet a cocaine dealer and buy a kilo for twenty thousand dollars. I was introduced to him by a source at the first meeting and had already met the guy twice more to negotiate a price. Now, at the third meeting, we were going to do the exchange.

The case agent had developed a good operational plan. He had picked the Rio Rico Resort, now known as the Esplenador Resort, as the location for the exchange. The resort offered good visibility, the parking lot made an excellent takedown location, and the agents could blend in with the guests and other patrons at the bar.

A good operational plan is vital to any exchange. I stress this with every case. Agents have to pick a site to their advantage; location, concealment, and visibility are crucial. The location needs to provide a place to prevent escape and an area to take down the crook when the timing is right.

I agreed to meet the dealer in the bar before he showed me the cocaine and the deal went down. Dopers love to rip the money and run, but this operation was well thought out and the case agent had the surveillance agents arrive about ten minutes apart. Some agents were stationed in their vehicles, some were out on foot in the bushes around the resort, and three agents were inside acting as patrons, one at the bar and two others at a table eating lunch.

I arrived last and went straight to the bar and took a seat about fifteen feet from the surveillance agent. I glanced around the bar, trying to be casual and not looking directly at the other agents. The bartender walked over and asked what I wanted. I uttered the immortal words, "Pepsi, please." He put the glass of Pepsi in front of me and I waited.

Even though I had met the guy before, I had butterflies in my stomach. I was nervous as hell but trying to be cool and relaxed as I sipped my Pepsi. The dealer showed up right at two, as agreed, and ordered a beer, and after some small talk he agreed to show me the cocaine. I threw a ten-dollar bill on the bar and we walked out to his vehicle. The outer surveillance units had observed his vehicle when he parked. I was hooked up with a body wire, which was being monitored by two agents in a van. During the final briefing before we left the office, the case agent went over his plan and I demonstrated the takedown signal for those who weren't able to monitor the wire. I would take my Chicago Cubs baseball hat off and simultaneously say, "It looks good. I'll get the money."

The dealer and I went straight to his vehicle. He reached inside, pulled out a small sports bag, and laid it on the trunk of his car. I opened the bag, and there inside was the kilo of coke wrapped in cellophane. I took time to examine it, then slowly took off my baseball cap and said, "It looks good. I'll get the money." Within seconds the place was swarming with agents.

The bust team rushed in from every direction, guns pointed at both of us, screaming, "Police, don't move!" To make things look real, they threw me to the ground and handcuffed me as well. I think the older agent who handcuffed me took delight in shoving me to the ground real hard. The dealer was arrested and transported back to the office for processing, where the case agent interviewed him.

Needless to say, I was excited. I had just made a major buy and had proven myself as an undercover agent. I drove back to the office delighted with myself. I entered the office and strolled to the briefing room, imagining a welcome of accolades and cheers. Wrong. Instead, the first words I heard were an old agent named George saying, "Someone get the FNG [fucking new guy] a Pepsi-Cola."

Then George, who had been seated at the bar on the surveillance, says, "Can you believe this kid? He's undercover in a fucking bar and orders a Pepsi."

I quickly learned not to make the slightest mistake, because agents eat their own. For weeks I heard jeers like, "Hey rookie, need a Pepsi?" Or someone would place a Pepsi, the trophy of shame, on my desk.

THE undercover (UC) agent works under the direction of the case agent, who started the investigation and knows the traffickers or violators but needs to do more investigation or directly incriminate someone with conversations or an overt act. Usually a source makes an introduction to a UC agent.

The source makes an introduction and the UC agent takes over, because we can buy the dope, drive the load car, participate in weighing the dope, and so on. Someone needs to focus on the totality of the investigation and keep the direction needed for a successful prosecution. The UC agent is usually living in the moment of the meeting with the crook, and needs to keep his or her head and push the crooks along to finish the negotiation.

In all my years of service I found maybe one in ten agents really capable of working UC. UC work is not structured; you fly by the seat of your pants, making up things as the conversation demands and being able to bullshit your way into and out of potentially life-threatening situations. The ability to lie successfully doesn't come from training; it comes from street smarts and sometimes a lot of luck. In Nogales there were only three agents who did real UC work: Clark, Ricardo, and me. In a small town there is always the potential for someone to know you, and you must be extremely careful never to get into a group where you might have arrested someone before. A lot of times UC agents would come from out of state, and we would work in other states as well.

One such agent was Clark. He could really work undercover. A slow, easy-talking guy, he could dress like a cowboy and you would think he was a true rancher. His Spanish was perfect, since his mom was Hispanic. Then he could put on slacks and a dress shirt and be just as smooth as a banker. His slow, easy way of talking put everyone at ease.

I was Clark's partner on a deal once where Clark was meeting a young Mexican guy to buy a kilo of heroin. Clark agreed to meet the dealer in Tucson at the El Con Mall. I was waiting in another vehicle and had eighty thousand dollars to be used for flash money. Sometimes dopers want to see the cash before they produce the drugs. Clark was supposed to see the heroin and give the bust signal for the takedown, but if the dealer needed to see the money first, Clark was going to call me and I would drive over and show the cash. The first rule of a drug transaction is never to keep the cash on an undercover agent in case of a rip-off.

The dealer arrived and Clark and the man just kept talking; the rest of us waited in and around the parking lot, wondering what the hell was taking so long. Finally, after a half hour, I saw Clark and the dealer walk over to the dealer's car and open the trunk. I radioed the units to stand by, expecting the bust signal and takedown to occur at this time. The heroin dealer took out a bag from his truck and Clark inspected the contents and continued talking; then the dealer handed Clark the bag and Clark walked over to his vehicle and placed the bag in the trunk.

I was on the radio giving a play-by-play account to the other agents, keeping them ready for the bust signal. Then Clark shook hands with the guy, and the dealer got into his vehicle and drove off. I radioed to the mobile units to keep a close surveillance on the guy, thinking he had not even arrived with the heroin and was going to a stash house to get the dope.

Clark then called me on my cell phone and asked me to drive to his location. I parked beside Clark and he jumped in my ride. Clark, in his easygoing, smooth-talking way, had exchanged pleasantries and talked about different parts of Mexico, one of which was where the man was from. They also chatted about ranching and other meaningless conversation, but the guy really liked Clark. In the conversation the dealer mentioned he also had about five hundred pounds of marijuana he needed to sell, so Clark said he would help the guy. The dealer was so delighted and taken with Clark, he gave Clark the kilo of heroin to hold while he returned to his house to get the marijuana.

Clark was one smooth hombre undercover. The poor heroin dealer returned and showed Clark the trunkload of marijuana, and game over. The signal went down and the guy was busted. The dealer was in disbelief when he learned Clark was an agent. He would have been less hurt if Clark had just ripped off the heroin.

LOUIE and I did a joint undercover buy in Tucson. We first met a Tucson dealer named Juan a couple of times at a restaurant to discuss buying five hundred pounds of marijuana. Juan told us he was waiting for a large delivery from Mexico. After several meetings and telephone calls, Juan finally agreed to sell us his load of marijuana when it arrived and invited us to his house to pick up the dope.

Juan told us to drive to the alley in the back of his house and he'd open the large gate so we could park inside his yard to load the marijuana. Louie and I were both wearing body wires, so the surveillance units could hear everything. Both DPS and Customs agents were covering us. It was the middle of the afternoon when we arrived. Louie and I decided to screw with the guy and have some fun; big mistake. We drove around the back of the house and honked our horn, and Juan opened the large gate so we could drive our vehicle into the backyard. Juan had a huge pit bull named Rocky tied up in the back. Rocky was friendly and was barking as if he wanted to play.

Once we were in the backyard, Louie told Juan, "Hey man, there are cops everywhere around here."

Juan smiled and told us, "Don't worry, that DPS vehicle parked down the street is where a highway patrol guy lives; he's no problem."

Louie smiled his boyish grin and said, "Seriously, there are cops everywhere. Hell, Juan, they're even in your backyard."

This was my cue. Louie and I pulled our badges and flashed them at Juan.

Juan just started laughing and said, "You guys are really funny; that's a good joke, guys."

We both looked at Juan and said, "The badges are real; we're actual police officers and you're under arrest."

Holy shit! In an instant Juan bolted for his house. Louie and I were right behind him, and all three of us hit the small rear entrance to the house at the same time. The space was a laundry room. Every cop knows that the most dangerous place to arrest someone is their house. Juan grabbed an automatic pistol from a shelf. Louie and I both grabbed Juan's hand. The three of us, with our arms upright holding the pistol hand, were a sight, like Olympic runners trying to pass a torch. Louie and I yelled, "Gun! Gun!" so the bust team would hear us and come charging to the house to help.

Body wires are a good and bad thing, depending on how you view them. The bust crew outside heard us say he's got a gun and immediately rushed to the house to help us. The bad thing is that everything said was recorded for court. Louie and I struggled with Juan for what seemed like eternity. With our free hands we punched Juan continuously. I hit him in the face, the chest, and then the neck, hoping to cut off his windpipe. I kneed him in the nuts. It was a test of wills to free the gun.

Louie was also hitting him, and we said shit like, "Break his arm. Kick him in the nuts. Shoot the fucker. Bash him in the head. Kill him," and God knows what else, but the yelling and cussing were all recorded. The truth was, if Juan had been a split second faster, he most likely would have turned and shot us before we could have reacted. When he grabbed the gun, the fear factor kicked in and we were right on his butt as he entered the room.

Juan finally dropped the gun and we dragged him into the backyard. Ricardo had jumped over the fence and was being held at bay by the pit bull. Ricardo had his gun out and pointed at the dog's head, ready to kill it if necessary. Juan saw the dog and Ricardo and dropped to his knees, pleading, "Please don't kill my dog, please."

Ricardo stopped his assault on the dog and gave us handcuffs to secure Juan.

The marijuana in the house was transported to the DPS station in Tucson, where the sergeant had us listen to the body wire. It sounded ten times worse than what actually happened. Juan was screaming, and there were numerous thudding sounds as we punched Juan and of course our elegant vocabulary. The DPS sergeant suggested that we make Juan a source rather than play this tape recording in court. It sounded like police brutality when we listened to the tape.

I was sent to work undercover on an investigation in Las Cruces, New Mexico. The case agent, Pete, was a friend of mine from El Paso. Pete and I wound up working in Mexico together years later. I was asked to pose as a heroin buyer from Chicago and negotiate several-ounce buys of heroin. The target amount was for me to buy a kilo. Heroin dealers are the least trusting of dopers. They are usually a family group. From the chemist to the transporter to the distributor in the United States, they are generally related.

I was introduced to the nephew of the chemist by a source from El Paso, Texas. I was going to deal with this guy to buy grams, then ounces, then hopefully the entire kilo of heroin. I met the guy and we hit it off. I bought the first gram, then a second, and then I asked to buy ounces. After I bought the first ounce for four thousand dollars and paid the dealer, we went drinking and I was able to convince a young man from Michoacán, Mexico, that I was a legitimate heroin dealer from Chicago. One trick of UC work is not to talk about anything that will screw you over later. Have a fake name close to your own; I always used Patricio, the Spanish form of the last half of my surname. I also said I was from Chicago, where I was raised. Keep things simple. Don't overtalk the situation and never be anxious. Most of the dealers are third-generation traffickers along the border and can pick out a narc from a thousand yards.

I told the dealer I really needed to buy a kilo because it was getting too risky for me to keep traveling back to Chicago with small amounts. I needed to make a big score and make the trip only every six months. The dealer's uncle in Michoacán, Mexico, was the chemist and processor, so the dealer said he had to travel home and check with his uncle. This caused a month's delay in the investigation. The young dealer traveled by the Mexican bus system, looking like a peasant farmer. He never drew attention to himself. Finally, after I'd been talking to this guy well into the third month of this operation, the crook called me and said that his uncle would help him and a kilo of heroin was en route.

I was delighted. I returned to New Mexico and the operation was set up. I was checked into the local hotel, and the backup units were in the adjoining room. The following day I received a telephone call. The dealer and his uncle were here and had successfully crossed the heroin into the United States right through the POE. I instructed them to come to the hotel, gave them my room number, and waited. Finally, the dealer and his uncle showed up and we were alerted by the mobile surveillance units.

The uncle said he was delighted that his nephew had met a good business partner. I smiled and patted the nephew on the back, addressing him as a compadre, a good friend. The uncle said he could accommodate me with a kilo of heroin every six months as needed. I nodded and the deal was sealed, and we would be great business partners. They would be the supplier and I the main seller of their merchandise. What could be better? I then asked if they had the heroin on them.

The old uncle took off his shirt to reveal the kilo of heroin strapped to his back and stomach with gray duct tape. It was divided into flat three-ounce packages so as not to be too bulky under his clothing.

I smiled, took off my Chicago Cubs baseball hat, and said the magic words: "Looks good, looks real good." In came the bust crew and arrested the pair. The dealer cried like a baby and said he couldn't believe that I had lied to him. He was genuinely hurt because he really believed we were compadres.

LIVING on the border where the demographics of the city are ninety-nine percent Hispanic and most people don't speak English has created some real language barriers. I received a call one afternoon about a load crossing at two in the morning. The source said, "*Mañana* at *dos*."

So at two A.M. I had the entire squad out waiting all night. The guys were pissed at me when no load came. The source had meant two A.M. the following day.

On another occasion, Layne was reading a guy his Miranda rights and instead of saying, "You have the right to remain silent," he told the guy in Spanish, "*Tienes el derecho de cagar en silencio*" ("You have the right to shit in silence"). The guy didn't know what to do. He thought Layne wanted him to take a dump in the holding cell. He kept asking Layne, "*Que, señor, cagar aqui?*" ("What, sir, shit here?")

Layne kept saying "*Sí*," staring at the old man like he was illiterate and had trouble understanding, until Carlos walked in and heard everything and couldn't stop laughing. For weeks, the narcotics group wouldn't stop laughing at Layne's new version of the Miranda warning.

Layne was a big man, an athletic kind of guy. He was slow to get pissed, but when he did, you wouldn't want to fight him. One evening, Layne had grabbed a guy smuggling a load and took him to the office to be interviewed. The guy didn't speak English, so we attempted to communicate in Spanish.

Layne proceeded to ask the guy, "*Cual es mi nombre?*"

The guy answered, "*No sé.*"

Again Layne asked the same question and received the same reply. Layne was really getting mad at the bastard and was about to jerk him out of the chair and pulverize the idiot. Layne was now yelling in English, "What the hell do you mean you don't know your name?"

Once again Carlos rescued the guy and told Layne, "He doesn't know your name. You're asking the guy what *your* name is."

Layne said, "Oh shit, I hope the guy doesn't know my name."

There were some key phrases that everyone learned and made mental notes on: *dale*, meaning "do it"; *mátalo*, which means "kill him"; and *córtalo*, which is "cut him." The command word *dali* during any vehicle stop or warrant caused suspects to be instantly thrown to the ground in a prone position.

FOR an experienced border agent, it is relatively easy to identify a trafficker's stash house. The windows are often covered with black plastic or aluminum foil. All the blinds are shut and no one comes in or out.

By the same token, homes that are used for alien smuggling can be equally easy to pick out. You can smell the unwashed humans and urine from the yard as they piss outside during the night. Sometimes the *polloers*, as the alien smugglers are called, will have eighty to one hundred people in a small house. The amount of garbage that accumulates is enormous. An experienced agent can often identify such a house while just walking down the street.

CUJO, THE KILLER DOG

I knew that large dope loads were being smuggled from the Short Street area. The highway patrol, the DEA, and our agents had seized several tons of marijuana from vans and pickups. I thought about the bullshit with Jose and his connection to Quemado and still wondered if he'd set me up. I had blown off looking for the shed after the shooting, thinking the whole thing had been bogus information. Too many loads had been caught coming out of the area, and I was starting to wonder. I knew there was only one way to find out. I had to go back in on foot and lie in and scout the area.

I decided not to tell anyone, especially the supervisor or Rene. He would have had a cow. I thought it would be better if I just kept my intentions quiet and walked around the neighborhood like someone who lived there. I wore a loose-fitting hoodie, buttoned up high like an East Los Angeles gangbanger. The shirt concealed my gun and radio as, once again, I started at the bottom of the hill and walked the trail up to Short Street.

This time I went in just before dusk; there was still plenty of light. I walked fairly fast and looked around every so often, keeping my head down. I wanted to look exactly like an illegal alien or, *wet*, as we called them. The term *wets* was started in Texas because the illegal aliens had to cross the river and were usually wet once they got to the United States. In Arizona we didn't have a river, and we joked here that the illegals should be called "M&Ms" or "Moist Mexicans," because all they got was dew on their clothes from the grass on the golf courses.

I got to the top by the border fence and walked toward a narrow row of three buildings, peeking into the first building. It was empty except for a bunch of spiderwebs. The second place was smaller and up a few stairs were a bunch of low-rent apartments on Short Street. The guy who owned these was a real slumlord. Once again, nothing but a few folding chairs and junk.

At the top of the ridge, on the hill, was another building. The driveway was really steep, and I doubted anyone could have gotten into this place. I was just about to walk up and peek into one of the windows when suddenly, from the other side of the shed, a huge mean-ass mongrel dog charged full speed to attack me. Thankfully, the dog growled and barked before he launched himself at me. As the dog lunged in my direction, I turned and ran. I drew my gun, preparing to shoot the damn dog. He caught me before I was out of reach and tore a large chunk of my pants just below my butt. Thankfully, the beast was connected to a chain thick enough to tow a semi. He was jerked backward as he took his first bite. He snarled and chomped the piece of pants leg to shreds.

I kept running full speed, afraid the beast would break his chain. Once I was far enough away, I turned around and the beast stopped barking. He looked quite content with his new chew toy. I looked like shit; half my right pants leg was gone and my behind was hanging in the wind. I glanced back at the shed and noticed that it had black plastic covering the windows so no one could see in. This fact, along with a killer dog tied to the shed, gave me no doubt that I had found the smugglers' storage shed.

I waited, crouched under a bush for about thirty minutes, hoping Cujo would relax and I might be able to sneak back to the shed to take a closer look. The problem was how to get close enough to either smell the dope or see inside with a light. I figured if I had to, I would use my flashlight to break a corner of the window and peek inside. Finally I started moving very slowly toward the shed, thinking I was in complete stealth mode, but Cujo had smelled my scent and moved like a lion to intercept me. I heard the chain dragging on the ground behind him. Tonight was not going to be my night.

I departed the area to figure out what I would have to do to outsmart the killer dog. He was vicious and had enough chain to go from one side of the shed to the other. This was one night I was glad I had a bag of extra clothes in the trunk of the car.

A couple of days later, at the POE on a duty call, I had a conversation with an old Customs K-9 supervisor named Matt. Matt was a legend, a mean, tough old ex-military dog handler. I told Matt about my problem with Cujo the dog, and Matt's immediate response was, "Just shoot the fucker."

I explained to Matt that he was tied to a shed where the doper lived. I couldn't just walk up there and shoot the dog. Matt then told me an old secret he and other military dog handlers used in Vietnam that was guaranteed to shut the dog up. Matt explained that he used to throw pieces of meat with a large treble fishing hook, the hook with three prongs, when approaching villages at night to shut the dogs up. The dogs eat the meat; the hooks stick to the tongue and throat and prevent the dog from barking.

"Christ," I said, "I don't want to kill the damn dog."

Matt answered in his usual rough fashion. "Who the fuck cares? Do you want to shut the damn dog up or not?"

I was still reluctant.

Matt finished by saying, "If you need any help, let me know. I'll kill the fucking dog for you." Walking away, he muttered, "Pissant pussy agents."

About two weeks later, I went in on foot again. I had asked Ricardo to cover me from Morley Avenue; I didn't tell anyone my idea. I'd confided to Ricardo about looking for the shed but decided it was best not to tell everyone.

Once again, I walked in dressed like a gangbanger and nonchalantly strolled toward the shed. As I approached the storage shed I could hear Cujo growling and barking as his chain dragged on the ground.

Instead of treble-hook-laced steak, I reached into my pants pocket and took out three pieces of raw meat in which I had inserted sleeping pills. Once again, seeing the tethered beast growling with saliva drooling from the side of his mouth made me think this dog should be put down. I had gotten the sleeping pills from a veterinarian one of the other agents was dating. Hell, I knew I couldn't kill the dog. I'm a dog lover at heart. It wasn't the dog's fault he belonged to an asshole doper. As I got close to the shed, I threw the meat to Cujo. I hoped that the pills would knock him out quickly so I could check out the shed. The dog ate the pieces of meat and then backed away. I saw him slowly find a spot and curl up. He growled in his sleep for a few minutes, then faded. This was my chance. I ran up to the shed, stabbed the corner of the window, and broke just enough to pull the plastic back and look inside with my flashlight.

There was the mother lode of at least four thousand pounds of marijuana stacked up in nice bales. I didn't dare try to get a search warrant with what I had just done, but I sure as hell was going to continue watching the shed. Any vehicles leaving the area were suspects for loads.

I wondered if this was the information that Jose had been telling me about before the shooting. Why the hell didn't he call back or say something? He had simply disappeared. Had he set me up? I was sure at the time he had, but now I wasn't so sure. Had Quemado found out about him talking to us? If so, then Jose was probably dead. I will always wonder what the truth was. Regardless, this was where the vans had been loading up.

I left the area and radioed Ricardo, using our ten-codes, to "forty-five at seventy-two in ten." This meant to meet me at Denny's in ten minutes. Our radio frequencies could be monitored by anyone who had a scanner. The local electronics store voluntarily gave anyone who bought a scanner a list of all the police and fire frequencies within a hundred miles. Our sources had already told us the traffickers were buying scanner crystals to monitor our frequencies.

We had a ten-code for every restaurant and bar in Santa Cruz County. We also developed a grid system for the areas of town. So if we were on Highway 82 on the east side, it was grid number four. This was the only way to prevent the smuggler from knowing where we were. At least if someone monitored our radio channel, they wouldn't have a clue where we were. I told Ricardo about the shed, and he agreed that if the dog died and we served a search warrant, they would know I broke the window and saw the dope. Better to keep quiet, watch, and wait for our chance to stop a van and get the driver to break and tell us where he got the dope, then return with a search warrant.

Within a week we seized two more large vans loaded with 1,200 and 1,600 pounds of pot. Then they stopped using the shed for a week or so. I figured this made a total of five large van loads taken off and around ten thousand pounds of marijuana.

A couple of days later, around ten at night, I watched a van being loaded and followed it to Grand Avenue, where the driver parked it in front of the Circle K store. The following afternoon around two, the van still hadn't moved. I didn't want anyone to know I knew where it was loaded or that I had it under surveillance, so I called a friend in the Nogales police department and discussed a ruse to take off the load. The local newspaper copied the police log every day, and anything on the police log was quoted in the newspaper the following day.

I arranged for the sergeant to pretend he'd gotten an anonymous call about the van, and then he would call Customs for a K-9 unit and turn the seizure over to us since they didn't work narcotics. Two marked police units arrived on the scene and milled around the van, and then, as arranged, the K-9 unit arrived. The

K-9 officer was Matt, who'd assisted me with Cujo. Matt was one old salty son of a bitch, and his dog, Rexx, a nasty German shepherd, was famous for biting anyone. Basically man and dog had the same attitude. Matt's G-ride was a white Chevrolet van. The back was equipped with a dog cage, and on the doors of his van were stick-on plastic placards of at least a dozen law enforcement agencies, each representing an officer Rexx had bitten.

Rexx was known to be the best narcotics dog at the POE, and Matt was known as the best dog handler. Matt was excited that this was an easy stat for his dog. The dogs and handlers are judged on how much dope they find per month. I had already told Matt that I'd seen the van get loaded, so it was a sure thing. Matt and Rexx circled the van once, twice, and then a third time, and each time Matt was more pissed off. Then he put Rexx away and said he didn't alert.

What the fuck! I had been watching this thing for more than twenty hours. I saw it loaded. Matt apologized profusely; he was mad as hell at Rexx and talking about killing the poor dog. He said he wouldn't claim the statistic for the load, but I told him he had to because I wanted the local rag newspaper to say that a dog alerted for the police after someone called in a suspicious vehicle. Finally he agreed. I heard later that Matt threw the training towel into oncoming vehicle traffic and Rexx was almost run over. Knowing Matt's temper, I wondered if he tried to deliberately kill poor old Rexx.

I heard a story about a K-9 handler who was pissed at his dog because it kept biting him. One day he took the dog to the roof of the airport terminal to play. Allegedly he accidentally threw the training towel too far, and it flew off the roof; the dog leaped off the five-story building in hot pursuit and didn't survive the fall. The K-9 officer said it was an accident, but no one believed the bullshit story. After all the stories I heard Matt and some of the other K-9 officers tell, I thought all K-9 officers were certifiably nuts anyway. K-9 officers will tell you they jerk off their dogs to promote some sort of insane loyalty. I love my dog as much as the next guy, but it will be a cold day in hell before I give my dog a hand job.

As we targeted the shack, we heard that Quemado was increasingly upset that he was losing so many loads, and he wanted someone to pay. Sources said Quemado was rounding up his mules and questioning them to find out if he had a snitch. He beat the hell out of everyone, but no one knew anything. Through the years I heard stories about traffickers torturing and killing employees they thought were snitches or *dedos*.

An agent's responsibility is controlling his source and knowing what the hell the source does. Agents allow sources to have only minimal participation with the trafficker's activities, such as driving a load in Mexico or counting money. When an agent hears of traffickers rounding up mules or torturing people, he generally asks the source how he knows. An agent's biggest fear is losing a source to the traffickers, and his second concern is that his source might be participating in the torturing.

Several years ago in El Paso, an agent found out too late that his source was torturing and killing suspected snitches and rival drug traffickers. The source, Ramirez Peyro, became known as "the House of Death Informant." The agent thought he had the greatest source in the world; Peyro had infiltrated the Vicente Carrillo Fuentes (VCF) drug cartel in Ciudad Juarez, Mexico.

Peyro had infiltrated the cartel so well that he was placed in charge of security. He had bribed Mexican police officers to make sure the dope loads weren't interfered with. Then he directly participated in torturing and killing three rival drug dealers. Some reports indicate that he was responsible for as many as twelve killings.

Peyro said he had no choice; he had to do as the cartel wanted or he would have been killed too. The VCF cartel interrogated everyone in a remote house equipped like a medieval torture chamber complete with chains and knives. Ultimately someone in Customs had the sense to get Peyro out after they heard he'd participated in murder. Mexican authorities were later directed to the "House of Death" in Ciudad Juarez and dug up twelve decomposed bodies.

Ramirez Peyro remains in solitary confinement in a U.S. federal prison. The Mexican government wants him extradited for murder. The controlling agent, his supervisors, and the entire El Paso office are still being investigated by Customs Internal Affairs.

I've lost a few sources through the years. It's not something an agent wants to admit to. No agent wants to be involved in or responsible for investigations that may inadvertently cause the death of an informant. The brutal truth is that drug cartels will kill anyone who gets in their way. They hire people who enjoy killing, and their brutality and torture methods rival anything seen in horror movies.

During the next six months I spent most of my free time watching the shed. The activity had slowed down, but a few more loads were taken off. I guess losing this much merchandise sent Quemado out of control and into a psychopathic rage.

I continued to watch the old man who controlled access to the marijuana stash house. He was a short, stocky, weathered old

Mexican guy, and he was ornery as hell. He had two younger guys working for him, but he was the boss. If anyone came down the dirt road by the shed, he ran out yelling and cussing at them to get the hell off his property. The two younger guys were always standing behind the old guy for backup. The old bastard tormented Cujo all the time; he had made sure the dog was mean. Cujo's only praise was when he savagely ran to attack people to keep them from walking within twenty feet of the storage shed.

As the marijuana loads entered and left the property, the old man directed the vans so that they turned around with the passenger door facing the side window of the shed. Then the workers loaded the dope through the window of the shed into the passenger door of the van.

One morning when I arrived for work, Ricardo handed me the *Nogales International* newspaper. The front-page headline read, "Elderly Man Gunned Down on Short Street." It was the same old man who was in charge of loading the vans and making sure the coast was clear for the drivers to leave.

Obviously Quemado and his henchmen had gone on a killing spree, executing everyone who crossed them or had anything to do with the storage shed. They blamed the old man for losing the loads. The old man's house had a nice Mexican carved wooden door with a large square hole at the top that opened up like a mini door to look out. According to the wife, someone knocked on the door, her husband went to the door and opened the peephole to look out, and someone opened fire with a machine gun right through the door. The old man took twelve bullets to the chest. The last thing he probably saw was the burned face of Quemado.

I knew that Quemado had bought a large white two-story

house in the elite subdivision of Calle Kennedy and now lived among the prominent socialites of Nogales, Sonora. His house had high walls in front and was guarded by his henchmen. Somehow, after all the seizures, Quemado seemed to disappear off our radar screen; none of my sources had any knowledge of what had happened to him. It was as if he had vanished in the night. I wondered if he had been killed as well.

OPERATIONS

OPERATION is the buzzword used to get funding whenever an agency has a long-term investigation that is going to take a lot of agents for surveillance. We write up a summary of the case, give it a catchy name after the word *Operation*, and send it to Washington, D.C., for funding.

Creativity is the key. Just like an artist, agents paint masterpieces with operational plans, outwitting narcotics traffickers and headquarters desk jockeys alike. A few of these great operations were Operation Casablanca, Operation Wagon Train, Operation Blue Lightning, and many others. Some worked great; others didn't. At times in our careers we actually outsmarted the traffickers and did some great investigative operations.

SINCE the marijuana harvest season runs through the winter, summers are usually slower and we have some leisure time on our hands. During this time we catch up on paperwork and spend days devising ways to outsmart the local smugglers. I wondered, *Why not our own stash house?* I came up with the idea of Operation Greenhouse. This wasn't going to be a farmer's garden, but a sanctioned marijuana shipping and receiving storage house.

The premise of the operation was that we would rent a house just outside the city and install audio and video equipment and then offer it to the local traffickers to use as a stash house. We'd have two agents work inside the house to receive and repackage the dope if necessary and transport it north as needed for a fee. I quickly went to town, writing up a formal request for money for two undercover agents to be assigned and money for rent, utilities, rental cars, and some modest furniture.

The concept was a good one. Major city police departments had used similar ruse operations called *storefronts*, such as pawn shops, to receive stolen merchandise. A lot of robberies were solved this way, and a bunch of petty thieves went to jail.

We finally received some funding, rented a house, and were ready to do business. We anticipated that we could operate and make a profit. We would charge the traffickers ten dollars a pound for storage. This would pay for rent, vehicles, utilities, and new camera equipment.

We began the operation on a shoestring budget and moved a few loads through the house. We received the dope, weighed it, and then had one of our sources drive it to Tucson in one of the rental vehicles we acquired for the operation. We equipped the vehicle with a tracking device and a kill switch, a device attached to the ignition and fuel supply that shut the car off when we hit the remote control.

Once the vehicle was dropped off in Tucson and another trafficker picked it up, we would follow it and then, as it approached a red light, hit the kill switch, shutting down the motor. Louie and Charlie from the highway patrol would use a marked patrol unit and pretend to assist the stalled vehicle, smell the dope, call a dog unit and arrest the driver, seize the dope, take our equipment off the rental vehicle and exchange it for a new one, and start the process again.

The operation was a success, but when harvest season hit we had to shut down. We were too busy with a hundred other loads. That was life on the border. No staffing, no time, and no support from above. We were mandated to handle the POE seizures, which took most of our time. Handling these seizures daily took the same amount of time as a major investigation, but the POE seizures and arrests were looked upon as meaningless busts and referred to as bag-and-tag cases. Everyone called the POE seizures "bag-and-tag" investigations.

As with most of our seizures and arrests, we never called the press and the seizures were not reported. We kept a lid on most of our investigations and tried not to have any leaks about what we were doing. This caused a lot of trouble for the drivers and stash house owners. The traffickers are paranoid idiots for the most part and were always concerned about the mules or drivers ripping off the dope and not paying them.

The only means of intelligence for suppliers was to read about dope losses in the newspaper or have someone drive by the parking lots of the various agencies to see if the vehicle was impounded. When the dopers in Mexico had no means to verify a loss of dope, they would call in the drivers and stash house operators and interrogate them. None of the local traffickers wanted to endure the beatings and torture, so at times, when we wanted a particular defendant to work for us after we raided his house, we let the guy go and waited for the shit to hit the fan. It didn't take long before the violator would be pleading with us to put something in the press so he wouldn't have to face the wrath of the traffickers in Mexico. A large number of violators became sources of information for us.

In one instance we heard that a storage facility in Nogales was being used to store about a thousand pounds of cocaine. We couldn't surveil the place, so we got a search warrant, raided a storage shed, and seized the cocaine. To be funny we wrote on the service copy of the search warrant that lists the items seized, "Dudes, thanks for the Coke," and we left our undercover telephone number and another line reading, "Call us if you want it back."

The traffickers were furious. They thought the warrant was a fake, and since nothing had been leaked out to the press, they began rounding up their crew and beating the shit out of them to find out where the cocaine was.

The traffickers went so far as to enter the United States and kidnap the brother of the police chief of Nogales, Arizona. The chief's brother's nickname was Fifty/Fifty, reflecting the view of some that he wasn't the sharpest knife in the drawer. He was involved with this group, and the traffickers thought that the chief had ripped off the cocaine along with his brother. They contacted the chief and told him that if he didn't return the cocaine, they were going to kill his brother. The chief called me and pleaded for me to put something in the newspaper. We did, and the brother was finally released after a good beating. Instead of quitting and learning a good lesson, he continued his career as a minor player in the dope business.

One source called and stated that her girlfriend was sleeping with a sheriff's deputy who was ripping off loads of dope and then driving them north to Tucson in the patrol car. Supposedly the sergeant and a young patrolman were involved. I worked the information but could never catch the guys in the act, so I met with the FBI and Internal Affairs, because arresting a deputy falls under FBI jurisdiction. We called the young patrolman in and questioned him. He held fast that he was innocent. I told him he had better watch his back, because the other sheriff's deputies would never believe that he didn't confess. Still he held fast to this innocence for about two days until he was threatened by members of his own department. He then confessed to his involvement and that of the sergeant.

REVERSE operations were when we duped unsuspecting smugglers into trading narcotics for guns or money. Every agency did reversals where the narcs pretended to swap seized narcotics for money, but trading guns was a unique twist, and these operations became known as Guns for Dope. Such cases were occurring all along the border. Smuggling guns south is as lucrative a business as smuggling narcotics north.

We had predrilled cable holes in most of the hotel rooms in town. We would stage a hotel room with video cameras and microphones and have a bust team in the adjoining room for cover. Then we put about a half dozen AR-15 rifles and numerous pistols, minus their firing pins, under the bedspread and lured traffickers to the hotel room. We sent out multiple sources to find a buyer—a wannabe, unsuspecting drug trafficker who thought he could be a tough guy if he had some firepower. The undercover agents flashed the guns, and then the trafficker would bring back a trunkload of marijuana or some kilos of coke in trade. Once the agents saw the dope, the bust crew would rush in and arrest the doper.

Meanwhile, outside we had several other mobile units watching for a rip-off. This was one of the few operations where we had to show our guns before seeing the dope. This was very risky and could have easily resulted in a rip-off attempt. However, we were cautious and never lingered in the room too long. Once the crooks saw the guns, we gave them several hours to return, and we made it clear that we wouldn't wait after dark because we didn't trust anyone.

It was amazing to watch the expressions on the smugglers' faces when we pulled back the bedspread and revealed the guns. Their faces lit up like a kid's in a candy store for the first time. Most of these guys were so eager to buy guns that we usually made an exchange within two or three hours. Needless to say, they were some really mad hombres once they realized that they had been duped.

IT was March, and anyone who thinks Arizona is always warm should think twice. March is very windy, and the temperatures drop below freezing nearly every night. A source called and said that a large load of possibly 1,600 pounds of marijuana was going to be crossed to a residence on North River Road. It belonged to a trafficker named Tuti, another young up-and-coming lieutenant for Jaime Figueroa-Soto. He was known to most law enforcement and was building a castle on a ranch that he'd bought on North River Road. We had pictures and were trying to get sources into his group to arrest him in the act, but he was a smart kid and we hadn't gotten anyone to roll over on his operation yet.

The source knew the location of the drop, but it was impossible to surveil. There were three houses together in a corner location, and each resident must have had several dogs. We tried to sneak in several times and were confronted by this pack of dogs. I didn't want a repeat of Cujo, so quieting them down was impossible. I scouted the area from every hilltop location, but I couldn't get a visual on the property. I decided the next best thing was to take a position along Highway 82 by the airport and watch the mules cross the road. The source stated that they crossed the canyon west of the airport. So I found a spot along the road just above the stash property and decided I would lie in, as we called it.

I assembled Joe, Rene, Tom, and Ricardo from our office and Louie, Charlie, and Harold from the highway patrol to assist in the surveillance. I requested a partner on the ground, and Tom quickly volunteered. We both dressed warmly—the nights had been freezing—but little did we know that tonight was going to set a record low. The source said the load would move from Mexico after dark, and we estimated that it would cross Highway 82 around ten P.M.

Around eight, Tom and I were dropped off along the highway, and we laid out our sleeping bags on the ground and waited. We checked in about every thirty minutes on the radio, more to keep ourselves awake than anything else. By midnight we still hadn't seen a thing, and the temperature had dropped to about eighteen degrees.

The surveillance units had already heard on the radio that the temperature was setting new records. I was just about thinking I was turning into a Popsicle and ready to give up when I heard movement. I checked my watch. It was after midnight. I could barely bend my arms to prop myself up to see. I told Tom I heard the walkers, and then, one by one, I saw the mules cross the highway about seventy-five yards in front of me. Our binoculars were so cold you couldn't see through them. Tom radioed the activity to the surveillance units. We finally had the load going to the residence. I counted at least twenty backpackers as they hurried across the road. After we were sure the last mule had crossed, we asked to be picked up. Louie arrived and drove us to Denny's. We were shivering from the cold. All I could do was hold the coffee in my hands and think that if Lola were here tonight, I would let her warm me up. I stayed inside until morning trying to warm up. We were waiting until first light to hit the residence, and I needed every moment to thaw out.

We assembled across the street at the Little Red School House, donned our vests, and briefed the units on the location one last time. Once we entered the driveway, which was a one-car entrance, two agents were going to the side and two agents to the rear, while Louie and Charlie would knock on the door and hopefully obtain a consent search. We didn't want to wait half a day for a search warrant. As we pulled into the property and the agents exited the vehicles, the half dozen dogs started barking, alerting the whole neighborhood. Then the mules who'd been asleep in the back shed took off. They scattered in every direction, running up the hill toward Mexico. We let them go. No one wanted to chase the backpackers.

The owner of the property acted stupid and confused and claimed he didn't know anything, he was just renting the property, and he consented for us to search the grounds. In the back of the property was a chicken coop loaded with hens too cold to get off the nest, and inside were the marijuana bundles. Without further ado we all grabbed a bundle and began loading our trucks with the prize haul. As the last bundles were loaded and we stood at the trucks admiring our latest seizure, we realized we were covered in chicken shit; the entire floor of the chicken house was layered in the gooey slime. The soles of our boots were full, and our jackets, pants, and hands all had the now-thawing shit on them.

Life on the border is full of wonderful surprises. As cold as it was, we had to practically strip out of our clothes before we got into the vehicles and departed. Everyone was laughing at each other, but somehow Rene remained spotless. How in the hell had he managed to be the only one not covered?

THE CARTELS

CARTEL leaders in Mexico are often made larger than life. Musicians sing songs about their exploits and they become idolized by young Mexicans, who dream of becoming a major trafficker to escape the poverty into which they're born. Traffickers win over entire towns by lavishing the people with gifts and throwing huge parties.

In the early 1900s a famous Mexican bandit named Jesus Malverde emerged in Sinaloa. He was said to be the Mexican version of Robin Hood. Jesus Malverde was hanged in Culiacán, Sinaloa, in 1909. Today he is revered as a saint by many of Mexico's drug traffickers. There are shrines erected to his likeness throughout Mexico where drug traffickers pray before smuggling. I have yet to arrest a drug trafficker from Mexico who doesn't wear a Malverde charm around his neck or carry a picture of Malverde in his wallet. I have done numerous search warrants on stash houses and found life-size ceramic heads of Malverde beside shrines in the homes.

Culiacán, Sinaloa, is the cradle where most of Mexico's top drug leaders have been born. Beginning around 1970, the first drug cartel boss to emerge was Miguel Angel Felix Gallardo. Gallardo sold chickens from the back of his bicycle as a boy, then worked the produce fields as a picker, and later he was a police officer. He was assigned as a security officer to the governor of Sinaloa, and Gallardo and the governor became close friends; the governor even baptized Gallardo's son, thus becoming the boy's godfather. Gallardo left the governor's staff to become one of the most powerful drug lords in Mexico.

Gallardo had total immunity from justice in the state of Sinaloa. Besides being best friends with the governor, he had completely infiltrated the police departments. Most of the police commanders were bought and paid for; in exchange, Gallardo was provided protection and intelligence on police actions so he could conduct his business. Gallardo had fourteen warrants for his arrest from different states in Mexico, but he remained free in Sinaloa.

Gallardo was the first drug lord to develop cocaine contacts in Colombia and Bolivia, thus becoming the number one cocaine trafficker in Mexico. He was ruthless and controlling. In 1986, during his peak of power, more than 1,400 people were killed in drug-related violence in the state of Sinaloa. Today, at a time considered the worst in Mexico's history for drug-related killings, there have been only five hundred murders in Sinaloa, perhaps due to violence spread throughout the border towns or the lack of reporting of killings during the 1980s. I've witnessed both periods and I think they're equally bloody, only now the violence is reported by the press every day.

Gallardo formed the first cartel or drug organization, and his list of lieutenants included Rafael Caro Quintero, Joaquin Chapo "Shorty" Guzman, the Arellano Felix brothers, Amado Carrillo Fuentes, and Arturo Beltrán-Leyva.

Caro Quintero, Chapo Guzman, and Amado Carrillo Fuentes all were very poor growing up and did fieldwork for a few dollars a day. Then they worked in the marijuana fields and rose to their positions of power. The Arellano Felix brothers, who were nephews of Gallardo, were the only ones who attended college in Mexico. Within the organizations there were a lot of blood ties by marriage, as in Mafia families.

I have driven the coastal highway in the state of Sinaloa numerous times. It is a beautiful state. As on California's coastal highway, you can see the ocean and the beautiful beaches. Sinaloa has tourist cities like Mazatlán where visitors relax on the beach, play golf, and sip margaritas. However, just a few miles inland is one of the most fertile farming areas in all of Mexico. Driving along the interior roads, I thought of farm country in Kansas and Illinois: large cornfields everywhere, along with fields of tomatoes, watermelons, and other crops. Unfortunately, right along with all the vegetables, a major portion of Mexican marijuana is grown in Sinaloa, harvested and transported to the border in semis right along with the real produce for entry into the United States.

Gallardo's lieutenants were given different areas of operation and the freedom to run them. In return, they paid a percentage of their profits to Gallardo. They worked together and supplied each other with product; the hunger for power and money controlled them, and they rose from peasant farmers to wealth beyond belief.

Caro Quintero had major operations in the states of Zacatecas,

Chihuahua, Sonora, Durango, and Sinaloa. He employed thousands of Mexican peasants to cultivate and work his fields. Some workers had come from Honduras. It was estimated that Caro Quintero's wealth surpassed $650 million.

The Arellano Felix family, with seven brothers and four sisters, controlled Baja California. Californians' insatiable taste for cocaine and marijuana made the Arellano Felix brothers rich beyond their dreams. This was an easy market; with Hollywood and the numerous gangs such as the Crips, the Bloods, and the Hells Angels, moving cocaine from Mexico was easy.

Chapo "Shorty" Guzman also controlled Sinaloa and Sonora. He stood five feet six inches tall but was ruthless and had a Napoleon complex. He was arrested numerous times and always managed to escape. Today he is known as Mexico's most wanted man.

All along the international border, in every border city, the cartels have hundreds of people working for them. There is a hierarchy of command: captains, lieutenants, enforcers who provide protection, financiers who take care of the money, and transporters and mules who move the loads north into the United States.

Amado Carrillo Fuentes, known as "the lord of the skies," moved drug loads by airplane. It was said that he moved four times more cocaine than any other trafficker. He was depicted in the Hollywood movie *Traffic* as the drug lord who had his face altered, and the rumor is that he is still alive. He's supposed to have amassed a fortune of more than $25 billion.

These traffickers have become the most powerful men in Mexico; no one really knows the level of their drug trafficking, money laundering, and political corruption of Mexican officials. Corruption has reached the highest levels in all government offices in Mexico. The list of corrupt officials includes congress-people, governors, army generals, federal judges, federal police, state police, mayors, and city police officers.

The city of Nogales, Sonora, has seen multiple individuals take over the plaza to run the distribution. Jaime Figueroa-Soto was the main captain who worked for Caro Quintero and Chapo Guzman and controlled the trafficking operations in Sonora and Sinaloa. Below him were numerous traffickers like Quemado and, after he disappeared, his replacement, the infamous El Jaimillo.

These members had different duties: recruiting load car drivers, recruiting corrupt law enforcement, buying cars, selecting stash houses, scouting and countersurveillance of the roads, and so forth. The enforcers of the cartels kept a tight rein over their operations.

Another associate was El Negro, who was an indiscriminate killer. He didn't give a shit who he killed. El Negro was sent to kill a rival drug trafficker in the state of Durango, Mexico. He located the man's house but he wasn't home, so to get the trafficker's attention, El Negro beheaded his wife and left her head on the kitchen table.

Then, for spite, El Negro kidnapped the trafficker's two young children, who were six and eight years old, in hopes that their father would show up to get them back. Negro had the kids in the backseat of his vehicle, but the kids were terrified and crying. No wonder, they had just witnessed their mom getting beheaded. After about two hours of driving, El Negro decided they were too much trouble, so he stopped on a bridge high above a river and threw them off one at a time. He enjoyed watching them fall a thousand feet into the ravine and the water below, killing them both.

These bastards all seem to be ruthless psychopaths, each feeding off the sick, disgusting traits of the others. Everything they did was to create fear and intimidate the Mexican people. The Mexican military, members of the Mexican Federal Judicial Police (MFJP), politicians, informants, and citizens always had the same quote when asked why they work with the traffickers: "*Que quieres la plato or plumo*" ("Choose the silver or the lead [bullets]").

Kidnappings in Mexico used to be the number one crime. The prominent citizens of Mexico hired bodyguards and took out multimillion-dollar insurance policies that could pay the ransom if a family member was kidnapped. Most of the kidnappings were committed by corrupt federal and state police officers working for the traffickers. They would kidnap rich, prominent citizens, and once the ransom was paid, usually millions of dollars, they bought cocaine and marijuana to sell to dealers in the United States. They quickly turned a couple million dollars into eight or ten million dollars in one harvest season.

A friend of mine from Hermosillo, Carlos Escalante, was a prominent young businessman. His maternal grandparents were best friends with President Reagan. Carlos was kidnapped and held for ransom. His family paid the kidnappers only to find him two days later, dead on the side of a road leading out to Kino Bay. The kidnapper, the ex-commandant of the state judicial police in Sonora, was eventually caught.

U.S. prisons are core recruitment centers for traffickers. Every time a member of the Mexican cartel is arrested and imprisoned in the United States or Mexico, the prisoners protect them, and then, in exchange for protection, they recruit the most violent offenders with associations on the outside to work for the cartels in Mexico. Once released, the inmates become enforcers and major distributors of drugs for the Mexican cartels.

During the past ten years the cartels have recruited thousands of members from the worst prison gangs in both the United States and Mexico. These vicious gangs include the Border Brothers of Arizona, the La Lineas of Texas, Los Negros from the Mexican prisons, and MS-13 from El Salvador.

The MS-13 gang leaders in El Salvador were the first to start cutting off the hands, feet, and heads of rivals or anyone who betrayed the gang. I believe there is a correlation between the ever-growing number of individuals being decapitated in Mexico and the MS-13 gang members working for the cartels. Decapitation is their trademark. This grotesque form of punishment and intimidation has no doubt spread to the other gangs. Even in the United States, MS-13 uses the same form of torture for its members. While I was in Washington, D.C., the police found a fourteen-year-old Salvadorian girl who was left to die after she had tried to leave the gang. Both of her hands had been amputated at the wrist. Luckily the girl survived.

THE SAN RAFAEL VALLEY

THE desert sun was starting to set. It was October and after a long summer of monsoon rains, the buffalo grass was knee high and had turned brown. The grass was concealing me as I crawled, cradling my shotgun in my arms in front of me, just like a soldier in an old war movie crawling toward the enemy. My actions could get me in trouble, but I wanted revenge. I was pissed off with this no-man's-land border zone. Only two people would be witness to my actions; one was an agent I trusted, and the other was a smuggler.

Earlier we had had another high-speed chase through the San Rafael Valley, and the driver had shot at us. Today I'd had enough; I wasn't going to just drive away and let his actions go unanswered.

I crossed the border into Mexico near where the smuggler had stopped his truck. He must have felt safe after the chase when he escaped back into Mexico. He had arrogantly parked his truck a short distance inside the Mexican border, probably as an insult to the American cops who had been chasing him. My adrenaline was flowing. I scanned the area as I got closer; with my shotgun at the ready, I raced the last few yards to the truck. The truck was abandoned. I couldn't see the smuggler, but I knew he was out there watching and he had a gun. I stayed low and went to the rear of the truck. There were bullet holes in the tailgate. I smiled; we had hit the truck when we shot back. The entire back of the truck was loaded with bundles of marijuana; I guessed approximately two thousand pounds.

I took a deep breath and hesitated for a brief moment; my brain was racing, and the rational side said, *What the hell are you doing?* But my impulsive side said, *What the hell, just do it.* I trusted my partner not to say a word, so the impulsive side won. I took an emergency road flare I had brought with me, took off the plastic cap, scratched the sandpaper side to the flare to ignite it, and laid it in the back of the truck between two large bundles of marijuana. It didn't take long for the bales to start burning.

Earlier in the afternoon, four of us had been working in the San Rafael Valley. In the last ten days at least a half dozen trucks had crossed the border, and at the first sign of surveillance they took off. Because of the remote open range, it's hard to follow anyone out of this area. We wrecked at least five of our government vehicles and had managed to stop only one load driver.

The drivers did whatever it took to make it back into Mexico. Our sources told us they were instructed to protect the loads at all cost. I had heard through informants that if the load drivers lost a load, they were beaten or had a finger cut off as punishment. Obviously this was a good motivational tool, because they were kicking our asses out here. These kids could compete on any racetrack in the United States.

Such was the case this afternoon. The driver fled at the first sign of seeing us, and after trying to stop the vehicle he turned around and headed south toward Mexico. The high-speed pursuit was on. We tried to force him off the road by bumping his rear end, but he raced on even faster. These drivers were good, which was probably why they were hired. There are a lot of racetracks in Mexico, and I thought the traffickers must have recruited the young racecar drivers.

Once again the bastard got away, but this guy was crazy, and after reaching Mexico and thinking he was safe, he stopped a quarter mile beyond the border fence and started shooting at us with a .22 rifle. We had stopped our vehicles well short of the border in anticipation of being shot at, which seems to happen often in the valley. Without saying a word, we broke out our long guns and returned fire. There, in the distance, stood the load driver at the front of his truck, feeling real macho and safe in Mexico, bragging to himself that he'd shot at the narcs.

His world changed quickly. First one agent then the other took aim and fired at the vehicle. The distance was too far away to tell how we did, but we could hear the sound of the rounds hitting the truck.

Most of us had AR-15s with thirty-round magazines. We always loaded the magazine with a tracer bullet every third round, so with three agents shooting at the same time it looked like fireworks going off. The driver fled on foot, running south and disappearing into a canyon a short distance away.

We decided to clear the area; one unit drove south toward

Sonoita, Arizona, and I decided I would drive west toward an area known as Washington Camp. As I was driving off, I stopped, thinking, *Not today.* This was the third time this month we'd chased a vehicle out here and it had raced back to Mexico. Not today; there was no fucking way I was going to drive off and leave the truck there. The lights went on in my head (perhaps they flickered); I thought, *What the hell, the driver's gone, the load vehicle is parked only about a quarter mile into Mexico.* The situation sucked and just didn't seem right; it was time for some old-time justice.

I told my partner to give me a few minutes and not ask any questions.

He said, "What the hell are you thinking?"

I said, "It's better you don't know."

Then he asked, "What are you going to do now?"

"Just cover me," I said. "You'll see what I'm going to do."

At least then if I got jammed up, he wouldn't get in trouble. If he didn't know what I was going to do, he couldn't stop me. I waited a few minutes to be sure the other agents were over the mountain and out of sight. I learned long ago that when you decide to do something outside the rule book, it's best not to have an audience.

I ran to the border and then crawled across the border slowly toward the truck. After I threw the flare into the truck, I waited just long enough to see the marijuana bales begin to burn, and then just as before I sprinted back north to the United States. I turned around when I got to the safety of my vehicle, and there in the distance was one big-ass beautiful fire. The scene was surreal as the truck and marijuana were engulfed in flames. My partner had covered me the whole time, his rifle aimed toward the truck. We looked at each other and I saw his sign of approval as we both grinned. Silently we drove off and didn't say another word about the incident. We both knew the war on drugs was a farce, but today we had won a small battle and achieved satisfaction.

Years later I learned that I wasn't the first agent to set a vehicle on fire in Mexico. Years earlier when Layne was a young agent, he was involved in a high-speed chase through the San Rafael Valley. In the excitement of the chase, Layne and his partner pursued a truck a half mile across the border, well into Mexico. The truck finally blew a tire and crashed into a ditch, and Layne and his partner jumped out and arrested the driver. They couldn't move the truck, so they off-loaded the marijuana from the truck into their G-ride, as many bundles as they could carry; they even filled the backseat next to the violator.

Suddenly Layne noticed another car approaching, and as they looked up, they realized that they were in Mexico. The second vehicle started shooting at them. Layne quickly returned fire, and the second vehicle sped away. Layne knew they needed to get the hell out of Mexico; they couldn't take all the marijuana in their vehicle, and they'd left about a thousand pounds of marijuana in the truck.

As they were about to leave, Layne's partner said that old Chevrolet trucks had a gas tank behind the driver's seat; he took a Buck knife, stabbed the gas tank several times, and watched the gas run into the cab and onto the ground by the truck. Layne flicked a match into the cab, and it exploded. Leaving the truck ablaze and the load of marijuana engulfed in flames, they quickly drove back to the United States.

They, too, were proud of themselves. They had arrested the load driver and recovered most of the marijuana. In their excitement, they radioed the office that they had captured one violator and recovered about eight hundred pounds of marijuana. However, before they cleared the San Rafael Valley, a Customs helicopter from the air unit in Tucson flew over the area and radioed that there was a huge fire in Mexico. Of course, being curious, the helicopter pilot flew over the site and radioed that a truck was on fire and there appeared to be marijuana burning in the back. Hell, the crew on the helicopter hovered so low they could smell the marijuana burning.

Nothing was said about the incident until the next day when they arraigned the violator in court. The U.S. Attorney notified the special agent in charge (SAC) that it appeared the defendant was arrested in Mexico, and bringing the guy to the United States could be considered kidnapping.

Layne and his partner were called up to the SAC's office and received one royal ass-chewing. The SAC told them they should go to jail for kidnapping, and this situation had created an international incident. The prisoner was ordered released from jail, and Layne was ordered to drive the guy to the border and release him. The thrill of victory turned into the agony of defeat. Layne's partner, who had ridden his motorcycle to the SAC's office, was so distraught that he wrecked his bike on the way home and broke his arm.

Layne didn't talk about this story often, but he said, "Remember, if you do something stupid, it's best to keep it a secret until the statute of limitations runs out."

* * *

THE San Rafael Valley stretches twenty miles along the border and encompasses the area east of Nogales from Washington Camp to the Huachuca Mountains. The headwaters of the Santa Cruz River originate in the valley and flow south into Mexico before reentering the United States by Kino Springs near the western city limits of Nogales. Three dirt roads connect to the valley from Highway 82. The largest ranch in the San Rafael Valley is the Sharpe Ranch. The old ranch house itself was used as a set in several John Wayne movies and was the ranch in the famous musical *Oklahoma*. The only barrier separating the San Rafael Valley from Mexico is a barbed-wire fence with several gates in it, as well as a cattle guard in the middle of the valley known as the T, which was a section of dirt road with the north-south lane in Mexico and the east-west road in the U.S. forming the shape of a capital T. This was the only area where the smuggler could drive through to Mexico without running into the fence. Years earlier, a local rancher had installed the cattle guard at the line to keep the onslaught of smugglers from cutting his fence or leaving a gate open.

The drug smugglers used several routes to escape detection. One road led them north past Parker Canyon Lake to Sonoita, Arizona. Another ran up the middle of the valley over Canelo Pass to Patagonia, Arizona, and back west toward Nogales. We used sensors to determine the direction of travel and would respond and wait for the load vehicles. Other times, when sources called, we lay in at various points to intercept the vehicles.

The traffickers were so brazen that they used semis to cross the dope through the San Rafael Valley. In one incident, two semis were caught with more than twenty thousand pounds of marijuana each. Smugglers used this area daily. The traffickers didn't hesitate to ram law enforcement vehicles or exchange gun-fire. For the most part, each agent worked alone until he needed help with surveillance and the load car was moving, but the valley was different. Because of the number of shootings and the deaths of two agents, the bosses mandated that no one worked the valley alone.

One tragic incident resulted in the deaths of two Customs agents, Bud and Bo. They were conducting surveillance in the San Rafael Valley and saw a truck cross the border. Believing the truck was probably loaded, they watched as it moved closer. It was around three in the afternoon, and with binoculars they could observe the bundles in the back. Bud and Bo were partially hidden in a tree line, waiting as the driver made his way north.

They radioed for assistance, and agents began responding from the Nogales office. The response time is easily thirty minutes. Slowly the truck approached; the driver saw them, and laid the pedal to the metal. They started chasing the driver north over the dirt road toward Patagonia. The dust from the road was so bad, they had to back off a couple hundred feet. The driver was traveling at up to eighty miles per hour. Then the driver made an abrupt U-turn on the dirt road and sped back south in an attempt to return to Mexico.

As the driver sped directly past Bud and Bo, he fired off a few rounds at them. Bud and Bo returned fire at the load driver and continued their pursuit. Dust was flying up from the road; they were now traveling faster than eighty on a single-lane dirt road heading back toward the border.

Without notice, the driver stopped. Bud and Bo realized too late that they were driving right into an ambush. They stopped right in front of the smuggler, who started shooting. Bud and Bo began returning fire from inside the vehicle. Bud grabbed his shotgun, but as he attempted to shoot it out the driver's-side window, he was hit and dropped the gun to the ground. The smuggler grabbed his shotgun and fired on Bo inside.

The load driver was shot as well but somehow managed to get to his vehicle and drive a short distance away before crashing into a ravine, where he died from his gunshot wound. Bud and Bo had radioed their position before the deadly shooting occurred. Sadly, they were found dead by the responding agents.

No one will ever know the exact truth, but the crime scene was examined over and over, and the investigating agents knew the San Rafael Valley and the perils of working on the southwest border. The official report contains a lot of second-guessing and *what-if*s, but you can't judge someone's actions under extreme circumstances.

After Bud and Bo were killed, the bosses mandated that surveillance in the San Rafael area required two agents, and for good reason. This hasn't stopped the shootings. Since Bud and Bo were killed, the agents and traffickers in the area have exchanged plenty of gunfire. Fortunately no one else has been killed.

TOM loved working the San Rafael Valley, and despite the policy that no one was supposed to work there alone, Hard Head Tom usually did. Tom would drive up to the edge of the valley, parking at the old cemetery by a place known as Lochiel. Seldom was there a day when a load vehicle didn't come across the border there.

One afternoon, Tom observed a Jeep Wagoneer illegally entering the United States through a ranch gate just west of Lochiel. It headed east toward the Huachuaca Mountains and the Coronado Pass. Tom began to follow the vehicle and called over the radio for assistance. Immediately other units from the area began to respond. Of course the supervisor went ballistic, knowing Tom was out there alone, but it wasn't the first or last time any of us had ever done it. The driver of the Jeep observed Tom and hit the gas. Tom activated the red lights and siren on his full-size Ford Bronco, but the guy drove faster and headed toward the area known as The T, crossing into Mexico about ten miles east of where he had entered the United States.

Tom knew the guy was headed there and tried several times to cut him off. Tom, with just his one arm, managed to drive, talk on the radio, and prepare for a gun battle. He was amazing. This was nothing new to Tom; he had more ability with one arm than most men have with both. He qualified with an AR-15 rifle, an automatic shotgun, and every pistol made. He was an avid hunter and sportsman and could shoot as well as anyone.

The smuggler refused to stop and crossed into Mexico at The T. Tom stopped at the border fence next to the cattle guard and watched. To Tom's amazement the guy drove only about a hundred feet into Mexico and stopped. What was this load driver doing?

Tom's first reaction was panic; he grabbed his rifle, anticipating gunfire. Instead, to his surprise, the driver climbed onto the top of his load vehicle and unbuckled his pants, dropping them around his knees, and flashed Tom a big bare ass. The crazy SOB was mooning Tom. The load driver began yelling insults in Spanish and giving Tom the one-finger salute. The final insult was when the driver grabbed his crotch and wagged his wiener at Tom, the Mexican sign for *Fuck you.*

Without thinking, Tom reacted to the gestures; he jumped into his vehicle and floored the gas pedal. The Ford Bronco sped into Mexico, covering the hundred feet before the smuggler could react; he watched in horror, pants around his ankles, as the Bronco slammed into his vehicle. Luckily Tom had applied the brakes at the last second just before hitting the Jeep. The load driver was thrown from the top of his vehicle and knocked head over heels onto the desert floor. Tom thought for a second he might have killed the driver; he grabbed his rifle, exited his vehicle, and approached the man, who was getting to his knees. The driver looked up in a daze to see Tom standing over him with an M16 rifle; he must have wondered, *Who the hell is this one-armed crazy person?* The man immediately attempted to run but tripped on his pants, tangled around his ankles.

He pulled up his pants with one hand as he tried to hobble off, fearing that the crazy American was going to kill him. Tom watched the driver shamble away and then began to laugh. Then reality hit. *Holy shit*, he thought, *I'm in Mexico.* Tom quickly looked around, jumped into the Ford Bronco, slammed it into reverse, and drove back to the United States about a quarter mile from the border for safety.

Then he checked out the front of his G-ride. It was none the worse for wear; the new dent just blended in with the dozen other dents and dings he already had on his vehicle from four-wheeling all over the desert. Within ten minutes, Joe arrived and made the usual inquiries about how Tom had seen the vehicle, where it crossed, and then, why the smuggler had stopped his vehicle so close to the border. Tom told Joe the story of the mooning smuggler standing on the top of his vehicle and said the guy lost his balance, slipped off the roof, and then walked away on foot for some reason. Joe and Tom waited and watched the Jeep for another fifteen minutes until the smuggler, realizing Tom had returned to the United States, returned to his Jeep and hauled ass into Mexico.

Tom never told the real story, and only a few knew the truth. For a long time the agents called the San Rafael Valley "Moon Valley." It's the little things that make agents smile and chuckle when they think about what really happens out in the field. Sometimes simple justice is more satisfying than a prison sentence, and it's achieved in small ways.

REFLECTING back, I know the older agents knew of our antics. They were constantly telling us not to do things because they had done the same crazy things, twisted and broken the same rules. They were simply wiser with age and trying to protect us. They had been fortunate not to have gotten in trouble, but the new generation of agents was changing, and the old rule of keeping your mouth shut was over. Internal Affairs had started a new campaign to recruit fresh new agents in the training academy. These new, young agents would be the eyes and ears for the Office of Internal Affairs and they reported misdeeds directly to them. These new spies were called field associates.

Once I became a supervisor, I often ignored similar acts of spontaneous rebellion by agents in my group when they overstepped the thin line between reason and reaction. They also learned quickly that it's best not tell your supervisor every detail of an operation. I was now the one who had to say no. I never told my agents about my own crazy antics for fear that they would want to do the same to copy me. I knew I had escaped death many times and had had a guardian angel up to this point in my life.

RIDE 'EM, COWBOYS

I was talking to a source who said a horse load was being crossed and picked up in an area called Rancho Grande, an old hotel site that at one time was going to be a resort for John Wayne but never got finished. It had burned down and all that was left were a few large quarry stones and bricks on a hilltop lot.

The lot was one of the highest points in the area, and you could see all the way to the Mexico border fence and beyond. It was a popular spot for stargazing and drinking. Hell, our group often drank there after a long surveillance—something the police referred to as *choir practice*. There was constant vehicle traffic coming and going, especially on the weekends. I checked out the area, and about thirty feet below the hill there were signs of horse activity and the usual signs of burlap bags and twine where the bundles had been tied to the horses.

I started checking the area every day, then took tree branches and brushed the area down to clear the old horse tracks so I would see new signs. I finally determined that the loads were crossing on a Wednesday night.

The idea of spending this much time for a small horse load was stupid, but for some idiotic reason I had decided I was going to catch the horses. I considered it a challenge. I once heard an old agent discuss how to catch horse loads in the canyons by Summit Motorway. The elaborate plan involved two sets of ropes with fabric flags tied to them stretched out on the ground and covered with leaves and sand. The location had to have lots of trees to make a square corral. Then, once the horses crossed some imaginary line, the agents pulled the ropes chest high on the trees, trapping the horses in a makeshift corral. The operation would take at least a half dozen agents lying in.

It simply wasn't feasible and never happened. To my knowledge no one had ever caught a horse-riding smuggler. I wanted to prove something, accomplish something no one else had been able to do. I was going to catch a horse. When I got a wild burr up my ass to do something, I had to try it.

I asked Joe to assist me, and he seemed really excited at the idea; he'd been buried with reports and needed a good stakeout for a stress reliever. I told Joe I had some ground rules before I would take him. I politely asked him not to bathe or apply cologne; I knew it didn't matter how well we were hidden, his cologne could be smelled a thousand yards off. Joe agreed, but I'm sure the thought of not showering drove him crazy.

Joe was a meticulous person; when he worked all day and had to work later on that night, he drove home for an hour to shower, shave, and change clothes before returning to work. Every time I worked with Joe and went to his house to get him, I had to wait for him to get ready. Joe jumped in the vehicle smelling like a French whore; his cologne saturated your senses. Joey the Arm believed in being well dressed, but he was also a professional. He took care of his equipment; he emptied out his Sig Sauer's .45 magazine daily to relieve the pressure on the spring, and his vehicle was always gassed up, oil checked and ready to go. The equipment in his vehicle's trunk looked like a display in a department store. Joe was the original Boy Scout in the sense that he was always prepared.

I was determined to get the horses; I really didn't give a shit about whether I caught the smugglers or seized the marijuana. No one in our office had ever grabbed a Mexican cowboy's horse out from under him. I knew this was dangerous; the cowboys carried pistols and rifles, and to lose a horse would be the ultimate shame. The operation had to be timed and care taken not to get shot or have the cowboy trample us with the horse.

Right at dusk we put on our camouflage gear, parked a quarter mile from the surveillance spot I had picked out, and walked in to wait for activity. I hadn't given much thought to intercepting a load vehicle, but I knew that the cowboy transporting the dope would be pissed if I took his horses. Being from Chicago, I knew dick about horses; I had done one-hour trail rides but nothing more. Riding horses was never pleasant to me. I assumed Joe knew about horses; hell, he'd been here long before me. That assumption was a big mistake.

I picked a spot I thought was going to be thirty feet from where the horses were tied up. We selected a good hiding position and waited. Joe didn't get into the field much and was real talkative and making jokes; he always made light of things and was easy to work with.

Within an hour I could hear the faint sounds of horses clip-clopping on the rocky trail, heading our way. Our concealment was excellent, and unless the traffickers had night vision, we wouldn't be seen. As the horses came closer and closer, Joe was getting more excited, and I had to motion to him to be silent. They came right up to within twenty feet of where we were. There was just one rider leading another horse. He was a true Mexican *caballero* ("cowboy"); he had the cowboy hat and Mexican boots with the angled heel. I had tried these boots on once in Mexico and never could figure out how anyone could wear those boots. I could see two burlap bundles on each horse. The horses knew we were there; they snorted and stomped, trying to back away, but the cowboy made the mistake of ignoring this signal of our presence. He looked all around but couldn't see anything. He unhooked the marijuana bundles from his horse, let them hit the ground, and then dismounted. After looping the horses' reins on a tree branch, he unhooked the bundles of marijuana from the saddle horn of the second horse. Then he picked up all four bundles and quickly took off to the top of the hill. He was easily carrying around 120 pounds of marijuana on his shoulders.

I motioned for Joe to wait. I didn't want to try to grab the horses too soon and risk a fight with the cowboy, in case he was armed. I also didn't want him to jump back in the saddle and be run over by a stampeding horse. There is nothing more danger-ous than a cowboy who can make his horse charge you and tram-ple you, or spin and kick the living shit out of you. I had heard these stories before from old-timers and wanted no part of it. I waited until I thought the cowboy was a safe distance away, then motioned for Joe to follow me. I quickly went to the first horse, a beautiful palomino, and motioned for Joe to grab the other horse by the reins.

I was excited that we had both horses as we led them up the hill to the top of Rancho Grande to see if we could find a load vehicle. Just as we reached the top, two cars sped off. I saw the cowboy standing there staring at us. He looked like someone caught with his pants down, sitting on the crapper. Reality struck him and he took off on foot toward Mexico. I could just imagine his cussing and yelling all the way to the ranch in Mexico. This cowboy wasn't used to walking in those stupid boots, either, and the terrain was very rough with hills and as rocky and hard to cross as the Mexican Sierra Madre. He'd have to explain to the owner of the ranch how he lost two good horses and saddles.

I guessed that the marijuana was loaded in the small pickup truck speeding away. I radioed for assistance, and Charlie from DPS responded. He managed to find and stop the pickup, but it was only a teenage couple playing kissy face and making out. They had been too busy fogging up the windows to notice anything, and when they heard the noise they got scared and raced out of the area.

So there we were, one agent from Chicago, another from New York, with two horses. No problem; we would just mount the horses and look cool sitting in the saddle when the other units arrived. Joe and I had both ridden horses before, no big deal. I took the reins, put my foot in the stirrup, and was going to throw my leg over to climb into the saddle. The palomino turned toward me and started trying to bite me. I moved away to avoid being bitten, and then he decided to turn in a circle. So there I was with my foot in the stirrup, moving like a merry-go-round; this pathetic circus lasted about ten minutes.

Joe was having about the same success with his horse. He would put one foot in the stirrup, and the horse would kick and buck. We spent fifteen minutes cussing and fighting those horses. We must have looked like comedians; it was definitely not our crowning moment.

Finally, Carlos arrived on the scene and we explained the situation.

Carlos laughed and said, "Just put your foot in the stirrup and get up." I said, "Really? If it's that easy, show us how a Texan does it."

Carlos quickly took control of the situation. He grabbed the reins of Joe's horse and told him, "Mount up."

Joe did, and the horse didn't move. Carlos grabbed the reins of the palomino and mounted up. Carlos slapped the ass end of Joe's horse and off they went. Carlos and Joe rode the horses back to the office. I was done with horses; I thought the palomino should be butchered and sent to a dog food factory.

As Carlos and Joe rode to the office, they came to a cattle guard and had to dismount the horses to go around the rails. Carlos told Joe, "Go low," meaning to go to the lowest side of the cattle guard. Joe thought Carlos meant he should crouch down, so on bent knees Joe walked like a duck, leading the horse. Carlos was still laughing his ass off when they got to the office. Joe was the brunt of many a good laugh later as Carlos demonstrated Joe doing the duck walk while leading the horse.

We put the horses in the vehicle compound and called it a night. Joe and I arrived early to the office to knock out the paperwork and try to figure out what to do with the horses. Yeah, it was a great plan. I got two horses, but they were not like a vehicle we could just tow off to the storage lot. The lot had the two horses and a hell of a lot of horse shit.

After some research we called the county livestock officer; he arrived with a horse trailer and rounded up the horses, and once again it was off to the next case.

DONUT'S BAD DAY

ALL of us have had that day when everything seems to go wrong, but when an agent has one of those days, the result can be disastrous, funny, and rewarding at the same time, depending on where you're standing.

I had received information from a source about a dump truck being used by a local group of smugglers. The traffickers had built a special compartment in the bottom of the truck that held two thousand pounds of marijuana. The hidden trapdoor on the bottom of the dump truck was activated by a hydraulic control. The traffickers would then load the top of the dump truck with sand. The source was really informative, providing the time of pickup, the address of a ranch in Tucson where the dope was going to be delivered, and all the names of the violators. Once we checked all the names in the computer, we discovered that the violator and address were already the subject of investigation by a Tucson agent named Don, who was new and had come from San Francisco, California.

Don was a nice enough guy, but any imperfections give you an instant nickname. Don's body was a thing to behold; he resembled a pear with legs and a shrunken head. His most distinct part was his large stomach, which looked like a donut attached to his feet and upper body. We nicknamed him "Donut."

The creator of *The Simpsons* must have seen Donut somewhere and taken a picture of him, because Donut and Homer Simpson are identical twins. Donut was quite impressed with himself. He arrived at the district with a holier-than-thou attitude, telling everyone that he thought the special agents in Arizona weren't up to his standards.

Donut had a source in the same group that I did, but his source knew the drop-off location as well, so we decided to use the Nogales agents to convoy the dump truck north to Tucson; then, with the assistance of Tucson agents, we would secure the ranch and Donut would write the search warrant and present the case for prosecution.

In Nogales, the narcotics squad watched the dump truck all evening, and at midnight they saw twenty-five backpackers arrive at the yard and slowly load the truck. The next morning, a Sunday, the truck was loaded with sand and departed the yard for Tucson. A helicopter was used for surveillance, as well as mobile agents in vehicles. The ranch was remote and accessible only by a single-lane dirt road. Once the dump truck got off the main road at Irvington in Tucson, the helicopter took over the surveillance and watched the truck arrive at the ranch.

The helicopter guided the agents, wearing raid gear marked front and rear with *Police/U.S. Customs*. They swarmed into the ranch. Each building was cleared and all the occupants of the ranch were rounded up and secured until Donut obtained the search warrant.

Because it was a weekend, Donut and another agent had to take his affidavit for the search warrant to the home of the U.S. federal magistrate on duty for her signature rather than go to the closed courthouse. They arrived at the home of the magistrate, a tough woman who was well respected by the agents. If they did their job right, she treated them well. It was a lovely Sunday morning; the sun was shining and she was in a great mood and welcomed the two agents into her home, offered them coffee, and was happy as she scrutinized the search warrant and asked a few questions and then signed it.

The agents were just about to leave when the doorbell rang and the magistrate invited the third person into her home. The younger man told Donut he had a phone call.

The magistrate said, "I don't believe I know you, young man. Are you a new agent?"

Donut answered for the man, saying the fatal words, "He's not an agent, he's my informant."

The magistrate told the informant to get the hell out of her house and then proceeded to admonish Donut for about an hour. The magistrate was only about five feet four, but she was a firecat. Hell hath no fury like a federal magistrate scorned.

Donut had just committed a cardinal sin. Had the magistrate not respected the hardworking agents who'd spent their weekend on surveillance, she would have shredded the warrant right then and there.

Back at the ranch, the agents waiting at the residence were getting pissed off. What the hell was taking so long? Finally Donut arrived, completely shaken up; he couldn't even concentrate. He got anything but sympathy from the surveillance group; instead he got another barrage of insults and bullshit.

The warrant was finally served. We searched all the outer buildings and property because supposedly there were large metal tanks under the horse stalls that contained additional marijuana. The owner had bought a water tanker truck, taken off the tank, cut access doors on the top, then dug out the hole with a backhoe and buried it in the corral. Supposedly the top of the tank was about three feet belowground. This was great, except there were two large corrals and about twenty horse stalls to check. The corrals and stalls were deep with horse shit. We dug holes all over the property, our eyes tearing from the ammonia smell of horse urine. We failed to find the buried tank. The Tucson agents decided to come back the next day with a backhoe to dig more.

Several subjects, including the ranch owner, were arrested. The agents gathered their gear and went home for a rest. It had been a long case, but a significant amount of narcotics were seized along with the ranch and dozens of vehicles. The traffickers were big-time and had been responsible for moving tons of marijuana from Nogales to Tucson.

Donut took charge of the ranch owner, who was his main target. He took the guy to the county jail for interviewing and booking. The federal magistrate, who was still making telephone calls, had contacted Donut's bosses and chewed their asses out. The shit rolled quickly back down the hill. Donut's supervisor and the assistant special agent in charge (ASAC) chewed him out. Donut was having the worst day of his life.

On this job shit happens more than we would like at times. Just

when Donut thought he couldn't have a worse day, the really bad
news hit the office. Donut, in his beleaguered emotional state,
completed the interview and booked the defendant into jail; however, Donut not only gave the jailer the crook's personal property
(wallet, belt, rings, etc.) but also accidentally included his own
investigative case notes and complete details about the entire investigation: the source's information, how the case started in Nogales, who called who—everything.

The defendant's lawyer arrived at the jail the next morning to
talk to his client and go over the case and bio data sheet when he
discovered the bounty of the entire investigative case. He seized
the moment and called Donut to cut a deal. The defense attorney
said he would reveal everything in court unless the case against
his client was dismissed. Once again Donut had to tell his supervisor the great news; it went back up the chain of command, all
the way to the top, and the shit rolled back down and landed on
Donut's head. The case was dismissed; the trafficker was released
from jail and told to take a walk, but unfortunately so was Donut.

The federal magistrate wrote a mandate to the special agent
in charge of Arizona stating that Donut was persona non grata
and wasn't allowed to appear in, testify in, or enter her courtroom
ever again. Within thirty days Donut was transferred back to San
Francisco.

The tradition in Customs is *fuck up and move up*. Within a few
years Donut was transferred to Washington, D.C., and promoted
to a GS-15 director level, the equivalent to an assistant special
agent in charge in the field. Only in the government service can
someone screw up being a field agent and be promoted to head
butt-kisser at headquarters.

Laughing at ourselves and the unfortunate situations we get

into is just human nature. These situations are often the best training aid. We learned from our mistakes and the mistakes of others every day. Hopefully, those mistakes didn't cost an agent's life. We laughed at our blunders, but we made damn sure to pay more attention next time.

OLD AND NEW FRIENDS

THE norm for new special agents is that your post of duty must be at least five hundred miles from your hometown. Ricardo was the exception to the rule. Prior to being an agent, Ricardo was a Customs inspector, working at the Nogales Grand Avenue POE. One of the principal problems leading to corruption at the ports of entry is the fact that they hire local people. Most individuals born and raised in a border town like Nogales, Arizona, have relatives on both sides of the border. In the Mexican culture, a second cousin is as close as a brother is to most gringo Americans. Local people often have relatives who work for smugglers. I have arrested the sons of several Customs inspectors for trafficking in narcotics.

Ricardo was really outgoing and loved to joke around, party, and drink. A friend of his seized this opportunity and asked Ricardo out for a night on the town. They went to one of the local hangouts and proceeded to party down. As the evening progressed, the friend finally asked the big question. He told Ricardo he was working for a group of smugglers across the line who needed to move lots of dope, and they would pay Ricardo big money, thirty thousand dollars per load, if he would let it through the POE.

Ricardo was caught in a dilemma a lot of Customs inspectors face: remain friends, say nothing and look the other way, or do the right thing? The corruption problem at the POE at the time was paramount. Every other inspector is local; they have family members on both sides of the border, and a lot of them are in the drug business. Ricardo shrugged his friend off and said, "Let me think about it."

For Ricardo, the decision wasn't hard. He wasn't going to betray his badge and oath of office. He was honest, he had served in Vietnam, and he was proud of the position of trust that the government had bestowed on him. He was not going to throw away his career and hard work for anyone.

But Ricardo knew that other Customs inspectors were passing loads. He'd heard rumors and knew that some were living well beyond their means. He suspected at least eight who were working the POE with him. So did others, but catching them was the hard part. Inspectors had a lot of latitude in how they performed their duties. They did not have to inspect every vehicle, and others were simply lazy or doing a poor job. Loads were crossing the POE every day undetected. The traffickers had the advantage of having individuals known as spotters at a bar known as the Border Tavern overlooking the POE.

Ricardo notified the Customs Office of Internal Affairs in Tucson and the local Customs Office of Investigations.

The Office of Internal Affairs turned over the case to the assistant special agent in charge in Tucson to investigate. The ASAC took his time and advised Ricardo to go slow and then set up a great operational plan. The ASAC was going to try to get all the players in this organization. Ricardo was sworn to secrecy; he was to tell no one, not even his wife. He was to report to work and wait for the friend to call again. Within a week the friend did call and asked Ricardo out again for another night on the town. Ricardo contacted ASAC, and a group of agents came down from Tucson to set up surveillance. Ricardo was wired up with a body recorder and instructed on how to proceed. He was to extract as much information about the group as possible without seeming too aggressive. Ricardo did just that; he drank and was as casual and cool as possible under the circumstances.

The friend told Ricardo he would give Ricardo half the money, fifteen thousand dollars, up front, and then the rest after the load crossed the port. He was overjoyed at having an inspector in his pocket, not realizing that everything he said was being recorded. After partying, the friend went straight south into Mexico to tell his boss about the wonderful news and brag about his success. Meanwhile, Ricardo spent most of the night getting debriefed by Don and translating the conversation from Spanish.

Two days later the friend contacted Ricardo again and said he wanted to meet in thirty minutes. Ricardo stalled the guy, saying he was home with sick kids. Ricardo immediately called Don and gave him time to get from Tucson to Nogales to cover the meeting and set up surveillance. Don arrived and placed the body wire on Ricardo. Things were moving as planned.

Don had already obtained a court order to get telephone records for the friend's cell phone and was tracing all the calls and identifying all the numbers. Through a local contact in the

Mexican phone company, we were able to get all the Mexican phone records. Don did a great job of surveillance, and slowly the trap was set.

Ricardo's friend paid the fifteen thousand dollars, and Ricardo gave him a front placard with leopards on it to use for the front of the load car. Arizona only uses one rear plate unlike most states. The traffickers would place the placard inside the windshield or on the front of the vehicle to identify the load vehicle as it approached Ricardo's lane. The very next day, the friend called and the first load was sent to cross around eight in the evening. Don and his crew set up a stationary surveillance, instead of a moving one, so as not to be burned by any heat vehicles. Usually the load vehicle is followed by a second vehicle known as a *heat vehicle* to see if it gets detained at the POE. In a stationary surveillance, each agent is parked and calls out the vehicle and direction as it passes them, in this case until it got on Interstate 19 and turned north.

As agreed, the first load vehicle approached and was crossed, and Ricardo made things look normal to the other inspectors. No one knew. The agents followed the vehicle to Tucson and the load was delivered. The load house was kept under surveillance. That night the friend called Ricardo and arranged a meeting to pay Ricardo the rest of the money. The meeting was videotaped and recorded. Ricardo received the rest of the money and advised his friend to cross three loads at once; the first car would have the leopard placard on the front, and the two cars behind would be loaded as well.

The friend was delighted, and the next day he paid Ricardo fifty thousand dollars for crossing three loads. That night at seven,

Ricardo was sent to the line, and the spotter in Mexico directed the vehicles to enter lane three, where Ricardo was working. The first car approached and was passed, along with the following two vehicles. Down the road they drove, into the waiting trap. Don had the highway patrol stop one vehicle, and the remaining two were followed to Tucson. Don and his group were waiting with a search warrant in hand. Then Ricardo contacted his friend to request the rest of the money. The friend came to the prearranged location but, to his surprise, was met by Don and several agents.

Ricardo earned the Commissioner's Award for his act of honor. He also earned something more valuable: the trust of the agents and, in particular, the trust of Don, who became an assistant special agent in charge and mentor to Ricardo.

Ricardo had developed a great source named Hector who provided detailed information on loads crossing straight through the POE. Hector was deeply involved in the organization and played the game both ways. He provided enough information to keep Ricardo and all the bosses in the office happy and also arranged for tons of dope from his organization to be smuggled through the POE. Hector provided us with at least two loads a week.

Hector worked directly for the Jaime Figueroa-Soto organization. He was extremely smart, and the loads he told us about belonged to the other organizations. He was eliminating the competition and crossing his own merchandise. One of the major players he told Ricardo about was Luis Villegas, a local kid who was all charm. Luis was a young, good-looking man, around twenty-three years old, who knew most of the inspectors because he had gone to high school with the young inspectors and police officers. Luis's main job was to recruit crooked inspectors for the traffickers. At this time it was estimated at least ten immigration and Customs inspectors were on the take and working with the traffickers to smuggle loads through the POE.

Hector was one of the first real sources to give up loads crossing through the POE, but then again he was eliminating the competition so his group would take over the plaza. Hector and Ricardo developed a great relationship, which boosted Ricardo's career. Hector would call and give Ricardo the exact vehicle description and license plate numbers and the time the vehicle was going to cross. Hector didn't always know the lane or the inspector, but we had enough to establish surveillance.

At this point we hesitated telling any supervisor at the POE about our operation. However, the district director was in charge of everyone in Arizona, so he was told, and then, of course, we had to tell the Office of Internal Affairs because it involved an employee. They, of course, had to tell the FBI, who claimed lead on any employees who were corrupt.

So the simple operation became larger by the day, and the FBI and Internal Affairs didn't have any resources to provide for surveillance or day-to-day activity, but Ricardo was instructed to call the second he was ready to arrest an employee.

When Hector called, the entire office rushed to get in place. Two agents had an eye on the POE to try to photograph the load vehicle entering. Surveillance units would be set up north of the POE; one unit was on Morley Avenue, and I parked on Crawford Street at the corner where Interstate 19 begins, just before Burger King.

We had a good routine going, and time and time again we successfully followed the load vehicles away from the POE and arrested the driver. At times, Internal Affairs told us to let the driver go if he cooperated and gave up information on a corrupt inspector. This wasn't a short-term operation; it lasted more than nine months. We had a routine; Ricardo would announce that Hector had called, and we dropped everything we were working on and set up at our surveillance locations.

One afternoon we rushed out to set up after one of these phone calls, and I went to the location downtown. I parked, reclined my seat, and began the waiting game. About ten minutes later a car pulled into the driveway of the business where I was parked, and a woman got out and went inside. About five minutes later she came back outside, walked up to my passenger-side window, and knocks on the glass. I rolled down the window and she said, "You can't park here; this is for customers only."

I said, "Ma'am, there are no designated parking signs, this is a public street, and I'm not blocking your driveway."

She became irate; it was obvious she had been drinking. She said, "You better move your vehicle or I'm calling the police."

I smiled, showed her my badge, and said politely, "I am the police; thank you for notifying me."

She stormed off. I watched her hips sway as she paraded back inside the business; she had a great backside. Within fifteen minutes I saw her coming back toward my vehicle. I was thinking, *What the fuck now, why can't this lady just back off?*

Once again she tapped the passenger-side window and said, "You need to talk to my sister; she's on the phone."

I answered, "No, I don't need to talk to your sister."

Then her tone changed; she smiled with a twinkle in her eye as she said, "Please talk to her."

This was a different approach; something about her smile was seductive. The wild-animal instinct in me had been awakened. I looked at her, thinking about the possibilities. She wasn't unattractive; she had long hair to the middle of her back and she was looking good in her high heels.

So what the hell, I said, "Okay." I radioed the units for someone to cover my location. Rene answered and said he would rotate to my location and cover I-19. I grabbed my portable radio and followed her inside. Sure enough, once inside, she handed me the phone. The sister asked me my name, and I told her, "Patricio."

She asked if I worked for Customs as a narc.

I said, "Yes."

She said, "Oh I know who you are. I've seen you at Mr. C's restaurant-bar." She told me her name was Sandra; I remembered her. She was smoking hot; hell, every guy wanted her.

Then she said, "Let me talk to my sister again." I handed the phone over to the sister, who said her name was Maria.

I made a waving sign with my hand saying good-bye and started to leave when Maria stopped talking to her sister and said, "Wait a minute." She laughed again and hung up the phone. Maria then walked up to me and said, "I'm sorry, I've had a few drinks at lunch."

"No problem," I answered.

"My sister told me all about you." Then without warning she leaned in closer to my neck and began kissing it.

I stammered, "I hope she said good things."

Maria smiled seductively and said, "No."

Oh boy, I thought. *I love that look.* I grinned then, and without saying another word, we started kissing and groping. Hell, I'm only human. I picked up the radio, called Rene, and said, "Alpha twenty-one oh six, I'll be off the radio a few minutes."

"Ten-four," Rene answered, "I'll cover your location." I

laughed and thought to myself, *If Rene only knew why he was help-ing me.*

Then she walked over and locked the front door, took me by the hand, and led me back to her desk at the rear of the shop. Maria placed her hand on the front of my Levi's and proceeded to unbutton them. There I was leaning back on the desk with my pants around my knees. She unbuttoned her dress and let it fall to the floor.

The next twenty minutes were wild and crazy. *Nothing like wild crazy sex in the middle of the afternoon while on surveillance,* I thought. When Rene called me on the radio for a status check, I stammered, "I'm code four and will be ten-eight in a couple of minutes." We finished, and I said, "Thank you very much," buttoned my jeans, and headed for the door to leave.

I had lost all track of time. Rene had parked right behind my vehicle and was scanning the area, wondering where in the hell I was. He knew I wouldn't have gone far from my vehicle. Maria put on her dress and led me to the front door. Rene saw me stand-ing in the doorway with Maria, her dress unbuttoned all the way down in front. She was definitely not shy; her breasts and most other body parts were showing. Rene's mouth dropped wide open; he stared at Maria in the doorway, then at me. I strutted to my ride as Rene watched, with his mouth still wide open. He rolled down his window and said, "How the fuck do you know her?"

"I just met her today."

"When?"

"Oh, about twenty minutes ago."

Rene's expression was priceless as he said, "How does shit just happen to you? Christ, you're the luckiest bastard I know."

Someone came on the radio telling us that the car was

approaching the POE and we should get ready. I jumped in my vehicle and the surveillance started.

The rest of the squad demanded full details later, after Rene kept telling everyone about seeing the naked lady in the doorway. I told the guys there are sacrifices for the job, some things that have to be done for the good of the government. I was just ensuring that we got a parking space for future surveillances.

THE next operation came up and I said, "I'll be in my usual parking spot."

The supervisor said, "Like hell you will. You're going to Walgreens on the corner of Morley and Grand Avenue."

My protests were met with a glare. *Walgreens it is*, I thought. The Walgreens store was two stories high, and from upstairs on the south, I had a great view of the entire POE.

Little did I know that Maria's sister Sandra would end up being the girlfriend of the trafficker El Jaimillo.

Following the seizure of more than twenty loads of marijuana and cocaine coming through the POE, Internal Affairs and the FBI were no closer to arresting any inspectors, or so we were officially informed. The reality is that the FBI treats other agencies like shit; they let you know that they are the intelligence-gathering agency, but they won't disseminate anything back out. They had been gathering bank records and had recruited some of the violators we arrested to infiltrate the group, offering the crooked inspectors bribes. The FBI was making this a long-term project; they wanted everyone who was crooked instead of just one inspector.

But somehow the word was out that Ricardo was responsible

for the loads being taken down, and Ricardo was transferred to the Air Investigations unit in Tucson with Don, which was no surprise.

ANOTHER character in the office was Jim, from New York. He spoke fluent Spanish and was always the schemer and comedian of the group. On one occasion, the POE had detained a man suspected of body-carrying heroin into the United States. This guy was interviewed by another agent, but after a lengthy interview the man said nothing and then demanded to speak to an attorney. On normal interviews this would be the end, but Jim was in the area and went to the POE to see what was going on.

He listened to the first agent's story and decided everyone was right; the guy had to be a body carrier. So in Jim's grand scheme of things he found a custodian's smock and said, "Let me try to talk to the man."

As the agents waited outside the holding cell where the interview was going on, Jim entered the room and introduced himself as "Dr. Jim." With his fluent Spanish, he told the man he had to examine him prior to release from the POE. Jim then pretended to feel the man's heartbeat, and then his back and stomach and his arms and carotid artery. Jim then told the man his heart was beating irregularly, and it was possible one of the pellets had broken inside him. He suggested the man go to the nearest hospital in Mexico and hope he lived.

The man asked if Dr. Jim really thought he was going to die. Of course the good doctor said, "Yes."

The man then pleaded to go to a hospital, and Jim said it was impossible. Since he hadn't admitted he had any heroin, he would have to be sent back to Mexico. The man pleaded to speak to an agent, to which Jim obliged and left the room. The man quickly confessed to swallowing twenty-eight pellets of black tar heroin and begged to have them removed.

This would have been great, except once someone asks to speak to an attorney the interview, per the Miranda rights, is over. The man was taken to the hospital, the heroin was removed, and he went to jail. Everything was fine until the man's defense attorney sent a summons out to speak with the POE's doctor. Jim suffered a few days off without pay for the incident.

JIM was one of those guys you like or hate. He was always the womanizer; his charm and looks seduced many a woman around Nogales. His wife soon found out about his extracurricular activities and busted him. In the heat of the battle, Jim gave up Ricardo and me as co-conspirators at large. Ricardo caught hell. I managed to escape because my marriage was already broken. Jim lost a few friends over this. One rule is that if you get burned, never include your friends. Ricardo still hung out with Jim, but I kept my distance.

ONCE, Ricardo needed a ride to one of his monthly National Guard meetings. His car was broken and he asked good old Jim to drive him that morning. The weekend warriors always assembled out front in the parking lot for a few warm-up exercises. Jim had picked up Ricardo right on time that morning, around five thirty, so as not to be late. Jim had on tennis shoes and a long bathrobe. Ricardo thought he looked stupid, but Jim just said it was early and he didn't have time to dress.

Jim pulled in front to the main gate and started honking his horn at all the guard guys to get their attention. The guys waved and watched Ricardo get out of Jim's car. Ricardo and the guard guys were all in full military camo clothing, looking all spit and polish. Ricardo, the Vietnam veteran, was proud of his military career. Just as Ricardo left the car, Jim honked again and then jumped out of the car and ripped off his robe to reveal a pink T-shirt and a pair of his wife's silk boxer shorts. Jim then waved like a girl and started blowing kisses to Ricardo and saying, "Love you. Think of me this weekend."

If Ricardo had had a gun, he would have shot Jim dead in the parking lot. Jim jumped in the car and quickly drove off. Of course Jim told everyone in the office, and when Ricardo came back to work, a pair of silk boxers was hanging on his office door for the world to see. Jim was eventually transferred to the Tucson office because of his crazy antics.

SUMMIT MOTORWAY

I got a call early one afternoon from a ranch hand who said he had been out looking for cattle and observed a smuggler leading four horses loaded with marijuana through a horse gate on the border at the dead end of Summit Motorway. This dirt road, located at the crest of the Atascosa Mountains, runs south to the international border, where cowboys and ranchers use a small gate to cross to round up cattle, and smugglers use the gate to cross dope. The ranchers on the Mexican side are six to eight miles south of the horse gate; the terrain is terrible, and these cowboys have to lead the horses straight up the mountain from Mexico, an eight-mile trip that takes a full day. The ranch hand figured the marijuana was taken to an area down along Ruby Road for easy pickup. I had worked the area a number of times and told the other agents where I was headed to check it out.

This area is fifteen miles west of Nogales, in a mountainous area surrounded by wilderness in the Coronado National Forest. Ruby Road runs west from Interstate 19 to Peña Blanca Lake, then turns into a one-lane dirt road that goes over the south end of the Atascosa mountain range to Arivaca, Arizona, an old mining town and later, in the 1960s, a hippie community. Summit Motorway is one of the dirt roads off Ruby Road.

I parked my G-ride and walked the known smuggling trail. I had been trained in tracking at the federal academy and had worked with the "Shadow Wolves" on the reservation. When I was a kid, my grandfather taught me how to follow signs when I was hunting.

I checked out the various trails that crossed Summit Motorway until I saw fresh horse prints. I tracked the horse trail for about three miles. Then, just as I walked around a bend on the downward slope of the mountain, I saw a cowboy come out of the deep wash and ride off like the wind.

I don't know who was more shocked, me or him. He had been well hidden and must have surely seen me tracking him. I watched him as he headed south, back to the border, probably a ranch in Mexico. He had most likely off-loaded the dope and then had his trail horses in a canyon above. I knew that the closest ranch south of the border was more than ten miles away, down really rough terrain. He wouldn't get there till daylight. I walked to the area he had just ridden off from and there, hidden under some cut tree limbs, was four hundred pounds of marijuana. I decided not to move the marijuana and to get help to watch the load and see if someone would pick it up.

Once back at the office I called the source again, and he said he'd heard the traffickers talking and they were going to retrieve the marijuana tonight. So I enlisted the help of Rene, Joe, and

Tom. I would be dropped off on foot at the marijuana load and then call on the portable radio when it was picked up, and the other agents would stop the vehicle. This was a simple wham-bam-thank-you-ma'am operation.

Tom took a location close to Interstate 19 at the last entrance into the Rio Rico housing area. Joe and Rene would take a position around the Peña Blanca Lake campgrounds. Rene drove me to the load site. The location I'd originally picked out didn't have any radio communications; it was too deep in the canyon. So Rene and I scouted around for thirty minutes until we found a radio signal. I was now about a hundred yards away from the load on a cliff above the stash site. This was not where I wanted to be, but Rene warned, "Don't move or we'll lose radio contact." So there I was, dressed out in camouflage with my face painted black, the usual ninja dress, in the mountains alone.

Rene returned to his position with Joe at the lake and started playing Trivial Pursuit in the car, while I was twelve miles away in the dark. It was worse than dark; as nightfall arrived, the mountain cast a darker shadow on the canyon below, and it was as if I were peering into a large black hole. I couldn't even see the road below, and worse, I could no longer see the stash site. If a vehicle came into the area, I had to know for certain that the dope was loaded, and by whom, for a good court case.

I took delight in breaking the news to Rene that I was changing position so I could see. I loved making him a nervous wreck. I just said, "I'm moving and will call once something happens."

Rene screamed his famous last words into the radio: "Don't move from your location."

Click. I turned off my radio.

Joe couldn't help but laugh; he knew that regardless of what

Rene said, I would move to another location to see the load. Rene continued berating me: *Reckless, crazy bastard; why does he always do this shit?*

Joe grinned and asked the next Trivial Pursuit question, "Who was the baseball team known as them bums?" Joe loved it when Rene was upset and turned red and was a nervous ninny, so every twenty minutes, Joe stirred the shit by telling Rene to see if I was on the radio. Joe's plan was to keep Rene distracted so he could win the game.

I crept in the dark to the bottom of the ridge and found a spot about thirty feet from the load with a great view of the dirt road. I settled into the middle of two manzanita bushes with a small-boulder-size rock in front of me. I crouched down, placed the shotgun on my lap, and waited.

I tried my radio again; no signal at all. I just figured if someone picked up the load, I would run back up the hill and call out the vehicle description and let the other units take it down, simple enough. I didn't have to wait long. Within an hour I heard a vehicle coming down the rocky dirt road; sound carries for miles in the desert at night. I saw two males get out of a truck, and then one began yelling out, "Luis, *venga*" ("Luis, come here"). The subjects milled around the area for ten minutes and then got into the truck and left. As the vehicle left, I could see that it had a Frontera, Sonora, license plate.

I realized that Luis, the cowboy, was supposed to meet them. They obviously had no idea where the dope was. Now what was I going to do? If they couldn't find the stash, there would be no reason to arrest them. I could think of only one solution. I went down to the load and carried the bundles up the ravine one at a time and placed them about fifteen feet off the road. I now smelled like a mixture of sweaty horses and marijuana from carrying the burlap bundles. My nostrils were overwhelmed with the smell, but I felt assured they would come back. Christ, a blind man should be able to find the dope load now. Besides, the smell of the dope reeked through the canyon. They should be able to smell it from a hundred feet.

I returned to my bush, piled branches around me again, and waited. Within an hour I heard another car coming. I could see two sets of headlights. Sure enough, both of the trucks entered the area and parked within forty feet of the marijuana. Two subjects came out of each vehicle, one carrying an AK-47. That was when every alarm in my body went off; my heart rate increased tenfold and every nerve jumped into warp drive. I was concealed under the manzanita bushes about thirty feet in front of the four traffickers. I now wished I were behind a boulder; the bushes provided no shield to stop bullets.

The smugglers were looking for a cowboy who had transported the load from Mexico on horseback. These guys were cussing the cowboy in Spanish ("*Chinga tu*" ["fuck your mother"]) and calling as loud as possible, "Luis, *dónde estás? Venga*" ("Luis, where are you? Come here."). But Luis the cowboy was long gone.

A guy with a pistol started walking straight to my surveillance location. I was crouched in the middle of the bushes. *Crap*, I thought, *he can't possibly see me, can he?* I had my pistol-grip 12-gauge shotgun in my lap, the safety off; I waited, motionless, knowing that if I was spotted, I would have only one chance to fire and then run for cover before the guy with the AK-47 opened up. He was the real threat; he could take me out easily. The guy with the pistol kept coming, to within five feet of the bush. I leveled the shotgun toward his midsection. I had two other pistols, a .45 in a shoulder holster and a .38 revolver on my ankle for backup. I knew that if I shot this guy, I would be in an all-out firefight. At a distance my shotgun was no match for an AK-47 assault rifle.

The guy walked right up to the front of the bushes. I thought he was going to start shooting. If I'd heard any type of metallic click, a bolt being pulled back, or a safety being switched off, I was going to let this guy have it right in the gut. *No*, I thought, *surely this can't be happening to me.* Then he pointed his two-inch snub-nosed pecker at me. No way in hell was I going to let this prick piss on my head. My mind raced. I would kill him first and tell everyone I saw something round and shiny that looked like the barrel of a gun pointing at me.

A lot goes through your mind in milliseconds. And then, just before the golden stream of reprocessed beer was about to flow and I was committed to shooting his dick off, someone in the group yelled to him. He turned and answered, "*Voy al baño*" ("I'm going to the bathroom"). *Yeah, on my fucking head, you bastard.*

To my great relief, as he turned around, the snub-nosed pecker wasn't aimed at my head as he let the stream flow. But I could smell the stench of his foul urine in the dark. The assholes yelled out again for Luis. I couldn't believe these guys; the marijuana load was twenty feet from them. These morons didn't even bother to look around; they just stood in the middle of the road.

So after more yelling, they drove off in the night; without wasting a second I raced up the mountain back to the original spot and called on the radio to have the vehicle with the gun stopped.

The units interviewed the four guys and arrested the gun-toting Mexican for possession of a firearm.

The whole group of agents then went to Denny's, the only all-night restaurant, to have coffee and bullshit about the day's events. I told the guys about the cowboy trying to piss on me.

Rene kept repeating his mantra, "I told you not to move, but you never listen. You're going to get killed one of these nights."

Joe had busted Rene's balls all night, getting him stirred up about the radio. Joe said every time Rene asked him a hard question, he mentioned my not having radio communications, and Rene would berate me for five minutes about always disregarding safety. That gave Joe extra time to ponder the Trivial Pursuit question.

THE west side ran from the POE on West International Street to the Mariposa POE. On the Mexican side, a road parallels the border as well. At the end of the road in Mexico, next to a cemetery, a large flood-control drain runs from Mexico into the United States. This drain is made of concrete and large enough to drive a big truck through. From this large conduit, hundreds of smaller three-foot storm drains connect from all over the city of Nogales.

At the corner of West International Street and Dunbar Street was a set of apartments rented by the smugglers on a regular basis. Usually one apartment out of the six was vacant and made a great lookout location. The apartments had one or two bedrooms, and from the front I could see the dead end of West International Street and an area known as The Corrals. From there I could see the Dunbar Street area and the houses along West International Street. For reasons unknown at the time, the bottom middle apartment was used most by the traffickers. All of the apartments had basic locks and were quite easy to pick and enter.

I would park my G-ride along the street and just walk straight up to the apartment, take out my little pick device, and gain access to the apartment upstairs. Sources kept telling us about the bottom apartment, and on a regular basis I would take up my position right above it and observe the smuggler carrying bundles of marijuana to a waiting vehicle. The loaded car would then depart, at which time the vehicle would be stopped and the crooks arrested.

This happened once or twice a week. The source would call, saying the smugglers were going to move another load from the apartment. At the time we just assumed the smugglers crossed through the fence and ran the marijuana to the house until the car showed up and then loaded the car. Finally, after several months, we decided that after the next car was loaded, we would simply raid the apartment and arrest the mules and everyone inside.

We had two options. One was to drive to Tucson and get a search warrant and raid the house after the load left; the other option was to just hit the residence while they were in the act of loading the car, and then we could enter the apartment on exigent circumstances. We chose option two: surprise the hell out of everyone and grab them all right at the complex. With another brilliant operational plan of action ready, we gathered our group. Two agents would be mobile; upon receiving the takedown order, they would drive into the rear parking lot and secure the back. Another two-man unit would block the street in front and grab anyone who tried to run back to the border. The rest of us would go to the surveillance apartment and wait inside and be the first through the front door to arrest and take down the ones inside.

All the units took their positions around nine at night. The load car arrived, and the driver parked it and went inside the apartment. Within fifteen minutes the action started. Three guys ran out the apartment door to the street and started throwing the bundles in the trunk. I gave the command: "Hit it, hit it."

The mobile units rushed to their position and we bolted out of our apartment, down the stairs, and toward the group below. One trafficker headed for the border fence; the other two went straight back into the apartment with the three of us right behind them.

I was the first through the door, yelling, "*Alto, policia.*"

The two subjects inside ran out the rear door and were grabbed by the mobile unit out back. The front door of the apartment was dark; no hall light or porch lights were on. I saw the smuggler in front of me disappear into the dark apartment. In the excitement, I rushed into the apartment and instantly dropped to my knees. I yelled to the agents behind me to look out. The two agents behind me slammed into my back as they came in.

I couldn't move; at first I thought it was a trap. I was standing, but in a three-foot hole. What the hell had just happened? Someone turned on the lights inside the apartment, and there I was in a small hole right at the entryway. I thought I'd broken my legs and, making things worse, the agents behind me had hit me like a football dummy on the way in. I crawled out of the hole; upon interviewing the violators, we learned that these guys were just about to dig the first tunnel from Mexico.

It was a crude tunnel about eighteen feet long and three feet in diameter, with no support and connected to a water drain on the edge of the street. Without thinking, we crawled to the end and checked it out. It went to the main large concrete water tunnel in Mexico. The traffickers had piled the dirt inside the apartment, and we simply dumped the dirt back into the hole, added a few bags of concrete, and poured water on top, and in our opinion the hole was filled up. Who would have thought this was the future of smuggling in Arizona? Little did we know that this same apartment would be used dozens of times more in the years to follow.

MARIPOSA POE/TRADE ZONE

JUST to the west of the Mariposa POE is the area known as the International Trade Zone. The area is the size of a large strip mall, with two streets and more than three dozen bonded warehouses. Semis flow through this area, making deliveries and pickups, all day and all night. It's a prime location for traffickers. One street in the Trade Zone runs right up to the border fence. The Trade Zone was, in fact, an international smuggling zone right under the nose of the U.S. POE.

On the Mexican side of the border, a dirt road ran directly behind the Mexican *Aduana* (Customs) station right down the hill to the south side of the Trade Zone. It was an open area with a few stands of trees and a livestock station and cattle pen. The smugglers would drive up to the house or under the shade trees and wait for a signal to cross.

At first the smugglers drove vehicles straight into the United

States by simply cutting the barbed-wire border fence and racing north through the Trade Zone. This was happening in broad daylight, two or three times a day. It seemed like we chased cars there every day and all night.

The government decided to stop the easy access, so a DC-10 Caterpillar dug a large trench along the border on the U.S. side. This trench was about ten feet deep by ten feet wide the entire length of the fence in front of the Trade Zone. We all thought this should stop the Mexican smugglers.

This idiotic thinking was shattered in about a month. A source called to tell me that a load was going to be smuggled in at the Trade Zone. He really didn't have any details, so I guessed that they were going to walk it over and load a semi. I had some extra time on my hands, so I decided to watch the area. I noticed two cars slowly cruising down the hill from the Mexican customs area; they were checking things out as well. One car drove around checking the area, and the other parked by a tree in the shade, just watching.

Then a pickup truck with four guys in the bed stopped next to the vehicles under the shade tree. The truck raced up to the border fence, and the four guys jumped out of the back, quickly took down the barbed-wire fence, and laid it to the side. Then, like a racecar crew at a pit stop, they ran to the truck and pulled out two large metal ramps. The ramps looked like they came from a garage, just like the ones you drive on to change your oil. These ramps were quickly laid across the impenetrable ditch on the U.S. side. I watched in disbelief, marveling at how fast and effective these guys were. In an instant they placed the ramps over the ditch at the right distance for the waiting car to cross. The driver of the load car didn't even hesitate. As quickly as the ramps were laid out, the driver drove straight to the fence and across the ramps, then sped north through the Trade Zone. I radioed for assistance and took off after him, straight down Mariposa Road. I followed and other units came to assist, and finally we stopped the load vehicle.

This scenario was repeated quite often during the next couple of months, with one or two cars crossing at a time. Sometimes we caught the vehicles, and other times they made a U-turn and hauled ass back across the border straight through Mexican customs, whose agents sometimes gave chase but mostly didn't, depending on whether they had been paid off.

Often, when we were outwitted, we tried to catch up quickly, so we rigged a remote camera at the POE and aimed it at the Trade Zone and the ditch area. We were able to use this camera from the office to monitor and react quickly to the numerous crossings. We also recruited a source who worked at one of the warehouses, and he called us about several loads being walked across—until he was confronted at gunpoint and threatened by a smuggler who said he had better not tell anyone or they would kill him. After that encounter, the source kept his doors closed and never called our office again.

At night the Trade Zone took on an eerie feeling; with all the buildings and vehicles parked there, it was hard to see the smugglers. They sneaked in from bush to bush and car to car to stash the drugs in waiting vehicles. On the Mexican side of the border was a high hill where the head traffickers parked to observe their smuggling operations. On several occasions a scout armed with a rifle and scope could be seen on the Mexican side, sitting high enough on the hill to watch and protect the smugglers.

During the height of activity at the Trade Zone, we called on

A look at Short Street with the international fence and Mexico in the background. Tom and I were pinned down by gunfire on this hillside.

The aftermath of a raid. We had just hit this ranch ninety miles south of Agua Prieta, Mexico. I'm leaning on the car. FROM THE AUTHOR'S COLLECTION

A ton of cocaine in the office prepped as the backdrop for a press conference.
PHOTO COURTESY T. SAUSER

Twelve hundred pounds of cocaine in the trunk of a vehicle.
PHOTO COURTESY T. SAUSER

Mexican military/army members cross the international border back into Mexico after being caught on the American side of the line.

At this produce warehouse in Mexico, the office was built on a hydraulic lift. When elevated, it revealed a staircase leading down to a thousand-square-foot drug-storage room. Five tons of marijuana were found there.

FROM THE AUTHOR'S COLLECTION

I'm demonstrating the entrance to an underground drug stash. This one was located underneath a bathtub that lifted up. The hidden room contained hundreds of weapons and millions in cash.   PHOTO COURTESY T. SAUSER

Richard Cramer, a fellow agent, and I holding Steyr AUG/A3 automatic rifles, standard issue at the time. We're also enjoying a cold beer after a long day's work.   PHOTO COURTESY T. SAUSER

other offices for assistance to work night operations. It was obvious that we were getting overrun with drug loads in this area and needed to contain the activity.

One night, I was parked in the warehouse area in a row containing other vehicles. I had the seat reclined and was able to peer over the dash to see the smuggling group staged on the Mexican side, waiting for someone to tell them the coast was clear. The group had sent a scout over to walk the area and see if any law enforcement was in the area. These scouts used two-way radios to communicate with the mules, and when the area was believed to be clear, he would give the order to cross.

The office was out in force that night, and we were staged down the road and inside the Trade Zone. We had information that a semi was going to be loaded with two tons of marijuana.

One of the Customs patrol officers (CPOs) and I were inside the Trade Zone, parked in separate vehicles about fifty yards apart. We were attempting to surveil the semis and hopefully see which one was loaded. It was about a half-moon and visibility was good. Halfway up the ridge on the Mexican side, we could see a figure sitting next to a tree holding a rifle. This was not good. We couldn't get out on foot or we risked being a target for the sniper. The Mexicans were at the most violent stage anyone had seen in years.

We saw two scouts enter the area, walking in separate directions. One took the hill overlooking the Trade Zone, and the other wandered through the Trade Zone checking around for any marked police units. These scouts were thorough, checking up and down the zone.

I noticed one scout coming down our row of parked vehicles

and trucks. He walked straight down the edge of the vehicles but didn't seem to notice us, and once he got to the end of the road, he paused and started talking on his radio.

Then he casually headed back down the road toward Mexico. He passed my truck, turned his head sideways, and gave it a hard look but never really broke his stride, and I assumed he didn't see me because he kept walking. I then watched him proceed slowly to the front of the CPO's truck, stop, and stare into the truck. In a flash he drew a pistol from behind his back, but before he could fire, the CPO fired first, shooting straight through the front windshield glass. The CPO was carrying a six-shot .357 revolver and fired three rounds. I was already out of my unit and running toward the CPO and the scout. I fired my pistol from around forty yards in full stride but missed.

The scout twisted and fell toward the ground. The CPO must have hit the scout at least once, but somehow he got to his feet and ran full speed toward Mexico. I thought he must have just tripped, because if he'd been hit, he wouldn't be as fast. I quickly stopped at the CPO's vehicle to ask if he was all right. The CPO waved at me and said, "Get him."

I gave pursuit to within about fifty yards of the border and stopped when I realized the subject had entered Mexico. I knew it would be too risky to pursue him any closer to the border. I also remembered the lookout with the rifle on the ridge. I maneuvered for cover and watched the ridge; seeing nothing, I returned to assist the CPO.

It was as if everyone disappeared in the dark shadows of the ridge. Obviously no more loads would be smuggled in this location tonight. We returned to our vehicles and debriefed at the office. The CPO was totally deaf and couldn't hear for about thirty minutes. He had shot three rounds from inside the cab of his truck; at that range the bullets penetrated the glass leaving three large holes, yet surprisingly the windshield remained intact. One round had creased the front hood of his truck.

THE U.S. Customs Mariposa POE offered more smuggling opportunities than the desert. It opened at six A.M. and closed at ten P.M. every day. So during the eight-hour period from ten P.M. till six A.M., vehicles would drive to the border gate as if they were turning around, stop momentarily to pick up several bundles, and speed off. If they were spotted, they simply drove as fast as they could to go outbound at the Grand Avenue POE. The Mexican customs officials were paid off and assisted with these smuggling activities.

One night the office heard that a border patrol agent was picking up the loads at the Mariposa POE. We were discreet in the operation and tried to rename the roads and the positions of our surveillance because the border patrol agents could monitor our radio frequency. After two hours of surveillance, a border patrol agent was observed traveling back and forth on Mariposa Road. He made at least two passes, then left the area. A short time later, another unit was observed cruising the side streets and parking lots. Finally one of our units was observed and the operation was called off.

The suspected border patrol agent was investigated multiple times, was reportedly taking bundles from seized loads, and finally was caught with cocaine, and he *still* has his job. Later on, he left the scene of an accident and was charged with multiple traffic violations. He beat the charges because the DPS officer took a blood sample from his vehicle without a warrant. His ex-wife even admitted that he stole loads of marijuana, but the guy is still employed today and lives in a large house in Nogales. To this day I still wonder what dirt he has on the higher-ups in the border patrol. Were some of the early bosses of border patrol just as dirty? One of the big disputes in investigations is that once a federal employee is identified as crooked, the FBI steps in and claims jurisdiction. The FBI may be good at some investigations, but they are few and far between.

I have but one motto when I think about the FBI: *I would sooner have a sister work in a whorehouse than a brother work for the FBI.*

LATE one night Tom was out cruising Ruby Road again. He followed a vehicle past the lake and watched it turn south on Summit Motorway. He had run the license and determined that the vehicle was from Phoenix, and although it didn't come back as a stolen vehicle, he figured it was. Many times stolen cars aren't entered into the system in a timely manner, and with only an hour-and-a-half drive from Phoenix to the border, a lot of vehicles get taken south into Mexico or are used to pick up loads at the border before the stolen cars are entered into the database. Tom decided he would watch the area for a while and stop the truck when it left. After about two hours of waiting, Tom was called back to the office and forgot about the truck. Sometime around noon he ran the truck again and it came back stolen out of Phoenix. He had enough reports to write and didn't need another. He let it go.

Around three in the afternoon I just happened to drive out to Summit Motorway; sometimes the only way to decompress from the job was to get out and drive around. The pressure of a bad marriage and constantly working add up with time, so a leisurely drive in the mountains refreshes you. I traveled down Ruby Road and turned south on Summit Motorway; at the end, about a hundred feet from the horse gate, was an old green Ford truck with a camper shell. I checked all around the area and there was no reason for this truck to be there. I ran the plate, and it was stolen. Shit; there was no way the locals would come out here and get this vehicle. A tow truck couldn't even drive up the rugged, steep mountain road; besides, I knew the Ford was going to load up after dark and drive out.

Then I decided to do another really stupid thing. I took out my CAR-15, which is an AR-15 rifle with a collapsible stock that makes it look like a machine gun, and crossed through the horse gate to invade Mexico. I had flown over the area but decided to see what the terrain was all about. I also thought that the asshole who had driven the truck here was on the Mexican side. I was very cautious and moved slowly from boulder to boulder, looking around with my binoculars. I scouted the entire area from the mountain peak. I could see ranches in the distance on the valley floor of Mexico below.

I hiked around for about two hours and found a huge cave about ten feet tall, sixteen feet wide, and more than forty feet deep. This was obviously the main hideout and stash location for the Mexican traffickers. I was amazed at the size of the cave, and even more amazing was the fact the entire floor was covered with burlap sacks from horse loads delivered to this cave. There must have been a million burlap sacks; the entire cave was about one to two feet thick with the sacks. This location was completely hidden from the U.S. side and couldn't even be seen from the air. I had flown over this area in a Black Hawk helicopter many times and had never seen it.

Those assholes, I thought. My Irish temper rose inside me. I wanted the bastards to know I knew about this cave and decided once again to make a little bonfire in Mexico. I lit match after match trying to light the burlap. I gathered up little branches and twigs and finally set the cave afire. If nothing else, the place would stink like hell. I retreated cautiously back to the United States.

I got to my truck and began to reflect about the so-called war on drugs. All I could think was how the bastards were beating us in this drug war. I then turned my attention to the truck. It was almost dusk, and someone was waiting to load it. Then I lowered my CAR-15, which was on full auto, and squeezed the trigger, emptying the entire thirty-round magazine. Anyone within five miles could have heard the sound of the .223 rounds tearing into the metal of the truck as the bullets ripped it apart. I knew I'd destroyed the engine and radiator, and at least *this* truck wasn't going to be used. The traffickers could probably see the fire from Mexico and most likely had a scout somewhere in the area watching me the entire time.

The following day, Tom returned to the area to look for the truck and discovered it shot all to hell and back. He knew I had run the plate the day before, but we hadn't spoken since I had been out in the field while he was in the office. He knew I would be in deep shit if it was reported. I did mention discovering the cave and was told to stay the hell out of Mexico. Rene got all over me. He was the protector and asked, "Do you have some kind of death wish? You're nuts going over there alone."

Tom was present and kept quiet. He knew more than anyone.

He could still see the smoke coming from the Mexican side and knew I had probably set the cave on fire.

It's hard not to lose focus in the battle on the drug-trafficking trade. The frustration of it becomes overwhelming and engulfs you. You're not just battling the traffickers; you're fighting the will of the American people, the entire justice system, the liberal Ninth Circuit Court, defense attorneys, and Washington, D.C. The smugglers have all the time in the world to wait out the agents. They have better surveillance equipment, more personnel, better vehicles. Agents are at the mercy of lawmakers who think antidrug agencies shouldn't have a budget, depending on the year and who is in Congress.

SHADOW WOLVES

SELLS, Arizona, is a small town about an hour's drive west of Tucson, Arizona, on the Tohono O'odham Indian Nation. The Tohono O'odham Nation covers 2.8 million acres and seventy-six miles of border with Sonora, Mexico. In 1972, by an act of Congress, the federal government and the Indian Nation agreed to the organization of a Customs patrol unit consisting entirely of Native Americans, called the Shadow Wolves. Each Shadow Wolf must be at least one quarter Native American, and the members come from nine different tribes, including the Tohono O'odham, Navajo, Sioux, Lakota, Blackfoot, Omaha, and Yaqui. The U.S. Customs office there consisted of three Customs special agents and sixteen Native American Customs patrol officers (CPOs).

The name *Shadow Wolves* implies the way wolves work in packs to track down their prey. The CPOs designed their own uniform patch showing a wolf in the shadow of a mountain.

When the Shadow Wolves are working they have to use the repeater channel because there are almost zero communication signals in their area. The old communications command center was known as Sector. Sector was a twenty-four-hour communications service center located in Florida. They handled all vehicle checks, including registration and driver's licenses; served as the national crime information center for wanted persons; and were the Customs agent's lifeline. Sector called in support, kept agents from approaching an armed and dangerous suspect, and sent aid to any downed officers.

In the early years we called Sector using a call sign, which designated the office and agent or patrol officer, such as A-2102; A stood for *agent*, P-2100 was the office code for Nogales, and 02 was the agent's number. Sector knew that 2100 was the Nogales office and 2102 was the call number to a specific agent; they had a typed list of the agents. One night a Sells Papa unit called Sector to report an airplane flying north over what he believed to be the international border. Sector didn't hear the specific call number of the unit. Sector inquired about the airplane and then asked how high the airplane was flying, hoping to get the airport to check on international arrivals. Then the Papa unit said, "Sector, airplane so high it looks like a fucking mosquito," followed by, "Never mind, Sector; I'm all fucked up."

Sector immediately called out on the radio asking the Papa unit to identify itself. "What's your call sign?" Cussing was not allowed by the FCC or Customs rules. The Papa unit coolly radioed back on the repeater and said for every office in Arizona to hear, "Sector, I'm not *that* fucked up."

* * *

SMUGGLING on the reservation is as active as anywhere in the district. The Shadow Wolves were great trackers, and they needed to be; the people they tracked were also Native Americans.

The Shadow Wolves referred to the smugglers on the reservation as "Carpet People." The Sells area is dry, sandy desert, and someone walking with normal shoes would leave an excellent trail to follow. The Carpet People tied large carpet squares to their shoes, which leaves a large flat pattern in the sand and is hard to detect. This has the same effect as snowshoes in the Great White North. They even dragged tree branches behind them to hide the carpet tracks. I went with the Wolves one time to track people, and it was damn hard.

In 1984, a CPO named Glenn Miles was following a trail out by an area referred to as the Damn. Miles came upon the Carpet People in the process of loading a vehicle with the dope they had smuggled across the border. He radioed for backup and then, in a brave attempt, tried to arrest the suspects and stop the vehicle. He was shot and killed, and the killer has yet to be brought to justice. The true story of what really happened died with Miles, just like the real story of what happened to Bud and Bo. Trying to put the pieces together is simply speculation based on experience by agents who came close to a similar fate. Miles was found dead, shot and left in the sandy desert near footprints and the tire tracks of a vehicle that was traveling north from the border.

Rene and I once worked an operation in the desert with Miles. We were using a large motor home as our base camp. We were enjoying the campout and cooking steaks we brought from town. It was a great time. We sat around telling war stories of finding smugglers and laughing about the crazy shit that happened to us.

Rene and I slept in the motor home, but Miles said he was an Indian and had to sleep under the stars. When we awoke the next day, the coyotes had raided our food supply from the cooler, and Miles took a real ration of shit. "Some Indian you are," we said. "Letting the coyotes come into camp and steal our food."

Miles was well liked, and after he was killed, agents were told to contact every source to try to ascertain information regarding the killing. Layne and I spent half the night calling informants. I advised the sources to concentrate on the group responsible. We wanted the killers and justice for the death of one of our own. We were going to meet the Mexican Federal Judicial Police (MFJP) in the morning at Sasabe, Arizona. Someone had information that the killers lived across the line in the little pueblo of Sasabe, Sonora, Mexico.

We left early and arrived at Sasabe before dawn, then waited for the MFJP to show up at the POE. The supervisory inspector was there, waiting to let us cross. We were prepared for anything; we dressed in black SWAT suits with Customs patches, S badges, and bulletproof vests. I had two pistols with extra magazines and my cut-off shotgun with a rifle string of shells. The other agents were also carrying two pistols each, as well as long guns. Rene had a Steyr Aug rifle, and others had Colt AR-15 rifles. There were twelve of us total, plus four MFJP agents. We were prepared for a full-scale battle and easily had more than a hundred and fifty rounds of ammunition each.

Just as daylight broke, we crossed into Mexico and drove the half mile to the pueblo of Sasabe, Sonora, Mexico. We parked by the town square, dismounted the vehicles, and spread out. The town consisted of a main street about one hundred yards long with small shops on both sides. As the MFJP asked questions, we patrolled the street with full gear. Soon the local citizens began walking around; they gave us a casual look and nothing more.

Rene, standing next to me, said, "What's wrong with this picture? These people aren't even concerned about us; it's as if they see armed people every day."

I looked around. Rene was right. Not a single person gave us a second glance. It was a spooky sort of feeling; the hair on the back of my neck began to rise. Did these people see armed guys here all the time?

Rene looked around again and then at me and said, "This just isn't right."

After about two hours of patrolling the pueblo and searching a couple of houses, we determined that the suspects were not in the town, and our incursion into Mexico was called off.

Within a week, the commandant from the MFJP in Hermosillo, Sonora, Mexico, called with another lead that one of the suspects was living in Santa Ana, Sonora, Mexico. We would be crossing into Mexico again to assist the MFJP. Santa Ana is about seventy-eight miles south of Nogales, Sonora, and is known as one of the major drug trafficking towns. Per capita it has more traffickers than any other town in Sonora. The area looks like the scene from the movie *Romancing the Stone* when Michael Douglas and Kathleen Turner meet the drug trafficker, with the river running through the farmland and fields everywhere. Except here every single person owns a 4×4 truck for moving narcotics. The MFJP doesn't like to spend too much time in this area because many of the local cops are on the take. Corruption is an understatement.

Later in my career, I had the opportunity to fly in a Mexican military helicopter over the mountain range of this area and was amazed to see more than a hundred short landing strips. This allowed small planes to land and deliver drug loads, which were then picked up by 4×4 trucks and horses.

Our group was called out to wait in the office for the Mexican feds. The plan was that we would meet in the Nogales office, travel out at first light, and raid the suspects' homes. Layne, Carlos, Joe, and I were selected to join the MFJP in Mexico. The meeting with the MFJP was delayed from eight o'clock to around midnight; they arrived at the POE and were escorted to our office.

The group consisted of five MFJP agents and three *madrinas* for the dirty work. *Madrinas* is the word for informants or crooks caught by the MFJP who have to work off their charges. They get to dress in the same black ninja outfits and carry guns, except they don't have badges. They are considered expendable personnel, or cannon fodder. They make entry into houses and if they get shot, it warns the real agents of trouble.

They arrived in a large extended van. The group had been detained by the Mexican army at a checkpoint outside Nogales, Sonora for four hours. The army finally released them but seized all their long guns, which were AK-47s and AR-15 rifles. This isn't an uncommon practice; if the Mexican army was on the take and a group of armed MFJP officers arrived from outside the area, they would assume a raid was going to take place, and therefore they would take the guns to protect the traffickers. They would then call the head trafficker. A few years later, while assigned to Mexico, I was held in much the same way in Los Mochis, Sinaloa, right in the middle of a freeway for three hours by local police who diverted the traffic off the freeway while I was held at bay in a Mexican standoff.

So now the group was armed with only a few handguns and was scared to launch their assault on the trafficker's stronghold in

Santa Ana. We offered to provide them long guns from our vault. Just when I thought things couldn't get any crazier, we finalized the operational plan and headed out to assault Mexico again.

We decided to drive a hundred miles east to Douglas, Arizona, cross into Agua Prieta, Mexico, to avoid the military checkpoint, then double back over the one-lane mountain road along the edge of the Sierra Madre range to the town of Magdalena, Mexico. This meant we had a four-hour drive before we even got to the town of Santa Ana to stage the assault on the suspects' residences. A normal drive to Magdalena, Mexico, from Nogales, Sonora, on Highway 15 would be about forty-five minutes.

We grouped up, with two U.S. agents and one MFJP agent in our vehicles and the rest of the MFJP officers in the van. So the journey began. We crossed through Douglas, Arizona, and into Agua Prieta, Mexico, without incident, then drove all night to the town of Magdalena. It was snowing in the Sierra Madre, which made the trip longer. We filled up the vehicles with gas and drove on to Santa Ana, Mexico. It wasn't quite daylight, so we decided to eat a quick breakfast around six.

As we were staging and waiting for directions on a side road, a local patrol unit cruised up and parked directly behind my vehicle. I was now driving a new seized brown Chevrolet Caprice with dark tinted windows and Arizona plates, registered in my fictitious undercover name.

The MFJP quickly ascertained directions to the first suspect's residence. The residence was an old, small ranch house located in the middle of a five-acre plot with barbed-wire fence surrounding the property and a padlocked gate to keep people out. The MFJP commandant positioned his men around the house. We were ordered to stand by our vehicles. American agents are not allowed to take any enforcement action in Mexico unless it becomes life threatening.

The MFJP commandant ordered the *madrinas* to hit the house. The poor bastards charged across the field at full speed, their AR-15 rifles at the ready. One *madrina* rushed straight to the front door and delivered one mighty kick to the door, then immediately fell backward, flat on his back, hitting the dirt. Simultaneous automatic gunfire erupted. Everyone thought the poor *madrina* had been shot dead by the killers inside. Suddenly, all bloody hell broke loose, and the MFJP agents all opened fire on the residence. It was a battle.

I was holding my shotgun, kneeling by the trunk of my vehicle and aiming at the house, as were the other agents. We all thought this was a full-scale firefight with the traffickers. The MFJP agents fired at least a hundred rounds at the residence, shattering the windows. The house was a shambles.

Finally, the commandant ordered his men to cease fire, and after all the smoke cleared, we saw a hand rise in the air. It was the first young *madrina*. It was as if he were rising from the dead. He hadn't moved during the entire shootout. It turns out that no one had shot him. He had his finger on the trigger and the safety off, and when he kicked the door, which was metal and opened out, he was knocked to the ground by his own force. The rest is history. He squeezed the trigger, firing a burst into the air as he fell to the ground. Then, as everyone else fired at the house, he lay frozen for fear of being shot by the rest of the group. *Holy shit*, I thought, *this operation is off to a great start.*

Only a military veteran could relate to the feeling of being in an all-out firefight. I will tell you that my asshole was so tight, you couldn't have driven a toothpick up it with a sledgehammer.

We tried not to laugh our asses off at the MFJP, but they were good sports and laughed at themselves. In less than an hour, we regrouped and were at a second residence where a second suspect lived. As the commandant pondered the assault on the house, the suspect drove up and was quickly snatched from his vehicle and carted off in the van.

We drove to a secluded area of town and were asked to wait as the MFJP took the suspect a short distance away. We heard yelling, a few screams, then silence, then more yelling and screams, which lasted about twenty minutes. The commandant came back to our location and said the interview had gone well and the suspect had willingly provided more information.

I had heard wild stories about Mexican federal police interviewing suspects. These interview techniques were described as beatings, electric cattle prods, jumper cables, and various forms of torture as seen in movies. This suspect was soaking wet from his shoulders to his head. I knew instantly what had happened; this was the Mexican form of waterboarding. This was my first observation of how Mexican police conducted interviews. Later in my career I witnessed dozens of other unique and interesting forms of interviewing during my tenure in Mexico.

In the Mexican version of waterboarding, the MFJP shakes up a soda-water bottle really well; then, as the suspect is held down, they squirt the soda water right up the person's nose. Just like waterboarding, the person believes he or she is drowning and usually confesses rather quickly. It seldom takes more than a few shots up the nose. The MFJP told me that if a suspect is real nasty, they mix chiltepin peppers into the soda water before shooting it up the suspect's nose. Chiltepin peppers are small, pea-sized peppers, so hot they burn your skin if you touch them.

The first suspect was placed in the back of Layne's 4×4 Ford Bronco—not the backseat area, but the small storage area. The suspect tried to look up, and the MFJP agent butt-stroked him with the AR-15. After one blow to the head by the MFJP agent, he stayed bent over. We weren't told the whole story, just that the suspect had confessed to knowing someone else who might have information about the murder. He was detained on general principle, or to see if he was lying about the information he gave the commandant. What followed were two more raids on other residences in Santa Ana and, without incident, two more suspects were picked up, interviewed in the same manner, and detained. Once again the two suspects were loaded into Layne's Bronco and provided with the same head-bashing as the first. Once again, we were told to follow the MFJP. The commandant drove to a house on the direction of one of the suspects, who said it was a stash house for dope. The house was abandoned; after a quick search following our raid we didn't find anything.

We were in need of a break and it was well after noon; most of the agents decided to relax in the shade. Joe and I were in the kitchen sitting on old chairs when we heard a strange sound, like the metal gong used by the Chinese monks for prayer. After hearing it three or four times, we decided to find the source of the noise. We walked out to the rear of the residence, where two MFJP agents were questioning one of the suspects. They would ask a question, and then, depending on the answer, one of the agents would hit the suspect in the head with a large two-gallon pot, producing the gong sound. You have to love the innovative interrogation techniques of the MFJP. During this time the other poor bastard was receiving the usual Mexican baptism of soda water.

This process took about an hour, and then we sent one of the *madrinas* for tacos at a street vendor and had a nice picnic lunch at the little house. The three suspects were now all in the small space in Layne's Bronco, all in the same bent-knee position looking at the floor. Then it was off to another residence in Altar, Mexico, west of Santa Ana. This residence was the same as the last three. More suspects were picked up, questioned in various fashions, and stuck in the back of Layne's vehicle. We were wondering, how many Mexicans can fit in the back storage area of a Ford Bronco? These guys looked like sardines in a can, all folded over and scared to move lest they get butt-stroked, which the MFJP guard did pretty regularly just for the hell of it.

Finally, after an endless day, we drove to the area just south of Sasabe, Sonora, the same little town where we'd started our search weeks earlier. We finally determined that none of the information the suspects had given the MFJP was valid. The commandant was certain all five suspects had told the truth. I knew if he had held the soda water to my nose, I would have confessed to anything. It was getting dark and the POE in Sasabe was closed. Luckily we contacted the U.S. Customs port director, who said he would go to the port and open the gate for us to enter. So what the hell were we supposed to do with the suspects? We didn't want them and the MFJP didn't want them, so we opened the door to the Bronco and told them to get out. The first suspect had been in his crouch position for more than twelve hours, the second two for more than eight hours, and the last two for around four hours.

We dropped them right there in the desert, about thirty minutes from the town of Sasabe, Sonora. Two barely got out of the Bronco; the next three had to be pulled out. Two agents literally lifted them out; they had been in the kneeling position for so long they couldn't stand or move their legs. They were pulled out and placed on the ground like little clay Mexican lawn statues, except they couldn't sit or stand, and they fell over sideways. They had lost all blood circulation to their legs. We handed them each a bottle of water, and without looking back, we drove off.

This was a long day and night. We were pushing close to working forty-eight hours straight and still had a two-hour drive home. So, without further ado, we drove to Sasabe and onward to our houses and sleep.

The Mexican traffickers were out of control; it was the most violent point to date. In Nogales, Sonora, the traffickers were battling it out on the street, gunning down rival groups at nightclubs and bars along the main tourist street of Ciudad Obregón. When the traffickers have power struggles, violence follows. We generally didn't care when they killed each other; it reduced the number of smugglers we had to deal with.

THE traffickers always seem to be three steps ahead of us no matter how many sources we developed. They moved multiple loads from every tunnel, canyon, stash house, or location before we found out. One such location was right under our noses, at the Morley Avenue POE which is about a hundred yards east of the Grand Avenue POE. The traffickers had been using this gate for at least two weeks and had crossed eight to ten vehicles per week with about four hundred pounds per vehicle.

Exactly three parking spaces to the east of the small U.S. Customs pedestrian gate on Morley Avenue, the traffickers had cut the entire section of international border fence along two metal posts. This cut went unnoticed by anyone on the U.S. side of the border. Luckily, a source called me to provide information about the traffickers' operation.

I told the guys in the office and we set up surveillance that same afternoon. We watched the operation unfold just as the source described. Around three in the afternoon, a marked Nogales, Sonora, police car parked next to the fence on the Mexican side of the border. Then around six, the cop moved his unit so the smugglers could cross the vehicles.

Sure enough, two Mexican cops arrived, driving a marked patrol unit with the number 32 on the roof and side doors. These were *transito* police in brown uniforms, best known for ripping off tourists or biting them for bribes; the border slang for this is *mordida* ("the bite"). They backed into the parking spot next to the fence and then walked away like they were on foot patrol. The entire block of businesses on the Mexican side consists of shady bars, strip clubs, and happy ending massage parlors. Just across the street, on the Mexican side of the crossing gate, is a strip club called Mr. Cherries. That was where the crooked cops went drinking till it was time to move their vehicle. This bar is where a lot of traffickers hang out; they have a perfect view of the Customs gate and can see out the dark windows when body carriers cross during the day. Once over, they would just wave as though saying good-bye to a friend on the Mexican side.

Rene took the "eye," or main surveillance position, on the second floor of the main Customs building, so he could take photos of the operation and call out descriptions of the vehicles when they crossed. Just after five thirty P.M., Rene radioed the units that the *transito* cops were walking back and had begun talking to three male subjects waiting by the fence. Within minutes the cops drove away and another vehicle took their place in the parking spot. Right at six, the stores along Morley Avenue began to close and the vehicle traffic in the area increased; shoppers were leaving and additional vehicles arrived to pick up the employees, just like a mall shopping lot at closing time. The Customs inspectors assigned to the little pedestrian gate closed and locked the gate and walked back to the Grand Avenue POE.

Then, right before our eyes, three guys grabbed two 2×4s, shoved them into the fence at the bottom, and pushed the entire section of fencing up high enough for a car to drive into the United States between the parking meters on the U.S. side. The smugglers had created a dirt ramp on the Mexican side and piled just enough dirt on the U.S. side to prevent the cars from getting stuck. I have to give the traffickers credit for always thinking of new ways to cross their merchandise.

In an instant the car merged with hundreds of others and the chase was on. Rene called out the activity and the vehicle description, but he couldn't see the license plate. Some days when you call out a vehicle description, such as "white Chevrolet Impala," it seems like there are ten driving around at once. This was the case today. We chased three cars till we found the one with a driver wearing a blue baseball cap matching the description Rene called out.

After following the vehicle to the Rio Rico area, we had the highway patrol stop it on Interstate 19. We didn't want to stop it ourselves and let the traffickers know the narcs were involved. This is the cat-and-mouse game that has to be played; if the traffickers find out that we followed and stopped a vehicle, they instantly assume a snitch is involved and usually shut down their operation. But when a border patrol or DPS unit stops the vehicle, they think it's some random stop for a traffic violation. Just the cost of doing business.

The next day we sat in the office, put our heads together, and revised our operational plan. I decided that the best position would be from inside the small Customs building itself. I informed the port director, who gave me permission to be locked inside the building when the Customs inspectors left.

Rene, in his usual safety-minded thinking, insisted that a unit remain parked along the street and be ready in case the traffickers discovered I was inside and decided to open up on the building with AK-47s or a grenade launcher. I loved making fun of Rene's mothering instinct, but I knew he always covered those *what-if* situations.

About five that afternoon, I parked my vehicle at the Grand Avenue POE, casually walked to the Customs building, and went inside. The inspectors knew me and had been briefed. Inside the building is a little bathroom with a small window facing east, giving me a perfect view of the crossing. I could see the license plate. It was a perfect surveillance point. So I stood on top of the toilet seat and watched the traffickers' operation unfold again. Tonight they crossed two vehicles, one racing through right behind the other. I called out both vehicles to the surveillance units and the race was on. The agents easily picked up on the traffic and followed them out of town. One was taken to Tucson, and the other was "killed on the highway" (our expression for a stop by DPS without incident).

Every operation has to end. After we'd worked the gate and taken down six vehicles, the smugglers realized that something was wrong, and instead of crossing daily, as they did the first two times, they waited three days to cross another car. After they lost that carload of dope, they waited a week before trying again, and two more vehicles were taken off. So they knew we were on to their operation and stopped crossing. Each night when I went into the Customs building, Rene became more concerned for my safety. He said he had dreams that the smugglers opened fire on the building, killing me.

The area by the Morley Avenue POE has seen its share of activity from the traffickers. Every few months a source provided new information about vehicles loading up along the fence. On one occasion they had dug a six-foot hole through the concrete to the U.S. side. Another trick was to have a vehicle drive along Morley Avenue and park over the storm drain, where someone was waiting to hand up dope from the storm tunnel below, or vans would drive up with holes cut in the floor so the packages of marijuana could be loaded straight up through the floor of the van. The traffickers are always thinking and adapting to our methods, and so far they have succeeded in staying several steps ahead of us.

The average person looks around Nogales today and sees dozens of cameras mounted on high towers all over the city and border patrol and police units on just about every corner. But the traffickers watch the cameras; they see them move, and they use the areas that are out of sight. They know which agent is working and which one is reading the newspaper in the patrol vehicle.

The traffickers work when the police units move; they wait for shift changes, because there is no overlap of positions. Day shift works eight to four and swing shift from four to twelve, so when the border patrol returns to the office, the traffickers have a thirty-minute window to run tons of narcotics through the voids.

The traffickers' intelligence network is incredible. No one thinks that they have any sort of system, but the fact is they have sources who are friends of friends, relatives, and wives of members of every law enforcement agency.

WORKING IN MEXICO

IN the late 1970s, the Mexican government, realizing it needed to do something regarding its drug problem, launched Operation Condor. Both the DEA and U.S. Customs agents worked in Mexico to assist in these operations. Ten thousand soldiers were sent into the Sierra Madre in the states of Sinaloa, Sonora, Durango, and Chihuahua. During this time, most of the drug leaders lived in their respective states on large haciendas and conducted their cultivation and harvest in peace. Once the Mexican army raided the villages, most dealers were displaced to major cities. The raids were unsuccessful, and the army general in charge of Operation Condor was ultimately arrested for helping the traffickers.

Around the end of November 1984, the DEA gave Mexican authorities information about a large marijuana plantation called The Buffalo. This plantation in the state of Chihuahua was approximately twelve square kilometers, and more than twelve thousand people worked there cultivating and harvesting the marijuana. Working on the marijuana plantation was not like factory work. Anyone who tried to leave was killed. This was a slave labor camp. Rafael Caro Quintero, a drug captain who worked for Miguel Angel Felix Gallardo, the godfather of drug lords in Mexico, was the known owner of the plantation.

Caro Quintero also had plantations growing in Zacatecas, Chihuahua, Sonora, Durango, and Sinaloa. He employed more than forty thousand peasants from Mexico, Bolivia, and Honduras to cultivate and work his fields. The MFJP had been tipped off about the plantation by DEA agent Enrique Camarena and a Mexican pilot named Alfredo Zavala. This information was quickly passed on to the drug traffickers, who were paying off the Mexican authorities for protection.

On February 7, 1985, both Camarena and Zavala, who was his confidential informant, were kidnapped in different places in Guadalajara, Mexico. The Mexican government failed to react to the situation and did nothing to arrest those responsible.

The U.S. government acted quickly, denouncing the kidnapping and initiating Operation Stop and Seize. The commissioner of Customs, William Von Robb, ordered every port of entry on the southwest border of the United States closed for twenty-four hours. Interstate commerce came to a halt. DEA credited this as the catapult that forced the Mexican government into cooperating with the Camarena investigation.

Everyone in our office was assigned to one of the ports of entry; we were in full raid gear with fully automatic weapons, standing guard at the ports. Traffic was backed up in Mexico for miles. Everyone was angry. Produce trucks were stacked up for five miles. But by the end of the twenty-four-hour period, Mexico had gotten the message that the United States would not tolerate the kidnapping of U.S. agents, regardless of whose country they were in. For two weeks following the closure of the ports of entry, every single vehicle entering the United States was fully inspected on the primary lane, causing major delays in international crossings.

About a month after the kidnapping, the half-buried bodies of Camarena and Zavala were found. They had been tortured beyond recognition. The official report said they had been tortured for days: broken fingers, arms, and legs; internal injuries; and cuts all over the bodies. They had been kept alive by a doctor who watched the brutal interrogation by the drug traffickers and MFJP.

An all-out turf war between the Mexican government and the U.S. government began. Information was provided to the media about the old drug lords and their relationships with Mexican federal agents and politicians. This became a catalyst to show the level of corruption in Mexico. Several MFJP commanders, agents, and police officers were jailed. The head of the MFJP in Guadalajara was jailed after he helped Caro Quintero escape to Costa Rica. Quintero was captured on April 4, 1985. It was estimated that Caro Quintero's wealth surpassed $650 million at his peak in the business.

In August 1985, after the death of Agent Camarena, the Customs Service decided to provide assistance and beef up our operations in Mexico. Eight agents were selected for a temporary duty (TDY) assignment to work in Mexico, assisting with the investigation and developing narcotics-related intelligence. The agents were chosen for their ability to conduct narcotics investigations and to develop and recruit sources of information, or informants. The special agent in charge at the time selected me to be the lucky one, or unlucky one, for this assignment, depending on your perspective.

The assistant Customs attaché and two senior special agents traveled from Mexico City to the United States to brief me on my duties and responsibilities in Mexico, and one senior special agent was to be my partner. We were going to work as a two-man team, collecting and analyzing intelligence, to support the DEA mission on looking for the group responsible for the abduction and death of Camarena. It had already been determined that Rafael Caro Quintero had masterminded the operation, but the DEA was seeking the members of the entire organization.

We were assigned coverage of the Mexican states of Sonora, Chihuahua, and Sinaloa. Our duties were to conduct narcotics-related investigations into the organizations connected with these areas. We would be working with the DEA whenever necessary and could share their office space, but they would be the lead agency on the investigation. Working narcotics was my specialty, so I was delighted to be chosen. I was told that I would be gone for six months to a year, depending on the investigations.

Rene said I was absolutely nuts for going. He had read all the intel reports, headquarters bulletins, and Mexican newspapers and listened to the news every day. He gave me the safety lecture and then said I had a death wish for going. Rene said, "There are no backup agents in Mexico, no radio communications; the entire MFJP and local police forces are on the take." He figured if the traffickers didn't kill me, the MFJP would.

Secretly, in the back of my mind, I envisioned finding Quemado and settling the score. I always felt that someday, sometime, our paths would cross again. I imagined a showdown in the Sonora desert like gunfighters of the Old West. Except I knew our shootout would take place in some dark alley or stash house he was guarding. I also knew he would shoot me in the back without hesitation.

A joke started that Layne, Carlos, Rene, Joe, Tom, and a few others in the office were collecting money for me before I left. I thought that was nice of the guys, so I asked Rene if the guys were getting me a surprise gift.

"Gift," Rene said. "Hell no, this isn't a gift. We're taking out a life insurance policy on your ass in case you get killed. As crazy as you are, we're betting on it, then we're going to split the $250,000 insurance policy."

The guys didn't wish me any harm, but the odds seemed good to them at the time. What the hell, a little extra money could be used by all.

I was driving the 1984 Chevrolet Caprice I had seized from a Nogales, Sonora, drug dealer. Three agents from Mexico were going to ride back as far as Hermosillo, Mexico, and then two would fly to Mexico City. We crossed the border without incident and started north on Highway 15, which runs from the border to Mexico City. This is the main reason Nogales, Arizona, is such a hotbed of activity for narcotics. The main highway goes through every drug production state: Michoacán, Jalisco, Sinaloa, and Sonora. The marijuana harvest season just happens to coincide with the production and harvest season of winter vegetables that are exported from Mexico to the United States. Mexico exports more than seventy-five percent of our winter vegetables from November through May.

I often attended functions and parties where the main owners of the local produce companies were present, and if they didn't know me and asked what company I worked for, I would tell them I was in the "green leaf produce" business. They would ponder the name and then obviously ask someone else where the Green Leaf company was and then point to me, and the fun started. By the end of my career, almost every single produce company in Nogales had heard my name.

Just to make small talk as I drove, I asked the attaché how far to Hermosillo, and he told me a twelve-pack. He instructed me to pull over at the first bright red Tecate beer stand at the little pueblo of Imuris, population four hundred. Mexico may be an underdeveloped country, but there are multiple beer stands in every village, pueblo, and town with at least five citizens. The attaché jumped out and purchased two six-packs of ice-cold Tecate beer. In Mexico they place the beer in plastic bags and fill the bag with ice so the beer stays ice cold to the last can. There I was, cruising down the highway with an ice-cold Tecate beer in my hand. *So this is what working in Mexico is like,* I thought. *I love it already.*

The older Customs agent I was assigned to was from San Diego, California; he was a few months shy of his fifty-fifth birthday, which at the time was mandatory retirement age for agents. He was hoping for some kind of special exemption, but it was never going to happen. I found out as time went by that he wasn't liked by the staff in Mexico and was liked even less by his fellow agents in San Diego. Within the first thirty days I found out why. Upon arriving in Hermosillo, we had another meeting with the local DEA agent in charge; upon our final briefing, the assistant attaché and the senior agent departed for Mexico City.

The following day I was charged up and excited about working. I knew the Mexican government was not assisting the DEA with the murder investigation, so it was up to the American contingent of law enforcement to develop sources of information to get the traffickers identified. The three big cartel members—Amado Carrillo Fuentes, Rafael Caro Quintero, and Chapo Guzman were the principal targets of the DEA at the time. I waited patiently for my senior agent to provide guidance. He had been in the country for more than five years, and I was sure he must be knowledgeable.

I met daily with Bill, the DEA resident agent in charge, to keep abreast of the situation. However, the DEA senior agent had other plans. He took the attitude that he was on vacation; he awoke late every day, had breakfast, and read the newspaper, and usually around eleven in the morning he was ready to go meet the MFJP. Then around two P.M. he had a nice lunch and had to have his martinis and relax. This guy was killing me with boredom. I considered him a lazy, useless ass, so I started hanging out at the DEA office and traveling with the DEA agents on interviews and learning the ropes from them. Within twenty days I was called and told to report to Mexico City because the Customs attaché wanted a meeting with me.

I arrived in Mexico City and was taken straight to the attaché's office, a large spacious office with a nice view of the Zone Rosa plaza. The attaché was a relaxed guy, wearing a suit as required in all embassies around the world, but you could tell he was a field agent. He cordially told me to sit and then asked if I wanted a drink and pulled a good scotch from his bottom drawer. He didn't hesitate or sugarcoat the conversation. He asked what the hell was going on in Sonora, because he hadn't seen one report yet. He said, "I was told you're a good undercover narcotics agent. What the hell is going on down there?"

I then relayed the daily activity of life with my senior agent and said, "I'm sorry, but he is the senior agent, and I was told he was in charge."

The attaché didn't hold back. He said the senior agent was a piece of shit and hadn't done a damn thing his whole career, let alone his time in Mexico. He then said, "You're going to be on your own from now on." He said he was recalling the senior agent back to Mexico City, then gave me a serious look and said, "I want you to get to work; I want some progress in this investigation and any other narcotics investigation." He wanted to put pressure on the Mexican government to let them know the U.S. Customs Service was working in Mexico.

That night I had dinner with the Mexico City agents, who briefed me on how to get the job done. I had been given my marching orders, and, being a good soldier, I didn't take the matter lightly. I had no concept of what was to come.

I flew out the next morning and arrived back at the hotel to change clothes and go meet the DEA. The senior agent was in the lobby of the hotel, checking out; he glared at me. Then, in a pissed-off tone, he demanded to know what had taken place at the meeting; he had been called in the night and told to pack and return to Mexico City. When he got pushy, I walked up to him and said, "Listen, asshole, you got your orders and I got mine." Luckily this lazy fucker was no longer my concern.

I quickly went to work. I met with every police agency in Mexico, trying to make contacts and recruit sources of information.

One of the worst sources I ever encountered, and unfortunately recruited, was an ex–MFJP commandant called Blind Tony. This source was running his own wiretaps on just about everyone. He had purchased his equipment in the United States from a spy store in New York and tapped the telephones of suspected traffickers in Mexico. He started bringing me dozens of audiocassette tapes on the head traffickers and their conversations. This source was a career informant who worked for anyone willing to pay. I found out later he was working for the FBI, ATF, DEA and me at the same time, taking the same information to all three agencies.

Blind Tony had developed and recruited his own group of subsources that he used to collect information, and then he filtered the information to me; when he was paid, he took half and paid his subsources half. His biggest drawback was telling everyone he was a subagent for the U.S. government. Blind Tony was an agent's worst nightmare. He had his own driver and bodyguard, and since he was an ex-commander, he and his driver carried guns in Mexico. But his tapes were effective, and the information gleaned from them proved invaluable to the DEA on the Camarena case.

I quickly developed more sources and started getting the MFJP and Mexican army to take down a few loads in transit to Arizona. I was adapting to my environment; I was going "native." I wore the dress of the Sinaloa cowboys: a white straw cowboy hat, exotic animal-skin cowboy boots, and matching Western belt. I had grown my hair out and had a full beard at the time. I was starting to act and think like the Mexican cops.

I carried two guns in Mexico, a Smith and Wesson .38 in an ankle holster and a Colt .45 automatic lightweight commander. Little did I know at the time (and I was never told by the embassy) that since I was a TDY agent, using an official Red passport, I didn't have diplomatic immunity; I basically had no protection from arrest or prosecution, and carrying a gun in Mexico is an automatic five-year prison sentence.

I had the embassy obtain a Sonora, Mexico, license plate for my vehicle. I had no office, and the DEA office was located on the seventh floor of a bank building in the center of Hermosillo. This facility was relatively safe and had underground parking for our vehicles.

I was required to call Mexico City once a week and give them a progress report. I sent my handwritten reports to them via embassy pouch. I was in Mexico, working alone with no oversight and doing everything to the limits of my mind and body. When I reflect on the situation now, I know it was absurd for an agent to work under those circumstances. I changed hotels regularly for safety. I knew to change my patterns and not to frequent the same places all the time, so naturally I became acquainted with every bar in town.

I became accustomed to the fast life in Mexico. I traveled all around the states of Sonora and Sinaloa by myself and developed a network of sources. I started working with one MFJP commandant named Christian Peralta. I felt that we had somehow developed a good working relationship. Still, I never trusted anyone and was on guard night and day. I tried to remember all the crucial rules: never use the same route of travel, never eat at the same restaurants, never develop a pattern that would lead to an ambush. I called for the room to be cleaned in the morning before I left, and then I placed a small, clear piece of tape on my door to see if anyone entered the room after I left. There was no way I would let the guys in the office get rich over my dead body. To say I was cautious was an understatement.

I provided Commandant Peralta with information gleaned from sources, and he started taking notice; he raided a few houses and took off numerous loads of marijuana based on my information. I also learned that drinking in Mexico took on a whole new meaning. It became a sporting event of sorts. Macho Mexican vs. Mad Irishman. I was in fairly decent shape, and drinking was becoming second nature to me. I reflected on the old saying, "God invented liquor so the Irish wouldn't rule the world."

One night, after I'd made a successful seizure of two tons of marijuana in a semi, Commandant Peralta called to say he wanted to take me out for dinner. We agreed to meet at nine for dinner at the Sonoran Steakhouse. Of course, being an American, I was early, but in Mexico being late is respectable, a cultural thing of its own. A half hour to an hour late is normal and acceptable in Mexico. I, of course, believe that showing up ten minutes early to a meeting is normal. I was always kept waiting for every meeting in Mexico, and I never got used to it. I waited forty minutes at the steakhouse for the commandant to arrive. I already had a couple of rum and Cokes under my belt. He showed up with an entourage, as was his custom: a driver and bodyguards in his vehicle. The subcommandant and accomplices followed in another vehicle, and there were at least four agents with them to act as bodyguards.

His guards exited the vehicle with AK-47s in their all-black ninja suits, followed by the commandant. Four guys stayed by the vehicles outside, and two stood behind the table for protection. Only commandant Peralta and the subcommandant sat at the table and ate. The meal started with a shot of tequila, followed by another, and then we ordered a Buchanan scotch while we waited for the steaks.

After dinner, as is the custom, you don't eat and run; we settled on at least two more scotches, and around midnight we had a brandy. It was a Friday night, and by now we obviously were feeling no pain. Commandant Peralta suggested we go out for a nightcap to his favorite watering hole. I had a slight twinge feeling about being set up, but the liquor had me relaxed, so I agreed. Was I about to be prey?

The commandant had one of his guards drive my vehicle and told the guy to go to a club known as the Boxaeo ("the Boxing Ring"). We parked in front at the entrance; the club bouncers began yelling for us to move our vehicles until the commandant's guards jumped out of the vehicle with their AK-47s and told the bouncers to shut up and get the hell out of the way. The bouncers were quickly moved to one side, and the three of us entered and took a table overlooking the dance floor, which was the exact duplicate of a boxing ring, only one side was open with stairs. The place was packed with people and a lot of single women. A waiter quickly came to the table, and the commandant ordered a bottle of brandy brought to the table with Cokes and a bucket of ice.

Let the party begin. Every drink needed a *saluda* of sorts, one to health, one to success, several to women; hell, we toasted everything. We quickly consumed the first bottle; the commandant took out his Colt .45 pistol and pounded it on the table in frustration as he tried to pour another drink from the empty bottle. One of his guards grabbed a waiter and chastised him for letting the bottle go empty and not replacing it with a new one. After that, the waiter hardly left our side and poured the drinks for us; our glasses were never empty.

The commandant was feeling no pain and quickly motioned for a table of young señoritas sitting two tables away to join us.

Why not, I thought. *I'm as macho as these guys.* The ladies obliged, and to my amazement they drank more than we did. We were now on bottle number three, and the ladies were flirts and encouraging us to dance. The bodyguards, of course, stood by the dance floor while we danced. God pity the first fool who bumped their leader while dancing; he would have been butt-stroked by a rifle. Needless to say, after a couple of dances no one else in the club danced when we did. The commandant was giving me instructions on how to dance in the Sinaloa style; the man extends his leg between the woman's legs, and the she hunches or rides his leg. The best way to describe this is the vulgar version of dirty dancing, more like dogs on a street humping. The ladies knew the dance well and were cooperating fully, singing the song as we danced. By now it was around three in the morning and the bar was just about emptied out except for our entourage. Bars stay open all night in Mexico; commandant Peralta and I were singing and hugging and were now *compadres borrachos*, drunken best friends.

As I was dancing, or attempting to, I felt my .45 automatic slide out of the waistband of my pants. I had just stuck it in the back of my pants with my shirt over it. In my drunken state, I made a feeble attempt to catch it before it hit the floor; no fucking such luck. I turned as it hit the dance floor and bounced; thankfully I didn't have it cocked and locked. *Son of a bitch*, I thought, *I'm not supposed to even carry a gun according to Mexican law.* I had been asked several times at checkpoints if I was carrying a gun, to which I always answered no. This should have been a very sobering moment, but I was beyond that.

There it was, lying on the dance floor for the entire bar and commandant to see. I stared at it and looked at everyone for what seemed like an eternity. The MFJP bodyguards had a look of panic and raised their weapons, ready to fire on someone, possibly me. In desperation I tried to pick it up, but in my drunken state I simply stumbled forward, moving left to right, and kicked it farther away with my boot. I looked up again, smiling; on the second attempt, I bent down, grasped the .45 automatic, and shoved it right in the front of my pants with the handle showing above my belt. I smiled and laughed out loud. I was proud of myself for just being able to pick it up.

I should have panicked. I looked over at the commandant; both he and the subcommandant were laughing their asses off. The commandant looked at me with the .45 automatic stuck in the front of my pants, slapped me on the back, and exclaimed, "*Ahorita tu eres Mexicano*" ("Now you're a Mexican"). Then he said, "That's how a Mexican carries his gun."

I was now considered an unofficial MFJP agent. By some grace of God I always managed to get out of these crazy-ass situations. I had just survived what could have been my last breath on earth.

Immediately after this, we left. I had to be driven back to my hotel by one of the guards. Hell, I didn't even know my own name at this point. The commandant insisted that one of the young ladies escort me to my room; she was instructed to take good care of me. Yeah, right; I spent the next two hours praying to the porcelain god and passed out in the bathroom. When I woke and managed to get into bed, the señorita was out cold, which worked for me. I still thought the whole room was spinning and I was going to die from alcohol poisoning.

I finally made it out of bed around four in the afternoon; I had already given the señorita some cash for a taxi and extras, and she

had left. I ate dinner and went back to bed. I had sealed my relationship with the commandant, and over the course of the next
several months I found myself repeating that evening multiple
times—with the exception of dropping my gun.

I wasn't a big tequila drinker before working in Mexico, but I sure
as hell adapted very quickly to my new environment. I decided
that the saying "Liquor is nectar of the gods" must be true, as I
developed a great taste for tequila.

I had been in Mexico for a little more than two months when a
source contacted me and said a semi was going to be leaving Culiacán, Sinaloa, loaded with mangoes and a concealed load of cocaine
mixed in the boxes. The source was present when the cocaine was
loaded in the truck; he provided the color of the truck, the trucking
company logo on the side of the door, and the trailer number on the
side and back of the trailer.

The source gave the exact time it had left Culiacán and the
estimated time it should pass through Hermosillo, Mexico. Supposedly the truck and trailer were going directly to the Nogales,
Arizona, border and would cross through the Mariposa POE. I
decided I would follow the loaded truck if I could locate it coming
through Hermosillo. I contacted Rene and Layne and told them
the whole situation. Rene told me again that I was crazy for working in Mexico and said he would never work across the line. The
one small detail I left out was the fact that the load was supposed
to be escorted by armed guards posing as Mexican federal agents.
Regardless, Rene and Layne set up an operational plan at the
POE to make sure the cargo was inspected.

I approached the DEA in Hermosillo, but they were busy on

other issues and were skeptical of the information. Besides, the semi was not supposed to arrive in Hermosillo until about dusk, and the embassy had a rule that no one was supposed to travel at night in Mexico. The roads are horrible and have no shoulders; cars stop in the middle of the road with no lights to fix flats, not to mention that cattle and horses are always on the roads. The DEA also had a rule that they could travel only in pairs, and the fact that there were supposed to be armed guards escorting the load was not too appealing either. The DEA advised me that I should not follow the truck; it was too risky.

No one ever said I was the most sensible agent, so I went to the edge of Hermosillo, where all vehicles enter the city. There is no other road around, and everyone passed this point. So here I was in Mexico, carrying guns illegally, with no diplomatic immunity. I was alone with no radio and a cell phone that wouldn't work half the time. I was about to travel after dark and follow a semi escorted by armed guards. I thought, *Life is good!*

At approximately six in the evening I saw the truck. It had the correct company name on the door, the trailer numbers matched, and—best of all, I thought—there was no escort. I did not see any vehicle following the trailer. I let the truck pass and slowly pulled out to follow it from several cars back. The truck navigated through Hermosillo using the truck route; once on the north side, it was again on Highway 15 traveling toward Nogales. I stayed back a good distance, blending in with other vehicles. Dusk had not yet come and it was still light enough to see, plus the full moon that night made the normally dark highway a lot more navigable. I was thinking everything was perfect.

About ten miles north of Hermosillo I noticed a truck coming up fast; it had to be doing about ninety-plus miles per hour. *Probably the Mexican Federal Highway Patrol*, I thought. As the truck passed me, I could see two subjects inside and three men in the bed of the pickup all wearing black military-style clothes, like the MFJP uniforms. The guys in the back were heavily armed with AK-47s.

Sure enough, just as the pickup reached the semi, it pulled in behind. Was the truck going to be pulled over? Not a chance. The pickup flashed its lights and took its place behind the semi. *Holy shit*, I thought, *the escort has arrived*. At this point I should have done the intelligent thing and just turned around and headed back to Hermosillo. But three hours later the semi, the pickup, and I arrived at the city limits of Nogales, Sonora, Mexico.

I followed the truck through the city to a warehouse district and observed the semi and the pickup pull into a large compound area. I drove around trying to find a location to surveil the compound; this was a bad-ass area of town and a worse area to conduct surveillance. Besides, it was already midnight and the area was silent; I would have stood out no matter where I parked. This would be like parking a car in the middle of a truck stop in the United States. I had reached the extent of this surveillance; to pursue the truck in this area was absolutely impossible. I even pondered the thought of approaching the area on foot. I realized it was suicide or instant death if I was discovered. For once I had reached my limitations and had to back away.

I broke off the surveillance and crossed the border to meet Rene and Layne. I briefed them on the truck and surveillance and the armed guards; they both said I was crazy for even following the semi. There was nothing more I could do; they posted a lookout for the semi and alerted the inspectors to conduct a thorough search when it crossed. I crashed out at the office on a couch until daylight.

I arrived back in Hermosillo around noon. I passed on the details and the location as the commandant listened carefully and then made several calls to his office in Nogales, Sonora, Mexico. He then said he would get back to me. I went back to my hotel to change and get some more sleep. Once again I changed hotels for security reasons. I didn't like the idea of the commandant and his men knowing where I stayed. The woman who had escorted me to the room had been to the lobby to call my room several times.

I trusted no one, not the MFJP or the army, and especially not the women they chose to set me up with. I knew I had one weakness: not being able to change vehicles. I was driving the only chocolate-colored Caprice in Mexico.

Around four P.M., I received a call from Rene, telling me the semi had finally made entry into the United States; a thorough search revealed that it was empty. I was mad at myself; obviously the dopers had off-loaded the cocaine. I wish somehow I had seen how, or what vehicle they off-loaded to. Later that same afternoon I returned to the commandant's office and inquired if he had gotten his group in Nogales to conduct a search warrant on the compound. He then sat me down and explained the facts of life in Mexico to me.

The commandant said, "Compadre, I like you, but you must understand how things work in Mexico. This is not the United States." He had made several inquiries and found out who owned the compound, and he knew who had escorted the truck to the border. He even told me the truck was probably loaded with cocaine. Then point-blank he said, "The truckload was paid off." He was given orders by his superiors to leave it alone.

That was the end of the story. Another lesson learned. To take any action would mean his removal or worse. He attempted to question me several times about how I knew about the truck and who had told me. I explained that I never reveal my sources either.

I let things calm down for a week or so. One afternoon I decided to go to lunch with Bill, the DEA resident agent in charge. We decided to go to Xochimilco, a great old steak house where the steaks are grilled in front of you and a woman makes homemade flour tortillas the size of trash can lids. To this day I don't pass through Hermosillo without stopping to eat there. Bill and I ordered and settled in to await our food when Bill leaned over and whispered to me that an ex–Mexican state police commandant had just entered the restaurant with three goons.

"What's the problem?" I asked.

Bill said, "I wrote the letter to the embassy for the guy's removal because he was corrupt and working directly for the head traffickers in Sinaloa." Bill thought the guy had been arrested or was long gone from Hermosillo.

The waiter placed the giant steak on the table. *Shit*, I thought, *I hope they have Tums to accompany the meal.*

Every time I looked over, the ex-commandant and crew were staring at us. Surely this asshole wouldn't try something here. Hell, the governor ate here all the time, as did every influential person in Hermosillo. Bill and I ate our meal in record time, hardly chewing the steak, but it was so good it melted in your mouth anyway. We summoned the waiter, paid the bill, and went to Bill's vehicle to leave. Looking through the glass window, we could see the group doing the same.

Bill started his Dodge Ram SUV and we sped off, laughing to ourselves and talking about the crooked commandant and all the things he was involved in: killings, bribery, and escorting loads of dope to the border, about the same as every other police officer in Mexico at the time. Then, without warning, we saw a Mercury sedan pass us, pull ahead to the next light, and stop. When the car stopped, two of the thugs got out of the rear doors and started walking toward us. Holy shit, our worst fear was happening. We were about to have a fucking shootout in Mexico on the main street. I pulled out my .45. I was cocked and locked, ready to fire, when Bill floored the Dodge and drove over the sidewalk and down an embankment, dodging trees and people.

Bill was on his radio, yelling for someone to answer. Finally one of the agents answered and Bill reported that we were coming in hot. He radioed the emergency and the need for assistance. I just kept watching the crooked commandant's vehicle. I had seen the two thugs run back to the vehicle, and the chase was on. We were now the hunted.

I had a gut-wrenching feeling. Bill drove his car like a madman as we cut cars off and made abrupt corners on two wheels. We had lost the car chasing us and I took over the radio, giving out our location block by block. We came in fast to the bank's enclosed parking lot, where the other DEA agents waited for us, long guns at the ready. The agents were positioned at two large concrete pillars, one at each side, ready for the firefight and assault to follow. We jumped out of the Dodge and took cover positions as well.

Thankfully, nothing happened, but the situation was too close for comfort, and everyone stayed in the office until after midnight, making phone calls and demanding that the ex-commandant be picked up. Commandant Peralta finally called and said the guy had been detained and was going to be sent to Mexico City to face charges. Both the DEA and Customs became concerned and were about to force Bill and me to leave the country for our own protection, but we brushed off the situation and said that since the ex-commandant had been arrested, the situation was resolved.

As much as I liked Peralta, I knew he simply had the other guy leave the city and back off. The last thing Mexico needed was another international incident caused by the killing of another American agent. The situation with Camarena had blown up in Mexico's face, and no one wanted another dead American agent, not even the head of the trafficking organizations. The last situation had cost them plenty, and they were in the business to make money.

A couple of nights later I was relaxing in the hotel lobby bar, listening to music, when Bill and two DEA agents came in looking for me. They had been working late in the office when my office called and asked them to check my status. It seems that a source had come to the office in Nogales and told Carlos, my supervisor, that he'd heard I had been killed in Mexico today. Wishful thinking on his part, or he was checking for the dopers to see if I was still in Mexico.

At the time, the DEA was conducting a major operation called Vanguard, which was the spraying of poppy fields in the states of Sinaloa, Jalisco, and Michoacán. I accompanied Bill on one of his rotations to Mazatlán, Sinaloa, to work the operation. The gist of the operation was that a small Cessna plane with two DEA agents and one MFJP officer would fly over the area and locate the fields; then another plane would spray chemicals on the poppy and marijuana fields, rendering them useless for production. This operation was short-lived after one of the sprayer planes was shot down by the traffickers and the pilot was killed. Operations were quickly suspended. However, the rotation wasn't uneventful.

Bill and I arrived at the airport in Mazatlán and were immediately photographed by the local state police, who were directly on the payroll for the traffickers. We were then followed to the hotel and kept under constant surveillance. The DEA agents assigned to the Mazatlán office picked us up at the airport and provided duty weapons, as we couldn't carry them on the airplane. Mexico is pretty tight about guns.

The Customs agents and DEA agents permanently assigned to Mexico had black diplomatic passports and were protected from search, seizure, and arrest. I couldn't screw up. It wasn't until I returned to Mexico as the assistant attaché in 1997 that I realized the seriousness of my actions in 1985.

Upon checking into the hotel, we didn't even unpack. I put the suitcase on the bed, put Scotch tape at the top of the door (my normal practice), and departed for dinner and drinks. Upon returning to the hotel, I discovered that my tape was gone. I pulled out my ankle gun and entered. Someone had visited my room and gone through everything. The suitcase was emptied out and its contents thrown around the room. The assholes weren't even discreet about checking. Hell, they wanted me to know they'd checked everything and were watching. I was betting they were looking for a weapon or some paperwork.

The first night was not your typical night in a Mexican resort. There was a prison break, and more than thirty murderers and traffickers escaped and killed several guards. So from the hotel bar we heard sirens and constant gunfire. At one point, the state cops stopped in front, wearing their black uniforms and automatic weapons, then ran down the street, firing at someone. Tourists ran from the lobby up to their rooms, and the hotel bar was deserted except for us.

The running gun battle went from one side of the city to the other and lasted more than six hours. For Bill and me it was exciting. For the tourists, it wreaked havoc. Some changed their itinerary for a quick departure the next day. I must admit, had I been a tourist with a family, I would have said to hell with Mexico too. Tourists then, like U.S. citizens today, read about the gun battles in the streets and the traffickers tossing hand grenades and decapitating police officials. Yet the warmth of Mexico and its people still draw me south of the border even today. I can't resist traveling there several times a year.

The following day things calmed down; since we were flying and didn't have duty, we decided it would be a good night to go out on the town. We decided to go to Boy's Town; yes, this is the place of ill repute, and here it took on a whole new image. The area was about two blocks long, with bar after bar. It resembled Bourbon Street in New Orleans. The street was barricaded, with local police at the entrance. Bands were playing, half-naked women were in the doorways and windows, and people were trying to drag you into every club for drinks and female companionship.

Bill and I stopped and grabbed two dozen roses and started handing out roses to every good-looking señorita we saw in a doorway. We strolled from one end of the street to the other without stopping until we were out of roses. Then we reversed ourselves and started back. At each club we visited, the ladies who got roses were delighted. We were poured free tequila and beers, and the señoritas promised ecstasy beyond our dreams. We had one or two drinks at each bar and flirted with the ladies; they were so thankful for the roses that we could have had sex with every girl, but we knew better. This was not a place where we wanted to get caught by the local police with our pants down. So after several hours of lap dances and fondling endless pairs of beautiful breasts, we left and returned to the hotel. Had we not felt like we were being watched the whole evening, I'm sure we would have escorted a couple of these ladies of the evening to our room.

At the hotel we decided to have a few drinks and sat at the bar. The hotel was on the beach, and the night was beautiful. It would have been great to be normal tourists, but we weren't. There were only three other people at the bar, and we struck up conversations. One American guy was there fishing, and a young couple from Canada had come here for their honeymoon. The guy was obviously a dopehead and his *eh* after everything he said was annoying as hell, but the wife was very attractive in a bikini top and wraparound Mexican shawl over her swimsuit bottom.

We started buying tequila shots, and then they bought *us* tequila shots. The fisherman gave up at midnight and went to his room. After every tequila the young wife got more friendly; obviously this wasn't true love with the new husband. The couple was ripped after about six shots. They said good night and departed; the husband was hammered and could barely walk.

Bill and I laughed. He wasn't going to be worth shit on his honeymoon night. We decided to have a final beer before we called it a night. Fifteen minutes later the wife came back to the bar in a tirade and told us her beloved husband had passed out and pushed her away in his drunken state. Well, what was a man to do? I consoled her. She had a tequila shot and asked if she could go to my room. She wanted to consummate her marriage with *some-one* tonight, and I guess I had the luck of the draw. How could a man say no to a proposal like that? I told Bill I'd see him in the morning.

It was an interesting night and the first time I saw piercing in private areas. Who knew?

We returned to Hermosillo the following day. I surely didn't want to be around the newlyweds, and both of us had plenty of work in Sonora.

THERE was plenty of activity in Sonora; narcotics were flowing through the city. Money laundering was prevalent everywhere. A lot of major traffickers had homes in the area that looked like Mediterranean castles. One took up a whole block, and others in San Carlos, Sonora, lined the beaches. All the traffickers had multiple ranches and traveled by motorcades equal to that of any head of state.

One evening the DEA agents and I were out drinking, feeling like we were really accomplishing something, when in reality we had not made the slightest dent in the narcotics trade. But we were too young and eager to know better. Every seizure felt like an accomplishment. So there we were in a Mexican bar known as the Rising Sun. It was set up like a British pub; the owner was married to a Mexican woman, and we felt comfortable. Besides, it was across the street from the University of Sonora and was frequented by lovely college girls. This soon became our regular watering hole; I made the mistake of frequenting the same place, becoming predictable. Little did we know we were usually under surveillance by the state police who worked for the traffickers.

Time moved fast in Mexico for me. Before I knew it, November had arrived. I went out to the Rising Sun and after drinking too much, I called it a night and headed back to the hotel. I was standing outside, letting the evening air fill my lungs, attempting to sober up a little, when something caught my eye. Someone lit a cigarette. I could see two guys just sitting in a vehicle smoking, but their attention was directed at me. I acted as if I hadn't noticed, but there was no doubt.

I was once again being followed. It's really unnerving to be the prey; there is no adrenaline rush, just a gut-wrenching feeling that settles into your stomach like a flu bug. Your senses aren't heightened like when you're hunting; instead your senses diminish and your judgment falters.

I got into my vehicle, figuring that I would drive around before going back to the hotel; I wanted to see who was following me, thinking it might be the Sonora State Judicial Police. I drove erratically and tried to lose the guys, and finally after several U-turns I did and drove back to the hotel. The following day I mentioned this to Bill and asked if the state police had started following them again. Bill hadn't noticed anyone, but to be safe he put his agents on alert.

I had forgotten the basic rules of survival; I'd let my daily pattern become predictable. I ate at the same restaurant, drank at the same bar, and took the same streets getting there. I was letting myself become a mark. I had always believed that I could go anywhere in the world; my philosophy was that if you don't look like a tourist, people won't screw with you and you won't end up becoming a victim.

Well, two weeks later I was back at the Rising Sun, drinking and having a good time. It was the middle of the week and I wasn't staying late. I ate and left the bar around nine, and again I noticed the same vehicle from a few weeks earlier. I also noticed another vehicle with a couple more guys inside. I felt cocky; hell, I had lost them once, and I could do it again.

I jumped into my Chevy and drove off, accelerating through red lights, hoping they would get caught in traffic. Not this time, no chance. It's harder to lose two vehicles than one, and I tried my U-turn maneuver to no avail. I then drove down multiple streets, hoping to lose them. I didn't want to lead them to my hotel. Then I made what should have been my fatal error. In my overzealous driving I got lost on a side street and turned onto a dead-end street. There are no dead-end street signs in Mexico. I locked up my brakes to avoid driving into a solid rock hill where the street ended. I quickly turned my vehicle around in an attempt to get out of the area.

No such luck; it was too late. The two vehicles had pulled across the street, blocking it. I had no idea where the hell I was. Shit, it didn't matter. I couldn't call for help; my car didn't have a damn radio. I watched helplessly as the cars positioned themselves at the other end of the street. For the first time in my life I was afraid; I thought, *I'm going to bite the bullet.* My life didn't flash in front of me, but I thought, *Fucking Rene was right again.* Time stood still. I don't know how many seconds or minutes passed; I simply said to myself, *This is it.* I resigned myself to the fact that I was going to die tonight on this dead-end street. But I would sure as fucking hell take someone with me.

I reached behind my back, took out my Colt .45 and placed it in the front of my pants, and grabbed the extra magazine from the glove box and put it in my shirt pocket. I rolled down all four windows, thinking I could shoot out of them as necessary. I was pointed toward the two vehicles blocking my exit, only now my fears had doubled. Two subjects were standing in front of the vehicles, and one looked like he had an AK-47 in his arms.

I decided this would be my one last crazy stand, like in a cowboy movie.

I put my high beams on, floored the Caprice, and raced forward; I was going to ram the bastards and go out in a blaze of glory. My adrenaline was in warp drive; I grabbed the .45 and held the steering wheel with the gun in my hand. I could have been placed in a mental institution at this point. I was in full survival mode and didn't know it.

It was kill or be killed. I had the gas pedal to the floor and was growling to myself as I sometimes do in anger. I saw the guys get ready, with their guns aimed at me. I was at full speed, holding the steering wheel tight, bracing for impact. Then, to my total disbelief, one vehicle moved out of the way. I was less than thirty feet from a total head-on crash. Why the hell they moved out of the way, I don't know.

I rounded the corner on two wheels and fled the area as fast as I could drive. I could only thank my lucky Irish stars tonight; once again I had narrowly escaped death. Perhaps the guys had a second thought or feared the crash would leave evidence and their car disabled. I believe that every one of us has a clock that has a predesignated stop time, and my time wasn't over yet.

I didn't even drive back to the hotel; I went to the DEA office and called Bill. I gave my account and we called the situation in to the embassy in Mexico City. That made two attempts on my life, and no one was ready to have another dead agent in Mexico. The following day I was advised that for my safety I was going to be pulled out of Mexico. My assignment was over for now. I was escorted back to the United States by the DEA agents. It had been a wild ride, but even *I* knew I had to leave.

INTERNAL AFFAIRS

ANY law enforcement officer who is worth his or her salt has more than likely dealt with the Office of Internal Affairs. Those of us in law enforcement have choice names for them: Headhunters, the Dark Side, or more descriptive words such as *assholes* or *pricks*. Regardless of how well you do your job, somebody, somewhere, at some time, will find a reason to complain. It's usually the general public, but there are jealous backstabbers in all offices whose feelings get hurt, or they feel left out and blame others for their lack of promotion.

When you become the subject of an Internal Affairs investigation, you're abandoned by the department and your co-workers place you under a microscope. A lot of agents crack under the pressure; they start drinking, beating the dog, arguing with the wife, and doing really stupid things in general. You become a social outcast; you're alone. You have to defend your actions surrounding the investigation, regardless of how good you thought you were or what a great job you did before.

If you're lucky, you might actually be interviewed by a head-hunter with at least some experience or an individual without an ax to grind against your department. The sad reality in the Customs Service and now immigration is that Internal Affairs has more than a few unqualified agents; many are absolute idiots who have never worked a major criminal investigation.

The entire southwest region was in turmoil. Corruption had engulfed the Miami, Florida, area a few years earlier, and now the focus was on the western states. This witch hunt was called Operation Blue Panel. It turned into a full congressional inquiry with endless hearings on corruption in various agencies.

Two senior agents who worked together at the Federal Law Enforcement Training Center in Glynco, Georgia, would soon become mortal combatants in a power struggle. These two butt-heads had worked together for more than twelve years, and the animosity was boiling over. Now, in an unfortunate turn for the Customs Service and the Arizona district, they both were in a position of misguided power. I will call them Big Bob and Little Bob.

Big Bob was promoted as the resident agent in charge of Internal Affairs in Tucson, Arizona. He was a huge man—six feet four inches, and over three hundred pounds. *Obese* would be a better term to describe him. Some agents are alcoholics; he was a foodaholic.

The U.S. Customs Office of Investigations was a hard place to work. It was a demanding job. Only those with the dedication and the ability to handle complex investigations got any respect from their peers or management. Disgruntled or lazy employees who didn't follow through on investigations were quickly admonished or written up by supervisors for failure to do the job. It seemed to us, then, that these were the agents recruited by the Office of Internal Affairs.

Little Bob was assigned to the Nogales office as the resident agent in charge (RAC). The two hated each other. Don was a small guy with a Napoleon complex, an alcoholic who treated women with total disrespect. His home life was a total disaster.

Nietzsche said, "That which does not kill you makes you stronger," but he left off the part about losing a hell of a lot of blood in the process.

Well, as I mentioned earlier, Anna, our secretary, had worked in the office for several years. One day she was sick, and a tow-truck driver came to the office to be paid for towing a seized vehicle. Another agent was covering for her, paying bills. He took the receipt, checked the file, and told the driver the bill had already been paid. After arguing with the driver, he started doing some research and found several strange-looking receipts and duplicate bills.

Little Bob demanded an immediate investigation; Internal Affairs was contacted and began to work with our agents. Anna, dear sweet Anna, was stealing from the petty cash fund to the tune of about forty thousand dollars and had been doing so for about five years, long before Don took over the office. She had quite the system. When the RAC was gone for a day or a week, the next senior agent or supervisor was placed in charge and became the acting RAC with authority to pay bills and sign receipts. This chain of command was like the military. Anna was smart and would wait for some unsuspecting agent to be placed in charge, and then she would present them with a duplicate invoice and tell them the RAC forgot to sign these bills.

Who wouldn't trust her sweet innocent smile and voice? She had just about every fucking agent in the office duped. Dear sweet Anna would take them a copy of a bill and have them sign it for payment. We ordered twenty undercover car antennas, but after three of us signed the fake invoices, we paid for sixty. Every time she shopped for personal items, she charged the office. She had quite the little scheme going on.

Two agents worked for months going through the receipts and traced the bills back over five years. Internal Affairs developed a different twist to the process; instead of arresting her and charging her restitution, they asked her to cooperate and make a video to use as a training aid. Bob must have hired a good writer to draft the script, because in the video dear sweet Anna put the entire blame back on the RAC and the agents in the Nogales office and alleged that our lack of due diligence was the cause of her stealing funds from the office. According to her, had we done an oversight of her purchases, she never would have been tempted in the first place. So she received no sentence and the entire office was described in a video as incompetent. I guess this defense should be used by every bank robber: "If the bank had had more security, I never would have robbed it."

Little Bob and the deputy special agent in charge (SAC) decided to visit the Douglas office for a couple of days to do an office inspection. For no apparent reason, Don left me in charge of the office as the acting RAC. I can't say I was happy about the situation; I wasn't the most senior agent left behind, yet I had to approve all the reports and hang around the office to field telephone calls and deal with bullshit all day. The office at the time had just hired four new agents, two rookies out of college and two agents who had been GS-13 agents with the FBI in New York: one named Fred, and a woman whose name I won't use. Only Fred was trainable; the other agent was a flower child who should have been fired within the first six months. She created nothing but turmoil in the office.

About two weeks earlier, Fred had responded to the port of entry and arrested a guy after the Customs inspectors discovered two kilos of heroin in a VW Bug. The registered owner of the VW had been trying to get it back through his attorney, who lived in Douglas, Arizona. This seemed strange since the VW was a piece of shit and was of no value. We inspected the vehicle again, found another two kilos of heroin, and decided to conduct a delivery of the car and arrest the owner. In Little Bob's absence, I had reviewed the drug arrest and seizure form and signed the bottom without noticing the one tiny little check mark that asked about publicity.

As the saying goes, shit happens. Customs sent out a press release about the extra two kilos, and then the attorney for the VW owner called and said, "Tell you what, keep the car."

Then Don called and said, "I want someone's head." He said, "Have that no-good, fucking ex–FBI agent Fred stay at the office; I'm going to fire him on the spot."

I could tell Don had been drinking, as he was slurring his words. Fred had less than three months on the job and by rights could have been released without cause based on the RAC's decision. Fred was about to be sick. I felt sick. I was taking phone calls every thirty minutes from Don and getting screamed at over the phone. Life sucked at this point.

Don was due back to the office by eight. Fred was a trouper, waiting in the office, thinking, *I'm about to be fired.* Then I decided to make a stand. I told Fred to go home.

He said, "Are you nuts?"

"Yeah," I answered. "I can deal with Don; get the hell out of here."

Fred hesitated but finally left.

At eight sharp, Little Bob and the deputy SAC arrived at the office. Don burst in the front door of the office, yelling at the top of his lungs, "Where in the hell is Fred?"

I was sitting in the secretary's chair by the front door and said, "I sent him home."

Then he yelled at me, "I told you to have him here. I'm going to fire him. Call him back to the office now."

I said, "No, I'm responsible. I approved the form in your absence, so I'm at fault, not Fred."

Don began yelling at me, and then the deputy SAC said, "Wait here." He and Don went into the office and closed the door to discuss the issue; after about ten minutes in real time, or eternity in my mind, they came out and said, "Let's go."

We locked the office and they led the way to Scotty's Pub, where they said, "You're all right. You're a stand-up guy; that was a gutsy move sending Fred home." They bought me beers and all was forgiven. Fred still got a minor ass-chewing the next day, but he had a job.

Meanwhile Bob was now on a roll after the incident with Anna. You would have thought he'd won an Academy Award. He approached the office in Washington, D.C., to set up a large task force called Operation Firestorm. Bob wanted to build an empire; his office at this time had only four agents. The Office of Investigations in Arizona had more than 260 special agents. Big Bob's goal was to have more than forty agents, and he recruited every agent who was disgruntled with the Office of Investigations and couldn't get promoted because of ineptness or incompetence. The timing was perfect. Big Bob went before the blue-ribbon panel, described the corruption on the southwest border, and said he would clean house.

Big Bob boasted to his agents that he was "the only law west of the Pecos." He referred to his agents as the Untouchables. He bragged that he could ruin an agent's career with just a phone call. Big Bob instructed his staff that he wanted the blood of an agent. In reality, I think he meant Don's head on a pole. It's amazing how power affects people; they become zealous and abusive and go over the top. Big Bob's pursuit of agents in the Office of Investigations was overzealous, to say the least. Any minor infraction was considered a cause for an investigation.

The special agent in charge of the FBI in Phoenix, Arizona, was interviewed about Operation Firestorm and Big Bob's comments on corruption in the southwest; he was quoted in the *Phoenix Sun* as saying that Big Bob was misguided and a loose cannon with no direction on how to proceed with internal investigations. That didn't deter Bob; he had built his empire of death agents and needed bodies to bury.

He selected a whole group of misguided agents to work for him. One agent had the IQ of a third-grader; other agents wrote his reports and Bob wrote his résumé for a promotion. They got rewarded for investigating an inspector who took an extra sick day or told off the traveling public. Almost everything they investigated could have been handled by a first-line supervisor. And these otherwise incompetent agents were now getting desk audits showing that they did a higher level of casework in order to be promoted.

Agents in the Office of Investigations had to work fraud investigations, narcotics investigations, money-laundering investigations, and neutrality smuggling of a magnitude to be considered a Class One investigation in order to get a senior special agent position. These cases involved the highest-profile violators; our agents had to write Title III wire affidavits, and the investigations usually involved multiagency task forces.

If I learned one thing on this job, it's this: don't align yourself with anyone. Agents who get promoted because they have a "godfather" and get dragged upward with promotions also find out that when the godfather leaves they are kicked out and roll faster downward. Such was the case with the several agents when Big Bob's reign of terror ended and the group of dimwits were disbanded. Some of Internal Affairs agents cried to every official in the government about how they were shut down because of their big corruption investigations. They claimed the corruption was at the highest level and might even include senators. They made themselves out to be the poor victims of a government cover-up and that they lost their jobs because they knew too much. There are several stories on the Internet written by bleeding-heart people who listened to their tale and believed them.

These dumb bastards were so brainwashed; they were like religious cult members who were incapable of self-thought. They believed everything they were told by Big Bob to be the almighty truth. When you go to a new office, the joke has always been, *Don't drink the Kool-Aid.* That phrase came about after the Jim Jones cult suicides—we knew the phrase was crude, and in poor taste, but . . . in our work it meant, *Don't believe everything you're told.*

This all goes back to the philosophy that there are two ways to get ahead: by working your ass off and doing the best you can, or by having a godfather who takes care of you. The choices are easy. The godfather route means you're promoted quickly, but if the godfather gets shot, you die with him. Getting promoted by working hard is a lot slower, but you can hold your head up and you'll sleep better at night without your nose up someone's ass. "He who kisses your ass the most will be the first person to kick your ass given the opportunity."

THE FIRST TASK FORCE

ABOUT the same time as the Internal Affairs group was started, the various law enforcement agencies in Santa Cruz County realized there was a major problem with narcotics in the area, so the sheriff, chief of police, DEA, border patrol, Arizona highway patrol, and Customs formed an advisory board called the Southern Arizona Border Law Enforcement (SABLE) group, where the chiefs could do lunch and talk shop to solicit cooperation between agencies.

Someone in Washington had decided that the way to approach narcotics was through the development of formal task forces. Everyone was already working together, but there was no formal paper to show who the boss was and collect data and stats for the bean counters. So throughout the southwest border area, formal task forces were established and funded by the White House. These new groups were called Border Alliance Task Forces.

Once the SABLE group was instructed to form the task force, they held a meeting and decided that each agency would choose someone to run the task force for one year. Well, it wasn't my lucky day; somehow I was chosen by the group to be the first Border Alliance Task Force supervisor.

The various departments allocated some great guys to the task force. The Arizona highway patrol assigned Louie, Harold, and Charlie. The chief of police assigned a patrolman, Guillermo, who later became chief of the Nogales police department. The DEA assigned a part-time agent, as did the sheriff. The border patrol assigned an agent named Al, who would become the officer in charge of border patrol in Nogales. Every person assigned was a great worker, and we were ready to kick ass and take names. I nominated Louie as my second in command and head bookkeeper.

By 1987 the Customs office was relocated into another space; the previous RAC (I say *previous* because at best they lasted two years) had requested a larger office as we expanded. The building was located on Mariposa Road next to another bar called Ryan's Pub. We shared the same parking lot and joked that we should dig a tunnel from the office to the bar. For a time it was the busiest bar in town, with live bands on the weekend.

Louie applied for grant money, the task force moved into its own building and set up office space with undercover phones, and we started making seizures on a daily basis. The amount of narcotics seized by the nine agents working on the task force exceeded the stats and seizures for every other department in the county. We were having a banner year of arrests and seizures, and so were other agencies such as the DEA and the state and local police.

Right around this same time, in 1988, the DEA had gotten some great leads on Jaime Figueroa-Soto. Figueroa-Soto had remained in seclusion until his teenage son started flashing money and went to a car dealership trying to buy a $120,000 white convertible Rolls-Royce to impress his girlfriend. The son asked to drive the car; the salesman laughed and said he wouldn't allow the kid to test-drive it. The kid pleaded and asked the salesman to take him to an ATM. The salesman complied, and the kid showed the salesman that he had more than $200,000 in his checking account. Still the salesman wouldn't allow the kid to test-drive the car. The next day the father and the kid went back to the dealership and purchased the vehicle. The father went on a rampage, yelling that the salesman had treated his dear little boy badly. Just because his son was a Mexican, he was not allowed to drive the car.

The salesman contacted a friend in the Phoenix Customs office, who in turn ran the name and realized the DEA had an ongoing investigation, and Figueroa-Soto was the head guy. The DEA, IRS, and Customs converged on the investigation and began tracking assets and gathering information to prove an ongoing criminal enterprise.

Several of the smugglers driving the vans had rolled over and identified Figueroa-Soto as the main trafficker. One customer was facing a hell of a lot of years in prison, so he copped a plea with the DEA and dimed out Jaime Figueroa-Soto as the main kingpin.

Jaime Figueroa-Soto was invisible to his neighbors in a ritzy Scottsdale, Arizona, neighborhood of million-dollar homes. Scottsdale was known as Snobsville to most folks because of the elite status of the neighborhood and the people who lived there.

IRS agents were called in, and within six months they showed Figueroa-Soto's wealth to be an estimated $40 million. Most of the money and phone records led back to the border as the source of his wealth in narcotics. The guy was linked to hundreds of loads and took a plea of twenty-five years in prison.

Following the arrest of Figueroa-Soto, my sources said that Quemado had dropped out of sight. They'd heard he'd gone somewhere south, to Sinaloa or Michoacán, Mexico. Everyone believed he was still working and moving dope, but his name didn't come up again in Nogales, Sonora, Mexico for years; when it did, with it came more violence than most could deal with.

The Channel 4 news reporter Lupita, in Tucson, heard of our operation and asked to ride along for a night with the cameraman. As it turned out, we had just arrested a guy who was supposed to make a four-hundred-pound marijuana delivery to Tucson. He had been paid to drive the load, but he didn't know the people and they didn't know him, so having an undercover agent delivering the dope was easy. I asked Guillermo to drive the load car to Tucson and make the delivery to the buyers. Guillermo had not worked narcotics before, so I decided to go along with him; I grabbed a cowboy hat and off we went to Tucson. We called the number and were instructed to meet the buyers at a Circle K store.

One Mexican guy showed up and asked Billy who the hell he was. Billy said he was told by "Jesus," the smuggler, to drive the load to Tucson and then call this number and showed the guy a piece of paper.

I jumped in and said, "Look, man, we need to deliver this shit. It's starting to smell in the trunk and I don't want to sit on it all day and night and risk getting popped by the law."

The guy nodded and, without arguing, said to follow him to a trailer park two blocks away and back the car into the carport.

Then we were led inside the trailer, where four Mexican guys were sitting in the living room. One guy had obviously been in prison. He had a tattoo on his forearm of two Bs next to each other, indicating he was a member of the Border Brothers, a Mexican prison gang. Immediately he said, "I don't trust fucking gringos," meaning my white Irish ass. He had that nasty prison look, like he had spent a hell of a lot of time lifting weights on his cellblock. I figured him to be the enforcer of the group. I didn't see any guns, but I was sure as hell he had one somewhere.

I stared back at him with my mean-ass Patricio stare and said, "Whatever, dude, I don't give a shit; I'll take my fucking dope and leave."

He backed off a little and asked how much dope we had, and I said, "About four hundred pounds." I looked around the dingy trailer and said, "Who's supposed to pay us?"

"Jose, but he isn't here."

"Fine," I said. "Do we need to wait for him to off-load the dope?"

"No, we'll off-load now."

I took the keys and unlocked the trunk.

So in broad daylight, Billy and I passed the bundles from the vehicle to the guys inside, and they placed them in the back bedroom. Once the car was empty, I asked Mr. Personality, "You got any beer?"

He said, "No."

So I said, "How about a collection for some beer until Jose gets back to pay me. I don't have any cash; I spent it to put gas in the car."

The meatheads dug into their pockets and put together about twenty dollars. I grabbed Billy and said, "Let's go get some beer."

We drove back to the Circle K; Louie pulled in and parked beside us, waiting to see if we were followed. We bought a twelve-pack and walked out to meet Louie and a Tucson DPS sergeant who was assisting with the case. Billy and I briefed them: five guys inside, no guns, but one subject looks like he just got out of a prison and is a Border Brothers gangbanger.

I told Louie to give us three minutes once he saw us go inside the trailer, and then Louie would give the command for the takedown and the raid team would rush in. Billy and I returned to the trailer, and I took the beer out and made sure every subject had a cold one in his hand. I wanted their hands occupied with beer rather than guns. I said "*Salud*" and looked out to see the bust team running to the door. Billy and I blocked the hallway to the rear of the trailer as the team rushed through the door. The gangbanger dropped his beer and was trying to get a gun from under the cushion on the couch when the team took him down.

He yelled to the others, "I told you not to trust a motherfucking gringo," and then he turned to me and said, "You're lucky I didn't kill you when you got here, motherfucker."

I looked at him and said, "Have a nice time in prison, asshole," as he was led away to the marked patrol units. I finished my beer and walked outside to relax. I told Guillermo I was proud of him and that he did a great job. As I looked around, half of the neighbors in the trailer park were standing across the street; some older residents yelled, "Good job." I guess they had been too scared to call the cops for fear of retaliation.

Lupita and Isaac, the cameraman, filmed the whole thing and were ready to launch the bust on the Channel 4 nightly news.

The telephone rang in the trailer and Louie answered it in Spanish. The caller wanted to know if the merchandise had arrived and Louie said, "Yeah, we got four hundred pounds."

The caller said he would be right over. Louie quickly assembled the team; we decided, *What the hell, we're already here, let's keep the game going.* The marked cars left the area and would wait for our orders to take down the car a block from the trailer after they picked up the pot. Before the first guy arrived, two more people called and wanted marijuana. This was the main distribution point for multiple dealers.

The first guy arrived and wanted five pounds. Louie and Billy weighed out the dope and handed it to the guy, and he paid us two thousand dollars in cash, a price he had agreed on earlier. We gave him the dope and he left, to be arrested a block away by the marked units.

Within twenty minutes the second guy arrived for his cut of the dope. He parked and came to the door and said, "What the fuck is up with your neighbors?" Louie and I looked out the window. We had been so busy inside, we didn't notice that across the street, two trailers down, about twenty people were sitting out on folding lawn chairs watching the trailer. Shit, they thought this was better than a drive-in movie. They had drinks and appetizers and were taking in the show. Louie quickly said they were bird watchers.

The explanation was good enough for this dopehead. He bought ten pounds and departed like the first guy. The neighbors waved to him as he left and he waved back, thinking, *What a friendly bunch of old farts.*

We stepped outside after he left and asked the onlookers to stay back for safety reasons. They clapped and cheered again. We watched as the crowd grew to about thirty people. This was a big night out for the snowbirds, Arizona's winter tourists, in the trailer park. By now it was dark and we decided it was time to end this game, so we radioed the bust crew to move in closer and we would take down the last person who was en route and call it a night.

The third buyer, a woman about fifty years old, arrived in a big Cadillac. She demanded to know what the hell was up with the people across the street. We told her they were stargazers and they did that every night. She was satisfied and inspected the marijuana, then wanted to know how much was left, and we told her about 375 pounds. She wanted everything. We acted dumb and said we couldn't sell all of it.

She handed us a bag with about fifty thousand dollars in cash and said she would pay the rest later. We pretended to protest at the small amount of money for the entire load but ultimately agreed. I put on my cowboy hat, and Billy and I proceeded to carry the entire pile of dope from the back bedroom to the trunk of her Cadillac. This was perfect; we wanted to end the operation and needed to get the dope out of the trailer and to the office, so using her Cadillac to transport it worked out. Needless to say, it fit well into the trunk. Since we weren't wired, as in most undercover deals, I had given the pre-bust takedown sign by taking off my cowboy hat and placing it on the top of the car.

The bossy old lady came out, proud of herself for getting all the dope at half price. She thought she had just screwed over some idiots and was now in a hurry to leave. So I closed the trunk and said, "Thanks," then placed my cowboy hat on the top of the car as I brushed my hair back.

She jumped inside and revved up the Cadillac as three marked units came roaring in with lights flashing. The neighborhood was alive; the group across the street cheered. We had nicely loaded all the evidence from the trailer to the rear of the Cadillac, and Billy got to drive it to the DPS headquarters in Tucson.

AFTER about six months of running the task force, I was called to a meeting with Don the RAC, Carlos, Layne, and Bob, the RAC of Internal Affairs. I was briefed on an investigation and told that everything said was confidential.

Bob said, "I hear you're a damn good agent and I trust you, so I'm advising you that Arizona DPS and my department are conducting an internal investigation on agent Louie."

I couldn't believe that Louie was crooked. I'd worked with the guy daily for more than three years. "No way," I said.

"Boy, just keep your eyes and ears open and report anything to me that's out of the ordinary. Every time you go out on surveillance, you're required to tell Layne or Carlos. Understood?"

"Yeah," I said.

After he left, Layne and Carlos said, "We don't believe it either, but you got your orders, okay?"

"Yeah, no problem," I answered.

I felt sick in the pit of my stomach. Could Louie really be working with the traffickers? Impossible. Layne said the threat seemed to be from telephone numbers he called in Mexico. I explained that he was trying to start a business and make T-shirts and raid pants in Mexico.

Layne said, "Just don't say nothing to anyone, got it?"

On many nights after working surveillance with Louie, I was tempted to say something, but I didn't thankfully.

We went about our business as usual, conducting surveillances, taking down multiple loads of narcotics, and thinking we were doing the best job possible. Finally, around the end of my term, about the eleventh month, DPS broke the news to Louie, Charlie, and Harold that the three of them were under investigation for corruption charges. The task force died a sudden death. The three were placed on administrative duty and were not allowed to work in the field. I was angry at the whole situation; they killed the task force, which had been so successful. I hated Internal Affairs for what they had done to the task force; I took the whole thing very personally.

I was called in to be interviewed by the DPS sergeant in charge of the internal investigation. I arrived and was kept waiting for thirty minutes in the lobby. They like making you sweat and treating you like a second-class citizen. Finally I was called into the interview room; the DPS sergeant and one agent from Internal Affairs were present. The sergeant placed a tape recorder on the desk and said, "I'm going to record the interview."

I said, "No, I would rather you write out the questions and then I'll write my answer."

He refused and said I had to be tape-recorded.

I said, "Sergeant, that might be your policy but it isn't a Customs policy. You had better read our manual. By federal guidelines an agent can refuse to be recorded, so if you want to ask me any questions, you will write them on a pad." I was feeling pretty defensive, so I added that I also wanted a copy of the questions and answers before I left.

This might not have been the smartest thing I ever did, but I was pissed off and I had read the entire Internal Affairs handbook that belonged to an old agent who had worked for them, so I was also feeling cocky, thinking I was smarter than both the idiots in the room.

The two headhunters left the room in a huff, and then about ten minutes later they returned and said they would comply with my wishes.

Comply, hell, they have no option, I thought. The entire interview lasted about a half hour; the questions centered on possible corruption of Louie and Charlie. When the questioning ended, I wrote my last answer and said, "That's it." I then looked across the desk at the sergeant and said, "Your investigation was bogus from the beginning. Your fucking department could have handled this sooner." I asked, "Why didn't DPS just call them in at the beginning and give them a polygraph? You screwed over my task force the way you handled the situation."

Right about this time, Bob the RAC entered the room and stood right in front of me, looking down at me sitting at the desk with his holier-than-thou attitude, and said that his office would handle internal investigations as he saw fit and that I wasn't aware of the seriousness of this investigation.

Then he said, "You can't have a copy of the notes; everything said here today is confidential and you're not allowed to discuss it until this investigation is over. You're under a gag order."

I went into a full maniac rage. I jumped up from my chair and stood face-to-face with Bob, causing him to take a step back. I raised my voice and said, "Only a federal judge can issue a gag order; this isn't court and I don't see your ass wearing a black robe."

Big Bob's face twitched; I had made him falter. So just for insult I said, "You fat-ass bastard, you couldn't find an investigation if it was shoved up your ass."

Big Bob raised his voice and said, "You can't talk to me that way."

"Fuck you!" I said. "You're all a bunch of idiots." Then, as a departing comment, I said, "You couldn't find your ass if you were naked in a round room full of mirrors." My blood pressure was boiling; it took every ounce of willpower I had not to punch the asshole in the face. In the hour it took me to drive back to Nogales, news of my outburst had arrived at the office before I did. A friendly agent in Internal Affairs had phoned the office and told them of my comments.

The following morning I arrived at work by eight thirty. A group of Internal Affairs agents were already waiting at the front door. Big Bob now wanted my head; I was told I was under investigation, but no one knew why. They demanded a copy of every Report of Investigation I had ever written. Then they wanted a copy of every travel document, followed by a copy of every payment made to a confidential source, and finally all of my payroll records and time cards. They left the office with eight boxes of records. I was now the subject of a full-scale Internal Affairs Red Book Investigation.

"Gee," I said, laughing, "I wonder what pissed them off?"

So in less than twenty-four hours I went from being someone who was trusted and considered a good agent to a lowlife scumbag on the Internal Affairs most-wanted list. In my opinion, I was being singled out because of the failed investigation into the DPS officers. I didn't have anything to hide, so I figured Big Bob would screw with me, find some pissant thing wrong, and I would get a couple of days on the beach to teach me a lesson. No big deal.

Finally DPS called Louie, Charlie, and Harold in for the big interview and polygraph examination. One by one they were polygraphed in depth by DPS. After spending a year conducting

their big investigation, DPS realized there was no criminal misconduct. All three passed the polygraph with flying colors.

Louie informed me that the three were later told by DPS col-
leagues that other officers had been told that if confronted in the
field, they had the okay to shoot Louie, Charlie, and Harold if
needed, because they were positively crooked. It's scary to think
that their own agency, Arizona highway patrol, had issued that
order without a trial or hearing. The whole investigation was
started by a confidential source who concocted the entire story so
that he could get some money. Yet the source was never polygraphed to see if he was lying.

The following day, Louie called and said the investigation was
finally over, so we decided to meet to discuss the affair. We knew
that Internal Affairs was still following us around, so we picked a
location down by the Santa Cruz River. I apologized to Louie for
not telling him about the investigation, and all three said, "Thank
God you didn't. Over half the questions on the polygraph were
about you. They asked if you ever told us about the investigation,
said anything regarding it, or even hinted of it, anything."

Louie said, "Big Bob wants your head."

I told them about my outburst at the interview with their sergeant and Big Bob. Everyone laughed, then said, "You better be
real careful; Bob thinks you're public enemy number one."

The tension and distrust that the Internal Affairs investigation
had caused between the four of us was over. A few hours of sitting
by the river drinking a few beers and hashing things out allowed
us to understand the situation we were placed in, and all the mis-
trust the stupid investigation caused us was forgiven. We drank,
hugged each other, and let it all out.

In August 1989, the special agent in charge of Arizona summoned me to his office for a meeting. I wondered, *What now?* I got along with the SAC, and he had always treated me well. At the scheduled time he called me into his office and said he had selected me to be a supervisor. Hell, I hadn't applied to be a supervisor; I was happy being a senior 13 agent. The conversation was very short. I said, "I don't want to be a supervisor."

The SAC said, "You don't have a choice. You are going to be a supervisor, period, meeting over."

This constant battle with Internal Affairs took its toll on me and others in the office. Layne, Little Bob, and I became the subject of several conflicts with Internal Affairs. I knew we were being harassed; I was a time bomb ready to explode, and explode I did on anyone and everything that got in my way. I got in a fistfight with the DEA's RAC over a surveillance in the highway patrol parking lot. I got in a fight with a local doper at a bar. I was ready to fight anyone. I drank more, worked longer hours, and seldom went home. I was now divorced and looking for a different woman every night as a conquest.

At this same time, cocaine trafficking was skyrocketing; Nogales went from large-scale marijuana trafficking to large-scale cocaine smuggling overnight. The push in South Florida was over. The traffickers figured smuggling through Arizona was the best way to get their product to California, where the demand was incessant. Nogales became the number two smuggling and distribution point for cocaine entering the United States.

Vehicles loaded with five hundred to a thousand pounds of cocaine were coming into the ports of entry daily. In one investigation, a van with a ton of cocaine was crossed through the POE at noon. The inspector never checked the vehicle. We became overrun at once. The players were the same but the product had changed, along with an increase in violence to protect the product. Corruption at the POE increased; the payoffs for passing loads were enormous. Payments to inspectors were said to be up to $100,000 a vehicle.

I felt that Big Bob spent the next four years trying to find some way to hang my ass on his office wall. Finally, I received a letter from the Customs Service saying the Internal Affairs investigation was officially closed. I was cleared of any allegations; sorry for any inconvenience, but these investigations are necessary for betterment of the service. I heard that Big Bob was removed from his position and that the Customs Service took away his supervisory responsibility and placed him in a back office somewhere to wait out his time till retirement. This ended one dark period in my career; not only mine, but those of a lot of good Customs employees.

After I spent years of my life under the microscope for allegations and rumors and spent days being interviewed, I became bitter and angry at the Customs Service. I was more alone now and, for the most part, never truly trusted anyone. I had fought to defend my actions and honor and felt like I was on trial for doing my job. I had received nothing but accolades, awards, and a wall full of certificates and plaques to prove my worthiness to the service. I was by no means an angel—I broke a lot of rules—but I'd learned a good lesson and a simple fact of life: people will try to kick you when you're down.

But during the hard times, you also find out who your true friends are.

SUPERVISION

I was back at Customs, in a new office with a plaque on the door that read SUPERVISORY SPECIAL AGENT. I was sitting at my desk with my feet propped on one corner, smoking a cigar, and contemplating my new position. Layne and I had started cigar smoking about three years earlier. The traffickers around Nogales had nicknamed me *El Puro*, the Cigar Man. I guess the reason I started smoking cigars was to enhance my bad-boy image and keep up a tough-hombre appearance. Then I discovered that cigar smoking gave me a few minutes of true relaxation. I was honored to have been chosen to be a supervisor, yet on the flip side, I liked working alone. I had more than twenty confidential informants working for me and was able to pick and choose my investigations. I wasn't sure how I felt. Who the hell *wanted* to be a supervisor? This meant more responsibility for the same pay. This was new territory for me. I had always been the guy *bending* the rules; now I was tasked with making sure the agents *followed* the rules.

Rene had been promoted to supervisor of the fraud investigation group. Layne, Rene, and I were now the three supervisory special agents in the Nogales Customs office. Rene, as a true friend, told me, "You're not ready to be a supervisor yet. I think it's a mistake."

The jealous prick, I thought. But the first two years proved him right. I wasn't ready, and I hated being a supervisor.

Ricardo was now working in Mexico City, Mexico; Joe was the RAC in Ajo, Arizona; Tom was assigned to my group; and Carlos had moved to Texas. Each of us had moved on and we were traveling down separate paths, yet somehow our lives remained tied together by a bond created over the last ten years.

Our office location proved to be disastrous. The traffickers quickly learned the location and did drive-bys constantly to check out our vehicles and try to recognize us. We had a fence installed to prevent anyone from seeing in, but it was pointless; from any location around the office we could be watched from the hillsides. For safety reasons, we almost never met informants at the office.

Meanwhile the bar next door got a real workout. Agents arriving early on Monday morning had to be careful not to run over all the beer bottles the patrons had discarded in the parking lot. The bar was a source of pleasure and misery for most of us. One RAC spent so much time at the bar, we joked it was his personal office, as he was usually drinking there before noon every day.

IN 1989, I took an old dilapidated couch that was falling apart and had it reupholstered in a blue Irish plaid fabric. I practically lived on the couch in the early years. Hell, during my divorce, when the shit hit the fan at home, I slept on that couch for weeks. Having Ryan's Pub next door was too convenient. I walked from the office to the bar, and after drinking at the bar, I'd persuade some woman to accompany me back to the office. The short fifty-foot stroll from the bar to the office was great. I used to laugh in the old days and say my couch had more DNA samples than a laboratory. The building was a government office during the day and a "no-tell motel" at night.

The government had finally realized that Arizona was overrun with narcotics and help was needed on the southwest border. Headquarters in Washington, D.C., issued an order to all the interior offices, such as Denver, Kansas City, Phoenix, and others, to provide a list of one or two names of volunteers to be transferred to the southwest border offices. If no one volunteered, the boss selected who would be transferred. Some of the RACs used this as a way of dumping all of their malcontent agents. I had not seen anything like this since Fidel Castro emptied the prisons in Cuba and sent all the murderers, rapists, political activists, and drug dealers to Miami, Florida. At least most of those crazies were kept in holding cells until they could be evaluated.

Before 1990, the Nogales, Arizona, office consisted of both Santa Cruz County and Cochise County, to include Nogales and Douglas. Nogales had twenty-five agents and three supervisors; the Douglas office was smaller and had eight agents and one supervisor. Both offices were a real mixture of individuals and characters. One transferred agent had previously been an RAC, until his son came into the office, took his service pistol from the desk, and shot a hole in the ceiling. He attempted to cover up the shoot-

ing and got into more trouble when he heard that his secretary
had some incriminating evidence in her desk. After trying unsuc-
cessfully to break into the locked desk, the moron tried to set the
paperwork in her desk on fire by throwing matches inside.

One agent was a flower child who didn't believe that anyone
should go to jail; everyone should go to a treatment center. Two
others had gotten in trouble in Denver after losing a fully automatic weapon. They saved their asses by snitching out their boss
for some violation.

Another was a total mental case who had filed three Equal
Employment Opportunity (EEO) discrimination complaints with
three different agencies in the last three years. Every time he got
in trouble, he went section eight and filed an EEO complaint. Of
course his prior supervisors said nothing. We called this the bung-
hole appraisal. A supervisor evaluates an employee and gives him
really high marks, knowing that the guy applied for a job elsewhere. Even when you call the office to ask another supervisor,
they lie to get rid of the guy. So the new office hires the guy and,
you guessed it, the receiving office takes it up the ass.

One wacko guy even changed his name to become more Hispanic. He bought bracelets from known drug dealers and knocked
up a barmaid who was a cousin of the drug trafficker Caro Quintero. The barmaid later went to his house and told his wife, "He
no love you, he only love me." This sent the guy over the edge,
and he blamed everyone in the office. Then the dumbshit broke
into the RAC's office and stole reports the RAC had written about
his misconduct. The following day the moron came into the office
with a copy of the stolen files and demanded an explanation from
the RAC. The goofball claimed someone had left the notes on the

windshield of his vehicle. The RAC advised the idiot about some-one breaking into his desk and then told him, "I fingerprinted my desk, and I will find out who stole my notes."

Mr. Wacko drove himself to a mental hospital, checked himself in, and claimed a section eight, and then he filed an EEO com-plaint saying he was discriminated against. He told his psycholo-gist he dreamed about scalping Layne and me. This made us both laugh because we had ex-wives who would gladly scalp us for him.

Another knucklehead came from Florida, and the first thing he told everyone was that he had gotten warts on his dick from his girlfriend, who was a hooker he brought with him. The guy was very likable, but his personal drama was endless. He showed up for work with scars on his head from broken plates and teeth knocked out by his girlfriend. Then she filled out every credit card application that he got in the mail and charged more than forty thousand dollars to his name.

A normal RAC office, or any law enforcement office, usually has only one screwball agent, who can be monitored and con-trolled. The list of deadbeats and Generation X agents who were forcibly transferred to Nogales was a supervisor's nightmare. The job was demanding enough without the added stress of a dozen wacko agents showing up at the office at once.

The ports of entry and the border patrol had increased their staffing as well and hired from the street without little or no back-ground investigation. One new agent hired by the border patrol was wanted for murder in New York; he had shot two men in a taxicab. Another new agent needed money, so he pawned his service-issued pistol and shotgun; every day he showed up for work without a weapon. There were reports of marked border patrol units robbing vehicles driving south with Sonora, Mexico, license plates. Santa Cruz County had returned to the Wild West it once was. The joke among law enforcement was, "If you want to commit murder, do it in Santa Cruz County because the homicides here are never solved."

All this drama coincided with the busiest time ever in Nogales. The cocaine-smuggling routes shifted from Florida to the southwest border. Just a year earlier, the largest cocaine seizures we made were one or two kilos. Overnight we were intercepting thousand-pound loads of cocaine instead of marijuana. There was so much cocaine, the smugglers didn't even try to conceal it; they loaded trunks of cars and drove them to the POE. The traffickers must have made Arizona the central distribution point for coke. We had two or three cases a day: air drops, mules backpacking in the canyons, and tunnels right under the Customs parking lot.

The first major drug tunnel discovered was in Douglas, Arizona, in 1990. The Douglas office had just been upgraded to an RAC office, becoming an independent station. The supervisors in Nogales were ecstatic, since we no longer had to drive to Douglas and take over the supervisory responsibilities.

A friend of mine who was a supervisor from Yuma, Arizona, was chosen to take over the Douglas office. For those who thought Nogales was a desolate, isolated border town, Douglas was a lot worse. Layne, Rene, and I were all offered the RAC position in Douglas, and we all turned it down. I viewed the agents in Douglas as a bunch of cowboy misfits. Every time I was sent there to supervise the office, I cringed. They had saddles in the back of their pickup trucks; they wrecked cars every week and really hadn't done any quality investigations. They seemed to drive around like the border patrol agents and run into smugglers in the desert.

The new RAC had been in place about six months when the

information on the tunnel emerged. He was good about keeping the information discreet and working the case as best he could with the agents he had. Unfortunately, another agent in Phoenix heard of the tunnel. He was born in Douglas and had some pretty good sources. In Phoenix, a supervisor from California was selected to be the new RAC. He was nicknamed "Mr. Greatly." He was very prim and polished; his clothes were straight from the dry cleaners, never a wrinkle, and he kept spare clothes hanging in the car. His office was pristine, nothing out of place. He seemed to me to have a compulsive disorder of some kind.

On several occasions when I visited the Phoenix office, I noticed that most of the agents were now dressing like Mr. Greatly. He demanded spit and polish. His agents were required to knock before entering his office and wait until he summoned them to enter, and then they stood like solders in the military until he made a decision. I enjoyed the fact that I didn't work for him. I would walk straight into his office, sit down, and shuffle his magazines around on the coffee table in an attempt to deliberately agitate him. When he got frustrated, I laughed and left.

Greatly was a demanding boss, yet he was one hell of an investigator. He developed some great undercover investigations such as Casablanca, an international money-laundering investigation dealing with drug traffickers, politicians, and Mexican bankers. I also worked on one investigation with him in which we took a Colombian trafficker out of prison and worked a major cocaine delivery from Colombia. He was innovative and had the ability to take an investigation six steps beyond what most agents thought normal.

Once the Phoenix office heard of the tunnel, they went to the SAC and immediately took the entire case over. In reality, the

Douglas agents weren't at fault; they were simply outgunned by a larger office with clout. Greatly was in the SAC's good graces and had proven his ability to get the job done.

Every office used different ways to accomplish the same task; each thinks the other is wrong, and Phoenix found fault with everything the agents in Douglas had done up till now. With Greatly at the helm, the investigation mushroomed into an international case. Headquarters was briefed, the commissioner of Customs was informed and demanded daily updates, and finally the drug czar at the White House was briefed. The investigation became a three-ring circus. Our favorite saying was, "Big cases, big problems."

The Tucson, Phoenix, and Nogales offices were mobilized to work the investigation. I can't recall all the nights I spent on the highway between Douglas and Phoenix with my group conducting surveillances on vehicles and suspects, but there were a hell of a lot. When time came for the actual raid on the warehouse, it looked like the Seventh Cavalry had arrived in Douglas; at least ninety agents from the three offices swarmed the town.

Just before the big raid, the Customs attaché office in Mexico City was contacted and asked to contact the MFJP for assistance. A unit from Mexico City was requested because of the corruption of the Agua Prieta, Mexico, MFJP office. A group of twelve MFJP agents accompanied by a high-ranking commandant was flown to the area to assist.

The raid was a blur. Agents served warrants on multiple residences and then hit dozens of residences. The entire population in Douglas, Arizona, was suspected at that point in time. One of my agents asked me who the main targets were and I said, "Just look at the Douglas telephone directory and pick a name."

My squad was assigned to execute the warrant on the main

warehouse, which was accomplished easily since it was a business and was closed for the night. To our surprise the entire tunnel was filled with water. But a source had said the traffickers had a way of filling the tunnel so it couldn't be entered from the United States unless the traffickers drained it.

The MFJP raided the Mexican residence where the tunnel was located in Mexico. This was a high-tech tunnel; the entrance was said to be in the game room, under the pool table. The room was about twenty feet square, with the pool table in the center. The carpet was removed around the pool table, which revealed an inset concrete slab about ten feet square.

The residence in Mexico and the warehouse in the United States were about 150 yards apart, with only the border fence separating the two. During the raids, I walked through a hole in the international border fence to the residence on the Mexican side. After looking over the room, someone suggested that we use a jackhammer to break the floor below the pool table. I called one of my agents, requested a jackhammer, and began the assault on the floor. It didn't take long to break through the four-inch concrete floor. Once I had busted a two-foot hole in the concrete, we peered into the darkness below and saw an entire room larger than the one we were standing in.

The ten-by-ten-foot section that held the pool table was set up with a large hydraulic lift identical to one in a mechanic's shop used to hoist vehicles. It was obvious that there was a control to lift the floor, but where? Every agent began turning on light switches, playing with remote controls and anything that seemed electric. Then someone twisted an outside water spigot to get a drink of water and the floor began to lift; we had discovered the switch.

The entire floor section lifted up, revealing a room with hydraulic lifts, generators for electricity, cables for towing a mining cart through the tunnel, and a flood and drain system connected to the main water supply. When the traffickers finished using the tunnel, they flooded it using a main water connection below a fire hydrant. When needed, the water in the tunnel could be emptied by means of a pump that used a drain on the curb of the street. It was the first high-tech tunnel discovered, and the following day rumors surfaced that a second tunnel existed.

The discovery was a media extravaganza; it headlined the world news for weeks. In the first three days everyone but the pope flew in to see the new wonder of the world. For us the pain and agony had only begun. The agents were working around the clock; time was of the essence. We interviewed suspects, sorted through mounds of records, and arrested new violators daily.

Being one of only several agents who had ever worked in Mexico, I was assigned to assist and coordinate the investigation with the MFJP, who were working a joint investigation in Mexico. During the first two days, information was received that the main stash house in Mexico was an old diaper warehouse. The MFJP agents from Mexico City raided the warehouse and discovered approximately ten tons of marijuana. While we were at the warehouse, the local unit of the MFJP arrived and demanded to know what the hell was going on. Then the MFJP commandant said that all the U.S. agents needed to return to the United States, as it wasn't safe in Mexico.

The following day we learned that the MFJP from Mexico City and the local MFJP, along with the state police, were fighting each other and had been involved in a shootout. The MFJP who had been helping us left and went back to Mexico City. We were told to stay out of Mexico until things could get resolved. I later learned that the marijuana in the warehouse belonged to Amado Carrillo, "the lord of the skies"; he had paid the MFJP for its protection and wasn't going to be interfered with.

Informants told me later that the marijuana was moved to another location and the traffickers were going to wait until we left the area. Losing the tunnel was simply a price they paid, but losing their drugs in Mexico wasn't going to happen. Amado Carrillo was the richest trafficker in Mexico; he paid off protection to the highest level.

Following the discovery of the tunnel, I spent almost two months in Douglas. I caught sleep when I could, an hour or two under a desk or a nap while someone drove, and I ate junk food and tacos in Mexico. Following the gunfight between the MFJP agents, a new special force of MFJP agents were called in. They were the elite Tiger Unit.

I was notified that I should go to the Agua Prieta airport to greet the new commandant of the Tiger Unit. I arrived at the airport, where more than a hundred MFJP agents were lined up by a hangar. The place looked like a military base; all the agents were dressed in black, carried automatic weapons, and had an embroidered image of a clawing tiger on their uniforms. As the commandant's plane landed, every agent came to attention, and I got chills, it was so impressive. This really seemed like one well-trained group. The Beechcraft King Air taxied into the hangar, and then in the distance I saw someone inspecting the men. The commandant started at one end and walked down the row, looking over every officer. As he came closer to me, I realized it was none other than my old friend Commandant Christian Peralta, the very same MFJP commandant I worked with in Hermosillo years earlier.

He finished his inspection and turned to the waiting American contingent. I couldn't believe it; the commandant shook hands with the other agents, and when he got to me he grinned and said, "*Que alegre, mi compadre*" ("I'm happy, my friend"), and we hugged the Mexican bear hug with slaps to the back; the *compadres borrachos* were reunited.

Things quickly became very serious. On the Mexican side of the border, the commandant was a no-nonsense guy. His unit rounded up suspects, who were quickly detained and interviewed. The commandant didn't like being lied to, and several suspects learned that the hard way.

Four suspects believed to be in charge of stash houses were detained and questioned one at a time. I was present at the interviews, and the commandant told them each he didn't like being lied to. Three said they knew nothing, but one guy said a stash house was located in a small village about twenty miles outside town.

Going on a raid with the MFJP is like driving the Baja 1000 road race. Tom and I were the last vehicle in the convoy of four Chevrolet Suburbans and one truck as we drove through twenty miles of dusty dirt back roads to the village. These maniacs drove at speeds approaching ninety miles per hour on a road that could safely be driven at twenty. We arrived in a cloud of dust; the residents probably saw us ten miles away. We waited in my vehicle for five minutes for the dirt to clear, and once I got out it was obvious that there would be nothing here. We had been led to a destitute village where the people didn't even have shoes.

The two suspects who had been brought with us had been riding in the back of the Suburban. The commandant ordered the idiot who told us about the village to be brought front and center.

The commandant asked why he lied. No answer. Immediately two MFJP agents held him while another beat him like a punching bag for lying. He was dragged back to the pickup truck and shoved into the back. The two suspects were told to lie flat in the bed of the truck. The MFJP agents sat on top of the guys lying facedown in the back of the truck, using them as seat cushions.

We departed the area, again traveling ninety miles an hour down the washboard road, leaving another massive dust cloud in our wake. The suspects lying in the floor of the truck were getting pounded by the road. As Tom and I followed the truck, we saw the MFJP agents punch and hit the suspect who'd lied with the butt of a rifle the entire drive back to Agua Prieta. Tom was assigned to take pictures of the entire operation and took some great photos.

We returned to the residence we used as a base command. It was a residence that we had raided earlier; the traffickers had used it as a communications center to coordinate air smuggling. This place belonged to Amado Carrillo's group. Few others used the high-band VHF radios, and the house had several radio towers mounted outside to communicate with aircraft.

The remaining suspects were taken to a vacant room and stood up along the wall. Then two MFJP agents dragged the suspect who'd lied into the room and threw him onto the floor. His shirt was torn to shreds. Hell, the guy's body looked like it had been through a meat grinder. He was a bloody mess; swelling and bruising had set in, his face was black and blue, and he was bleeding from dozens of cuts. The guy was moaning and whining like an infant and had the dry heaves. The remaining three guys froze and stared at their friend lying on the cold concrete floor.

The commandant entered the room and everything became

silent; then he turned to the three standing suspects and said in a normal tone, "I don't like liars; I will ask you one last time where the stash houses are."

The three suspects looked like little kids in school; two of the suspects quickly raised their arms to speak and gave up every drug dealer and known stash house in Agua Prieta. They also led us to a massive grave where the thirty laborers who had dug the tunnel were buried. These poor peasants had been kept in a house for months and not allowed to leave until the tunnel was dug. Then, once it was finished, they were loaded into a large truck, taken out to the desert, and killed. The traffickers wanted to make sure that there were no leaks about the tunnel.

It was two different worlds. In the United States the suspects would have said nothing and asked for a lawyer, and the case would have ended there. In Mexico, I witnessed more than my share of interviews and interrogations. American agents weren't supposed to see the abuses for fear that we would talk about them; now Mexico has a civil rights division to prevent such abuses, and the MFJP agents are supposed to obtain a search warrant like we do.

Things in Mexico are not always what they appear to be. When you read about the MFJP making giant seizures of drugs, you don't realize that more often than not the narcotics seized are sold back to the traffickers. This is the Mexican system of checks and balances; the traffickers bribe the MFJP before they set up operations, and then business is booming and the amount of drugs smuggled is enormous, so the MFJP make a large seizure, sell it back, and demand a raise in their monthly bribery fund. Who can blame the Mexican police? They make less than three hundred dollars a month; they either cooperate or die. The Mexican way of life for most police is "the silver or the lead."

Let's say I'm a Mexican cop and I make ninety dollars a month. A trafficker offers me another two hundred dollars a month, tripling my salary, and all I have to do is take a long siesta—but if I say, "No, thank you," I get killed. Not even the Godfather would have refused that offer.

IN the United States there are still corruption problems at the various ports of entry. We don't admit it and it takes forever to investigate the corruption, but it exists and will continue to do so until the government makes each inspector, border patrol agent, and law enforcement officer take a polygraph before being hired, and every three to five years to deter the weak who get tempted.

The sad reality was that when the cocaine push started, corruption at the port was at an all-time high. There must have been at least twelve immigration inspectors who were known to be on the take. There wasn't a day that a source didn't say a load was passed at the POE by a crooked inspector. In the six years between 1996 and 2002, nineteen immigration inspectors and six Customs inspectors were fired, arrested, and prosecuted for accepting bribes and trafficking in drugs through the ports of entry.

It was believed that several of these were recruited by a local trafficker named Villegas. Villegas worked for El Jaimillo, who seemed to be the head of the plaza in Nogales, Sonora, Mexico. Luis had gone to high school with some of the new inspectors and had recruited them to work for him. We also had sources working for Luis who provided us with the time and place of his cocaine deliveries.

It was a winter day around two in the afternoon; the wind was blowing and it was raining and visibility was terrible. We had established surveillance around the stash house and were waiting for the load van to arrive. We wanted to catch the driver, and hopefully Villegas as well, when the dope was delivered to the house.

The van crossed right through the Grand Avenue POE with four thousand pounds of cocaine stacked up in a panel van, the kind a repair man drives, that had the rear of the van sealed off from the driver's compartment. It drove up and was waved through the POE and never inspected. The van pulled into the driveway of the house and we initiated our raid. The driver saw someone and ran out the back door and disappeared as we approached. Villegas then fled to Mexico. I demanded action from the MFJP in Mexico: a raid on El Jaimillo's house in Calle Kennedy and several other major stash locations. I asked that a few agents and I accompany them. So once again I was armed and raiding houses in Mexico and pissing people off. Sometimes becoming too visible isn't good; your name gets tagged in the newspaper and you're on the nightly news being interviewed, and you become the target of choice for the traffickers. I had multiple price tags on my head.

THE war on drugs can never be won when you're betrayed by the guys standing next to you in the trenches on the front line. The power of the traffickers and their unlimited supply of money are often too much for individuals. The sad reality of life is that there are Customs inspectors, border patrol agents, DEA agents, and immigration agents who have fallen to the lure of easy money. We became so busy with corruption cases that we didn't concentrate on the main suppliers; hell, they were off the radar. The offer of women and the fast life and up to fifty thousand dollars to allow a load to cross the international border or a checkpoint over-whelms them. One immigration inspector had $300,000 cash in his closet when he was arrested.

THE office worked for the next two years, trying to investigate the corruption at the POE. We were being saturated with co-caine loads being crossed through. We joined forces with the FBI, the DEA, and every law enforcement agency that would assist. The FBI initiated a Title III wiretap and finally, after an extensive investigation, twelve immigration and Customs inspectors were arrested for corruption, charged with allowing illegal drugs to cross, selling border crossing cards, money laundering, and tax evasion.

The years spent as a first-line supervisor were a blur; I worked night and day. The traffickers dug so damn many tunnels that when a confidential source called, we prayed they wouldn't say the dreaded T-word, as we called it. Because of the international drama following the Douglas tunnel investigation, if a tunnel was mentioned, it required twenty-four-hour-a-day surveillance and monitoring. We brought in remote cameras, mobile homes, and surveillance vans and sat on the holes until we decided to termi-nate the investigation and fill the hole with concrete. Most of the time we had confidential sources telling us when the dope was crossing in the tunnels and what car was used for the pickup, but that wasn't good enough for Washington, D.C. They demanded around-the-clock surveillance when the ugly word was mentioned.

We investigated too damn many tunnels and had to conduct endless surveillances that lasted for weeks on end. I hated the mention of tunnels. After about twenty-plus long-term surveillances, I told my group not to mention the T-word unless they knew it was a large and significant tunnel.

The Nogales drain system, with hundreds of three-foot storm drain pipes running from one end of town to the other, was a maze. Most tunnels were less than twenty feet long and were exits out of the main water drain under Grand Avenue. The little moles rented houses next to storm drains, dug down four feet and over ten feet to the curb, cut into the metal drain pipe, and dragged the dope from the main drain to the house.

To date, more than seventy-five tunnels have been discovered in Nogales, and at least another twenty that we never told people about. Among these, only about ten were well-constructed tunnels connecting a business or residence in Mexico to a business or residence in the United States. These tunnels have been discovered in churches, the Elks Club, the center for the blind, and about every downtown business in Nogales, Arizona.

When the press heard of a tunnel being discovered and came for pictures and a story, we always fed them the same line: *The tunnel is new. It was just discovered and this was the first load taken off.* The press knew we were lying, but in reality we worked the damn tunnel from inception as it was being dug. Informants told us about it, we waited and worked it till the last load was taken off, and when the traffickers decided not to use it anymore, then we called the press.

The agents in the Nogales office were the best at recruiting and handling confidential informants. I preached source recruitment and development at every office meeting. I used a simple story to explain why we need informants. I used the game of golf as a tool, telling the agents to imagine you're playing golf on a new course. The course has no signs, no markers, and no scorecard to look at; the only one who can tell you is a caddy. He knows where the green is and the yardage. He carries your clubs. But it's still up to you to strike the ball and putt on the green. In our world, the informant is our caddy. He guides us, tells us how to navigate the border terrain, shows us where the traps are, and so on, but we still have to catch the smugglers. They are both games you love and hate.

The agents in the office effected hundreds of arrests each year and seized massive amounts of drugs. The Nogales office was the leading office in the United States for drug seizures and arrest. Regardless of how hard we worked, the traffickers simply increased production every year. The volume of narcotics crossing the border was staggering. Some days we worked three to five operations a day, with some of these operations taking place simultaneously. Then the agents had to respond to the ports of entry to handle the arrests and seizures there. The ports generated ten to twelve seizures daily.

Rene had taken the position as RAC of Sells, Arizona, and was the boss of the famous Customs Patrol Shadow Wolves. I was driving around one day with Layne, and he turned to me and said, "Boy, I'm retiring. I've had enough."

I thought he was kidding around and said, "Yeah, right, bullshit."

Layne said, "You just reach a point; you'll find out someday. Everyone knows when it's their time to walk away."

So by default, or because no one else wanted the position, I was promoted from supervisory agent to resident agent in charge (RAC) in Nogales. I went from supervising ten agents to supervising thirty-four agents. I was now accountable for the actions of the entire office. Sounds great, except a supervisor and RAC are the same GS-14 pay grade and make the same salary.

I lasted about two years before the stress and anger of dealing with the bosses above and the new Generation X agents who had been forced to transfer to the office took their toll on me. I requested a transfer; I needed out of Nogales.

With the major advancements in technology, surveillances had become easier; tracking devices connected to laptop computers helped us follow cars to their delivery destinations. We could watch houses with remote cameras using line-of-sight communications like satellite TV. We now watched stash houses live on laptop computer while sitting at the office.

About two weeks before I transferred out of Nogales, I went to the border regarding another tunnel from a business in Mexico to an apartment complex in the United States—the same apartment complex on West International Street that had been used twice before for tunnels. I was supposed to tell the press the usual story: the tunnel was just discovered, this was the first seizure, and so on.

I had crossed the border to meet with the MFJP and look at the tunnel when I was photographed by the Mexican press standing over the tunnel. I was holding a cigar. It was in my trademark pose and I asked that the picture not be used. Yeah, right; the next day there I was on the front page of the *El Imparcial* newspaper. I was identified by name, with a caption saying, "The boss of DEA in Nogales is known for his expertise in tunnel investigations." I joked with the DEA agents about my new title, head of the DEA.

I realized that the significance of the photo was truly untimely about a year later. The idea of having my picture on the front page of the newspaper two weeks before I transferred to Mexico, identifying me as the head of the DEA, could not have been worse timing.

BEFORE becoming a supervisor, I volunteered for temporary investigative assignments to a dozen places, including New Orleans, Los Angeles, Puerto Rico, Georgia, Texas, Miami, and Bolivia. These thirty-day, ninety-day, and six-month details provided an escape and freedom from the day-to-day routine and challenges of Nogales.

I took a position as RAC in Hermosillo, Sonora, Mexico. Even though my first tour of working in Mexico had ended in threats, working in Mexico again had always been in the back of my mind. The allure of Mexico, with its culture and hospitality, seemed to call me. I loved working in Mexico. I had worked in and out of Mexico during the last ten years, but living there was a whole new experience. I was older now and a much more experienced agent. I would actually have an office and a house to work from, instead of living in different hotel rooms and hiding. I looked forward to working full time again in Mexico. The political climate seemed a lot calmer, the Mexican agencies and the U.S. agencies were getting along, and cooperation was at an all-time high. What could possibly go wrong?

I had a large staff that consisted of a secretary and me. I didn't care. I was exhausted from the mayhem of years in Nogales. I was happy for a change of pace. In Mexico, the RAC is also called a Customs attaché/senior Customs representative. This position is great; you run the office and conduct investigations. Fieldwork was my expertise. The happiest time of my career was being a senior special agent in the field, working my own investigations.

At this same time a good friend of mine, Pete, was promoted to be the new Customs attaché in Mexico City. Pete was an old friend from the El Paso, Texas, office and a border rat just like me. He had worked his way up the ladder and was no stranger to the problems on the border. Pete, like me, was burned out from the daily life in the El Paso office. The investigations of the House of Death informant were still underway, and a half dozen agents were under investigation for leaving a load of marijuana during destruction.

All marijuana is destroyed by incineration at a Tucson facility. The group of agents from El Paso, Texas, brought over several tons to destroy and threw it into the incinerator and left, figuring it would eventually burn up. Well, an employee of the plant decided this was his golden opportunity. After looking into the incinerator, he dug into the burning pile, and retrieved about four hundred pounds of slightly charred marijuana. The happy guy loaded it into his truck and left work early to enjoy his newfound fortune.

No one said this idiot was the sharpest knife in the drawer. The dumbshit forgot that some of the slightly charred marijuana was still burning, leaving a large trail of smoke from the camper shell. The worker passed a police car, and the patrolman was knocked over by the odor. The cop said it was like a scene from a Cheech and Chong movie. The officer quickly pulled the truck over to find that the guy was so stoned he could barely drive; he had inhaled so much smoke that he had no clue what he was doing.

This incident started a full-scale Internal Affairs investigation on misconduct and a new policy on how agents assigned to the destruction detail had to watch the dope until the last ounce was burned. Seriously, who would think some knucklehead would drag burning marijuana out of a thousand-degree blast furnace? One more lesson learned the hard way. The Customs Service had agents assigned around the world, but it took less than twenty-four hours for rumors to spread. So when an agent or office did something stupid, we all learned from it and were thankful it wasn't our office.

Pete and I found out later that the RAC was leaving his position in Texas. One day I got a call from Pete, and he said he wanted me to get rid of an old Pontiac. I asked the secretary if she knew where the car was and she said, "You'll have to ask the prior RAC." I found out that he had given the government vehicle to an informant, who sold the car.

The Hermosillo office needed an enema; it was on the chopping block, and headquarters was debating on whether to close it for lack of activity. I didn't wait long to stir up a shitstorm. I terminated the secretary, hired a new one, and spent the better part of the first year reorganizing the office, meeting a multitude of Mexican commandants from every agency and traveling the states in my jurisdiction. I knew that to be effective I had to recruit and develop a cadre of confidential sources. I soon realized that not everything had changed. I found a few individuals I had known in the past.

The RAC of the Hermosillo office was in charge of coordinating investigations of narcotics smuggling, weapons smuggling, child pornography, and money laundering in Mexico, just as I had done in the United States. My jurisdiction covered Chihuahua, Sonora, Sinaloa, Durango, Nayarit, Jalisco, and Baja California. I covered the border towns from Big Bend National Park in Texas, west to El Paso and Ciudad Juarez, then the border towns in New Mexico, and on to California to San Ysidro and Tijuana, Mexico. I guess this information was left out of my tourist travel guide when I applied for the position.

I also failed to evaluate the fact that my jurisdiction was also the main jurisdiction of the worst drug cartels in Mexico. Caro Quintero was still in prison in Mexico, so his brother Miguel was running the operation. Caro Quintero lived like a millionaire in prison. He had a tunnel built that led out of the prison; he went to nightclubs and restaurants and had women brought to his cell. He dined on the best china and had the best restaurants deliver to him in prison. He was still running his empire via cell phones and telephone lines installed in his jail cell.

Amado Carrillo, "the lord of the skies," controlled the distribution of most drugs moving into and out of Mexico; he was considered the number one trafficker at this time. It was estimated that he owned more than twenty-two private 727 airliners and hundreds of small aircraft to distribute his drugs. Carrillo's wealth was believed to exceed $25 billion, and he was considered untouchable. He had property in almost every state in Mexico and was constructing a mansion in Hermosillo, Sonora, one block away from my assigned residence. Thankfully he died and never finished it.

I was in Mexico for less than a month when a 727 jet landed at Bahia Kino, a small beach community fifty miles west of Hermosillo. The jet landed at the small airport, overran the runway, and sank into the sand. The jet was loaded with ten thousand pounds of cocaine and was stuck so badly the traffickers just left it buried. My sources said agents from the MFJP and state police helped off-load the cargo and escorted the load of cocaine to the border for distribution.

The Beltrán-Leyva cartel was also active in Sonora and Chihuahua, and the list of traffickers operating in my area could have filled the Tucson telephone directory.

Chapo Guzman was also in prison. He had appealed his prison sentence and had hired the same prominent defense attorney, Francisco Alatorre, from Hermosillo, Sonora, who had been the defense attorney for Rafael Caro Quintero. Francisco Alatorre had a law office in San Diego as well as in Mexico City, but after the Caro Quintera case, the government took away his visa and about two million dollars in cash that he was paid by Caro Quintero for attorney fees. I was introduced to Alatorre by another attorney. I didn't know who the hell the guy was. It was an old Mexican ploy: *Can you help a friend?* When I checked on the name, I found that Alatorre was barred from ever getting a visa or entering the United States again.

Alatorre expected this news but appreciated that I checked. I was invited to lunch with him several times along with other attorneys in Hermosillo and enjoyed his conversations. Alatorre had a secretary in his office who reminded me of Luscious Lola, only this señorita was classy and was dressed to the nines every day. I gladly accepted offers to visit Alatorre's office. I listened as he explained the complexity of his famous clients and gained some insight about the dark circle they lived in. Alatorre was very sly; he tried several times to offer me token gifts, such as a watch and a pair of handmade shoes. I declined the offers. I knew he was testing me; he wanted to see if I could be bought. He figured if I took a small gift, then I would likely accept larger gifts or cash bribes.

During the course of the next year I had several meetings with

Alatorre. He explained how he was given gold-handled Colt .45 pistols by Caro Quintero as payment for his loyalty. These are the pistols on display at the DEA headquarters. Today, in the middle of the afternoon, Alatorre was driving when two gunmen pulled up to his vehicle in another car and fired three rounds point-blank into his head. Alatorre died instantly. He was killed immediately. Rumors emerged that a rival trafficker had him killed and ordered the hit. Two years later, he was released from prison and regained his empire.

Once again, I thought that by seizing narcotics and attacking the money of the cartels. As the Mexicans say, I was trying to be myself. I need to prove myself again as a working agent. It had been nine years since I'd worked my own investigations. I could once again work without hindrance.

The Arellano Felix brothers controlled Baja California and were considered the largest cocaine smugglers in Mexico. Working for the Arellano Felix brothers was Theodore Garcia, known as "El Teo" ("the Enforcer"). He left a trail of dead bodies in his wake throughout the Baja California area.

El Teo was the most feared man in Baja California. He tortured and killed randomly. His partner was an individual known as El Pozoler ("the Stew Maker"), who disposed of the bodies of the people that El Teo killed. The Stew Maker took the bodies and dissolved them in fifty-five-gallon barrels of caustic chemicals. When he was finally arrested, more than three hundred bodies were found in barrels stacked up in a warehouse, in various stages of meltdown from the chemicals.

I traveled to Tijuana on many occasions and always hated it.
The place gave me the creeps. Staying in the hotels in Tijuana
was outside even my realm of safety.

ONE day I stopped to get a hamburger at a Burger King in Hermosillo. It's a modern city of about five hundred thousand people
and has every fast-food chain, just like the United States. As soon
as I walked in the door I saw Villegas, the fugitive from Nogales,
Arizona. Villegas was responsible for crossing dozens of loads,
and the big load of four thousand pounds of cocaine in the van and
bribing Customs inspectors. The bastard was sitting with several
people but definitely saw me and made eye contact. As he was
leaving, I motioned for him to come over to my table. I said, "We
need to talk. If you give up the dirty inspectors, I will work on
getting you a deal."

The conversation was aborted because the guys with him
walked over to see what was wrong.

Christ, I thought, *I could have just as easily run into that fucking psy-
cho Quemado. I doubt he would have just chatted with me.* I think that was
when I realized I was very vulnerable, and alone. Sure, there were
four DEA agents at the American consulate, but they were just as
busy as I was and always traveling. I knew that to survive this tour,
I needed to wise up. I had been out of the field too long and was
taking simple things for granted.

I started thinking about my first tour in Mexico. I had always
used different routes daily, and I never ate at the same restaurant.
I began to think about how that tour ended, and I realized that
perhaps things weren't any better now than they were ten years
earlier. I had to change my habits quickly before I became a mark.

During my tenure in Nogales, I had met a Mexican army colonel in Nogales, Sonora, Mexico, and we had become close friends. Colonel Sanchez was a tough old guy from the state of Jalisco, Mexico, the birthplace of tequila. He was also one tequila-drinking hombre; on more than one occasion I had the pleasure of being invited to his little house on the military base in Nogales, Sonora, and emptying a bottle or two of tequila while his wife fed us her special Mexican dishes. The colonel felt honored to have me at his home; he served carne asadas and invited his young captains and lieutenants. The colonel took on all comers who attempted to show their tequila-drinking prowess.

Tequila should have a warning label, and one should be allowed only a three-shot maximum. It also never has the same effect twice; one time when you drink it you're mellow and simply pass out quietly, and then the next time you're ready to fight the entire world. Just as in John Anderson's cowboy song, "Straight Tequila Night." Few words can describe the international bonding that results from consuming tequila as it occurs in Mexico. Two strangers can become best friends for life after consuming a bottle of tequila together. Colonel Sanchez and I were two old warriors fighting the drug war because it was what we did, without question.

On many occasions I developed information about stash houses in Nogales, Sonora, and went directly to Colonel Sanchez. He mustered his troops and we raided the house in a matter of minutes. He would laugh and say, "Drugs are the responsibility of the MFJP; we don't have the authority, but not to worry." He showed me a faded old piece of paper; it had turned yellow from age and was kept inside a plastic folder to prevent it from falling apart like dust. The search warrant had been signed by a Mexican federal judge about fifteen years earlier; Colonel Sanchez held it proudly and said, "No one ever asks to read it."

He knew that I had transferred to Hermosillo, Mexico, and introduced me to a colonel there who, in turn, introduced me to an army general in charge of the state of Sonora.

Ricardo had taught me well regarding Mexican culture and the fine art of dealing with officials in Mexico. The biggest mistake most DEA and Customs agents make in Mexico is that upon meeting a Mexican official, they immediately ask for something. American agents think that just because they have a badge, they should receive help. Nothing is further from the truth.

In Mexico, first you eat and drink, and after a couple of days of getting to know each other, then it's okay to talk shop. It's like a dating game; there has to be a courtship. Always let the Mexicans make the first move. When I was first introduced to the general, we made small talk, and then he asked, "What do you want?"

I said, "Nothing at all."

He didn't expect that. But I learned that he had an interest in photography of desert cacti and that he liked twelve-year-old scotch. I made it a point to buy a nice book with photos of cacti and his favorite scotch. Then, in a month, I asked for another meeting, where I presented him with the gifts. He expected that I wanted something, to which I said, "Nothing. I am in your country as a guest, and if I can be of service, let me know."

About a month went by and he called for a favor. He needed a travel visa for his wife's sister, and I made the arrangements through the State Department. The State Department official had tried to contact the general for the last four years without any results. The consulate general issued the visa herself, and he was honored. The general was now on the hook because in Mexican tradition, a favor begets a favor. I was now off and running, as multiple sources were providing me with information on several traffickers, and the information resulted in the seizures of semis full of marijuana. I had sources providing information on ranches where the marijuana was grown. U.S. agents assigned to work in Mexico have no authority to arrest or make seizures; the information must be passed on to a Mexican law enforcement agency. I chose working with the Mexican army. I did provide some small loads to the MFJP, but the majority of the loads I gave to the general, who dispatched his army.

One source gave me information about a ranch that resulted in the seizure of twenty-five tons of marijuana. I was invited to witness the destruction and given the ceremonial torch, a mop soaked in diesel fuel to light the plants on fire. I felt I was really making significant seizures and preventing the dope from getting to the border. The response I received from Washington was that it didn't matter because the marijuana was seized by the Mexican government.

Then, one day in 1999, I received a telephone call from a supervisor in Tucson who told me someone had made a death threat against me. My first reaction was to think that it might have been Luis Villegas or Quemado, but the supervisor didn't have the name of the trafficker and said he would call me later. I brushed it off, saying, "What else is new?" Hell, I had received several death threats while working in Nogales.

Then, three hours later, the assistant special agent in charge in Tucson called me and said that the FBI had a Title III wiretap operating and had overheard a conversation between an unidentified male and Jaime Gonzalez Gutierrez, also known as El Jaimillo, the trafficker in Nogales, Sonora, who had risen to a place of power after the fall of Figueroa-Soto. The same El Jaimillo whose house I'd raided in Nogales, Sonora, and the same guy who had Sandra, the best-looking woman in Nogales, Arizona, as his squeeze. Who says money can't buy everything? El Jaimillo and someone in the Beltrán-Leyva organization were intercepted on the wiretap discussing a hit on me. El Jaimillo wanted me dead. He knew my full name, my address in Hermosillo, and what vehicle I was driving.

I wasn't given a choice. I was told to pack a bag and get the hell out of Mexico ASAP.

After raiding El Jaimillo's residence a couple of years earlier in Nogales, Sonora, I had thought he was arrested by the MFJP in Hermosillo. Hell, the arrest by the MFJP back in May 1997 made the newspapers. I had heard that he offered the police a hundred thousand dollars to let him go. I guessed that he'd bought his way out or paid the prison officials to let him go. According to the wiretap, he was pissed off because I had been hitting his deliveries pretty hard and seizing a lot of his dope before it reached Nogales, Sonora.

I was told to pack enough clothes for about two weeks. I called a few contacts before I left and told them I would be leaving for an uncertain amount of time. One of these was the Mexican army general. I briefed him on my situation, and he said, "I'm sure everything will work out so you can return."

The entire DEA group escorted me to the border in Nogales, and the next day I flew to Washington, D.C.

I had to wait, idle, in Washington, D.C., while the Office of Investigations and the Office of Internal Affairs investigated the death threat. I had no idea if, or when, I was going to return to

Mexico. Ricardo was now working for the Office of Internal Affairs in Tucson and kept me informed on the situation. I was called into the Office of Internal Affairs in Washington and asked if I had concerns about returning to Mexico. I said no and was allowed to return to Mexico the following week.

Somehow things just have a way of working out. Upon returning to Mexico, I heard that El Jaimillo had been found dead; someone had executed him. He had been shot twenty-eight times and his bullet-ridden body was bound with duct tape; he was wrapped in plastic and stuffed in the trunk of a vehicle. Someone notified the Nogales, Sonora, police of a suspicious vehicle, and when they opened the trunk they found his body.

I reestablished all my contacts with the MFJP office and military upon my return. I was invited to a meeting with the Mexican army general. He greeted me and said, "I'm glad you're back." Then he spoke in a different tone of voice and said, "You don't have to worry; the person who threatened you was taken care of."

Then it looked as if he smiled. That look and that statement said something together. I wanted him to clarify his last statement, but I dared not ask any questions. What the hell did the smirk or smile mean? Did the general just tell me that he had had El Jaimillo killed, or was he just telling me about the death of El Jaimillo?

During my next meeting with the general, he invited me to his office and presented me with a special gun permit signed by him to carry a pistol. This had never happened to any U.S. agent working in Mexico. I was now the only agent officially allowed to carry a weapon in Mexico. DEA agents were begging me to ask the general for a permit for them. But the permit was a one-of-a-kind special favor; I knew that to ask for another would be offensive.

* * *

I continued my assault on the traffickers, and, based on constant information about air smuggling and short landings by the hundreds in the state of Sonora, we finally persuaded the Mexican government to allow Customs to place an Air Interdiction Unit in Hermosillo, Sonora. The detail was known as Operation Halcon.

I'm not sure what was more difficult, getting the Mexican government to cooperate or persuading the Customs pilots to move. They were already in Mexico but had been assigned to the airport in Puerto Vallarta. They lived in large, luxurious two-bedroom condos with ocean views and sat around drinking beer all day. They hadn't flown an actual intercept mission in more than a year.

The air program in Mexico consisted of one U.S. Citation Interceptor jet equipped with nose cone radar and filming equipment to track and record aircraft suspected of transporting drugs. The program was sanctioned by the Mexican government, and they had a military pilot on board with the Customs pilots. The Mexican military provided a Beechcraft Queen Air and a Black Hawk helicopter to assist once a suspect's plane landed.

I flew into Puerto Vallarta to help the pilots and mechanics pack up the airplane hangar, then drove the pilot's vehicle back to Hermosillo. I was given an eight-man Mexican military escort back to Hermosillo, Sonora. We drove the first day to Mazatlán, Mexico, and then were given a new group of soldiers to escort us the rest of the way into Hermosillo. In the afternoon we stopped in Los Mochis, Sinaloa, for gas. The military guys were all dressed in black fatigues. At the station we stretched our legs and drank soda for a few minutes. While we were there, I noticed a city cop at the station but gave it no thought.

We hit the road again and were about fifteen minutes down the highway when we were surrounded by thirty police vehicles; the military escort jumped out and surrounded my vehicle. We were, quite literally, in a Mexican standoff. The young military lieutenant met with the chief of police but could not convince him that we weren't going to raid a house in his territory. The standoff lasted more than three hours. While we were parked in the middle of Highway 15, traffic was diverted off the freeway and around us. It took calls to Mexico City and the State Department before we were finally released. The entire state of Sinaloa was bought and paid for by the traffickers, and they were making sure that we were just passing through and not going to raid anything in the area.

The Customs air group was relocated to the Holiday Inn in Hermosillo. The one-bedroom suites with no view and no ocean were in the back of the hotel. The weather was so hot in Hermosillo, you could fry an egg anywhere. Temperatures in Hermosillo reach more than 120 degrees in the summer. Siestas are still honored in the state of Sonora; the MFJP commandant worked from ten A.M. to two P.M., then went home for a siesta till six P.M., then worked till around midnight.

In spite of the complaining and moaning, the pilots flew, and in the first week they identified three targets and the Mexican military seized three loads and three aircraft. The pilots had stats to justify the move. I assisted with tail numbers and identified the pilots and the trafficking group responsible. By the end of the first year, more than thirty-four planes were seized. Not every aircraft was seized when it landed. Dozens escaped, and a couple were trailed back to the fields where they loaded; on one surveillance back to Los Mochis, a plantation with more than thirty tons of marijuana was observed and raided by ground forces who destroyed the crop.

One night after the pilots returned from flying, they stopped to eat at the Mexican restaurant Sanborns, which is like a Denny's. One pilot noticed that they were being watched. Sure enough, two Mexican men kept staring at them, and when he went to walk around the store in the front, one of the men followed and watched his every move and even followed the pilots outside when they left the restaurant.

The pilots called me, and then Washington, D.C., called me, because they had reported the situation to the highest level. I had to get the MFJP to stand guard at their hotel and escort them to the airport the next morning. I was told to write a new threat assessment for the area, which I downplayed; the pilots, of course, wrote their own and made the area seem like a war zone. Then the State Department had to write one to even out the two to the satisfaction of everyone.

Less than two weeks later, the pilots went to the same restaurant and once again encountered the suspicious Mexicans. But they immediately called me, and I called the MFJP. We all responded and surrounded the restaurant. We had instructed the pilots to wait until we were set up before leaving the restaurant. We called them and said to come out, and sure enough, as they left, the two guys followed and were greeted with about ten automatic rifles pointed at them. The two guys literally pissed themselves as they were thrown onto the sidewalk, and then they were cuffed and whisked away to MFJP headquarters.

The poor bastards were interrogated to no end. It seems that they weren't trying to hurt the pilots; the two Mexicans were gay and thought that the one pilot was the most beautiful hunk they

had ever laid their eyes on. They couldn't help but admire his
blond hair, blue eyes, and bulging muscles. They were in love and
referred to the pilot as *El Guero Dulce*, which meant "the candy
sweet blond American."

I wrote the full report and sent it to everyone I knew, including D.C. and the State Department. The pilot quickly earned the
nickname *Nalgas Dulces* or "sweet ass," and the rest of the pilots
hesitated before they cried wolf to headquarters again.

THE mountainous area south of Nogales, Sonora, between Imuris
and Magdalena has hundreds of flat hillsides that are perfect for
landing small aircraft. The traffickers line the dirt hilltops with
buckets of oil and kerosene and make landing lights for the planes.
There were times after the first year of doing the air intercepts
when, if they knew they were spotted, they torched the entire
plane and the load of marijuana to burn any evidence.

In a year's time around 2001, there were an estimated 1,200
fades in the border area. Fades are when an aircraft disappears
off the radar. This is known as a short landing just before the border to off-load the drugs. The Air Interdiction Unit seized a total
of thirty-seven aircraft, twenty thousand pounds of marijuana,
and two thousand pounds of cocaine. Thirty-seven out of 1,200 is
a low number, but the traffickers had an unlimited number of pilots and an endless supply of stolen aircraft at their disposal. In
the United States during this same time, the theft of small aircraft
was at an all-time high.

The same year, I had seized a record amount of marijuana,
more than 270,000 pounds. These seizures were the result of very
good sources of information. My one-man shop had beaten the

total number in pounds seized by the entire Nogales, Arizona, office during the same one-year period.

I was continually traveling to the border to assist other offices. Ricardo had finally gotten out of Internal Affairs and had taken the position of supervisor at the Nogales office. With the exception of Tom and a couple of other agents, the entire office had changed. Half the agents had rotated out and gone to other offices or Internal Affairs; some transferred to Tucson and Headquarters.

I got a call one day from a source known as "Dr. Nogales" who said an airplane had landed at a ranch near Agua Prieta, Sonora. I contacted the MFJP and then asked if anyone from the DEA wanted to go with me. The DEA agents all said they were busy and didn't want to drive the three hours to the ranch.

I called the commandant, who just happened to be a Mexican army colonel on loan to the MFJP. In Hermosillo, there were three different commandants of the MFJP. One guy, called "The Yankee," was in charge of the entire state and all federal crimes; another commandant was in charge of terrestrial airplane loads; and finally, DEA worked with a commandant who ran a vetted unit of men who had taken a polygraph to prove they weren't corrupt. At least they weren't corrupt at the time they took the polygraph. The three commandants didn't trust each other, and all thought they were over the others.

I learned early on in Mexico, always choose the army. The terrestrial commandant not only was in charge of the air smuggling, but he also had the responsibility for drugs seized at the main military checkpoint just south of Benjamin Hill on Highway 15 running north and south.

The source was an ex–Mexican military captain who didn't have a problem meeting or working directly with the commandant. He rode with us and guided us directly to the ranch. This was no ordinary ranch; it was a large spread that had a small-aircraft landing strip, three ranch houses, several horse stables containing dozens of quarter horses, and a roping arena. The search revealed more than two thousand pounds of marijuana in a horse shed. The caretaker on the ranch was arrested. To my surprise, the commandant questioned him in front of me. The caretaker must have thought I was an MFJP agent, and he offered the commandant seventy-five thousand dollars to release him. The commandant made a big deal out of telling the caretaker no, but I'd bet that if I hadn't been along, the commandant would have accepted the money and left.

The commandant called the military base in Agua Prieta, and thirty soldiers arrived to secure the ranch. The local MFJP agents from Agua Prieta, Sonora, arrived to assist as well; they seemed nervous as they looked around. They informed us that this ranch belonged to Amado Carrillo, "the lord of the skies" himself. This ranch was well known to the local MFJP. Hell, they were most likely paid to protect the ranch and provide security for the loads when they landed the planes here. The raid by the commandant in Hermosillo had taken everyone by surprise.

I reported the seizure to Pete in Mexico City, who reported it up the chain; taking off a load from a top trafficker was big news. Pete told his counterpart in the DEA, who was pissed and demanded to know why I didn't include the Hermosillo DEA agents. I had, and the DEA/RAC in Hermosillo got his ass chewed for not going. The DEA attaché told Pete he needed to curtail my enforcement activity because my bold actions were going to get me killed. He told Pete he would be directly responsible for my death. Pete was a good friend and became worried sick that he needed to slow me down. Everyone still remembered Enrique Camarena getting killed for taking down large plantations and pissing off the head traffickers. I assured Pete that I was all right. He trusted my instincts and ability.

Good old Dr. Nogales, the source, was riding high. He was paid quite well for his endeavors and continued to provide information on ranches with acres of marijuana, and, as always, I passed this information to the colonel. Then Dr. Nogales called to report that loads of heroin were being smuggled via the trucks coming from Michoacán, Mexico. He didn't really provide much more detail, but I made some notes and wrote a brief intel report.

About a week later, Dr. Nogales arrived at my office with an official MFJP report about the seizure of five kilos of heroin at the Benjamin Hill checkpoint. He stated that it was all his information, and since he had contacted me weeks earlier, I took the seizure at face value, paid him $2,500 from my petty cash, and told him I would request another $15,000 from Mexico City as his payment for the seizure. I then wrote my report. I contacted the colonel and invited him to lunch to show him the report and told him that Dr. Nogales was a great informant. The colonel read the report, then said that Dr. Nogales had had nothing to do with the seizure of the heroin. I had been duped; I had trusted the source and taken his information at face value. The commandant called in the captain in charge of the checkpoint and demanded to know who the hell released the official MFJP report to Dr. Nogales. The poor agent who released the paper was arrested on the spot. I contacted Dr. Nogales and asked him to come to the commandant's office. When he arrived, I fired him on the spot as well for lying to me. He protested, but between the commandant and me, he broke and confessed to his scam of working with the agents at the checkpoint to split money by giving him reports so he could screw me. I told the good doctor, "Adios, and don't come to my office again."

It seems that the good Dr. Nogales later showed up at the Douglas, Arizona, office and told some new baby agent who didn't know shit that I had cheated him out of thousands of dollars I owed him for the heroin seizure. The shithead agent called Internal Affairs and reported that I was ripping off sources for money from seizure payments and—you guessed it—I was under investigation again. Timing was on my side this time. Several agents who had worked directly for me in Nogales were now working for Internal Affairs. They interviewed the agent in Douglas, Arizona, and then demanded that the source take a polygraph test. The Internal Affairs agents who were assigned the investigation agreed that I was a mean, grumpy bastard, but they never doubted my integrity. Dr. Nogales was brought to the Internal Affairs office and wired up for the polygraph, and before the machine was turned on, he broke and confessed to making up the entire story to get money from the rookie agent in Douglas. Professional sources know how to work the system. I always told my agents, "Never trust a source. Especially when it concerns another cop. When in doubt, polygraph the bastards."

Pete called me back to Mexico City for a conference, so I boarded the Aero Mexico flight in Hermosillo. Before I boarded the flight, I noticed a caravan of three Suburbans arriving at the airport under heavy guard. A man who was traveling in the convoy was whisked into the airport and allowed to go directly to the plane. I thought the guy looked familiar but couldn't remember where I had seen the face.

Then, about halfway to Mexico City, I almost choked on my drink when it dawned on me who the guy was. It was Miguel

Caro Quintero, the brother of Rafael Caro Quintero. The minute the plane landed, I called the office at the embassy and reported the entourage. No one was available to intercept him, and once again he disappeared.

IN my quest to develop sources of information, I was asked to help an attorney I knew obtain a visa for his sister. Little did I know at the time that his sister was the owner of several strip clubs in Hermosillo. The State Department called me and demanded an explanation of why the woman should be given a visa. The short answer was, *Where do you think the traffickers spend thousands of dollars in cash a night?* The visa was granted. The brother-and-sister duo ended up opening six strip clubs and provided information on the high rollers who entered and spent five thousand dollars in cash a night. The bouncer out front copied the license plate numbers and listened for the names.

The fringe benefit of my new source was that I always had a welcoming table to enjoy the eye candy. Since I had the dubious duty of entertaining Mexican officials and visiting U.S. law enforcement, the clubs were a great refuge for entertainment. The visiting agents all pleaded with me to take them out. I was like a celebrity. The naked women greeted me by name and rubbed their breasts against me and lined up to hug me. Being an agent in Mexico did provide some wild excitement. The TDY agents called me "the Lord of Titty Bars."

I learned that by virtue of having fake business cards identifying me as a plastic surgeon specializing in breast enhancement, I was often given the delicate task of touching hundreds of delightfully soft, ample breasts in order to make a personal recommendation, a job I took quite seriously. I also loved to visit the FBI agents in Mexico City; I would take a handful of their business cards and hand them out later at the various strip clubs. I figured it might help the agents' reputation.

Following a tip from the bouncer I had documented as a source, I was able to get information on a high-rolling trafficker that resulted in the seizure of two thousand pounds of cocaine in Cuidad Obregón. Then, just as before, some unknown trafficker made a death threat against me. The second threat wasn't as specific as the first, and I persuaded Pete to allow me to stay in Mexico. This threat was reported by none other than my old source Blind Tony.

Within six months, Operation Casablanca, the large money-laundering investigation, broke open. Several bankers and politicians in Mexico were involved, creating a big scandal. Once again I was told to pack a suitcase, only this time the Mexican government was going to give all Customs agents in Mexico the boot. We were all on standby to be kicked out of Mexico. It took about ten days for things to settle down and we were allowed to stay, under political protest by Mexico.

HEADQUARTERS TOUR

NO good deed goes unpunished. I couldn't escape a mandatory headquarters tour required of managers. I was assigned to the staff of the commissioner of Customs. I didn't think things could get any worse. I imagined myself sharpening pencils or opening doors for upper brass as my punishment for my past indiscretions.

I reported to my new office in Washington, D.C., on August 1, 2001. I rented a nice high-rise condo just across the Potomac River and the Key Bridge, close to Arlington Cemetery. From my condo balcony I had beautiful views of the White House and the Pentagon.

I was assigned to an office known as the Office of Border Co-ordination. The office was staffed with individuals from various divisions of Customs and the U.S. military; all were GS-14 or GS-15 employees. There were three inspectors from field operations, one inspector from the immigration service, two Coast

Guard commanders, one army colonel, and two special agents, one of which was me.

Timing is everything. Forty days later, all hell broke loose; September 11, 2001, was a day to remember. We saw the news of the first plane crash, then the second, and then the Pentagon was struck. The entire office was evacuated; the fourth plane was still missing and believed to be headed back to Washington, D.C. The entire metro area was in gridlock. Bridges were closed, metro trains stopped running, buses and taxis disappeared; the entire city was in chaos.

We stood outside the building; there was really nowhere to go and no way to get there. We went to Harry's Bar, our favorite watering hole, and solemnly we watched the events unfold on the news like the rest of the nation. When I finally arrived home late in the evening, I stood on my balcony and saw the Pentagon smoldering. It was a very eerie moment.

In January 2002, I was sent to Moscow, Russia. My task was simple: persuade the Russian government and the Russian customs service to identify suspected Middle Eastern terrorists arriving from Iraq or Afghanistan into Moscow via commercial airlines and forward the information to the U.S. Customs Service. How hard could this task be, right? Well, the cold war was history, but the attitude wasn't.

I called the travel office, booked my flight, took orders from everyone in the office for vodka and hats, and departed for Dulles Airport. I was somehow booked on a separate airline than the other eight members from various departments in headquarters accompanying me on the trip. I had a two-hour delay in Germany and was the only American on the flight from Germany to Russia. I went through Russian customs and immigration, then stood in the airport terminal waiting another thirty minutes, because I expected an embassy car to pick me up. Finally, I went directly to the taxi stand at the airport, grabbed the first taxi, and departed for the hotel. The Russians must have thought I was a new spy in town. I noticed a car following my taxi; hell, I had spent enough time being followed by the police in Latin America to know that the Russians were following me.

If the Russians weren't suspicious before, they quickly became suspicious as hell. I must have hired the only taxi driver in Moscow who didn't have a clue where the hotel was. The poor bastard was so lost, the normal twenty-minute drive from the airport to the hotel took two hours. The taxi driver stopped twice to ask people for directions, and then he stopped and made a telephone call for directions. This must have made the KGB go insane.

Finally, upon arriving at the hotel, I checked in and was told I would have to wait a few hours for my room to be assigned. Why the hell did I need to wait two more hours when I had been expected four hours earlier? The rest of the staff had been picked up by the embassy driver upon arrival and checked into their rooms. They had eaten dinner and were asleep, except for a couple of people. I noticed that two stocky Russians had followed me inside and were at the front desk. I was tired, aggravated, and hungry. I walked down the street, had dinner, drank shots of vodka, and looked at the lovely scenery. The ladies in Moscow are hot, and I thought, *Wow, I could like Moscow.*

The next day I went to the American embassy and called Russian customs to meet the director, but I couldn't even get a janitor to meet me. Every time we called, the director was out, and then he was reassigned and a new director was taking over. The embassy conducted a sweep of my hotel room for security purposes and found two live microphones and one live video feed in the room. To say the Russians were suspicious was an understatement.

The mission wasn't a total disaster; I had a great time, and I hooked up with an allegedly "retired" KGB colonel in the hotel lobby who showed me the finer art of drinking vodka as well as the sights of Moscow.

THE four years in Washington, D.C., were definitely eventful. I rode the metro to work every day armed with two extra magazines, halfway expecting to shoot some extremist suicide bomber. I wasn't alone; half the people riding the metro were armed, and I think if someone even started saying suicide prayers he would have been shot.

Then, just about when we thought things couldn't get any worse, the Washington, D.C., snipers appeared. These two crazy psychos just decided to shoot people at random locations throughout the entire D.C. metro area. Everyone was scared to go outside and walk to the bus stop in the morning. These assholes shot fourteen people at random.

In 2003, because of the events of September 11, 2001, the government reorganized and formed the Department of Homeland Security. This reorganization was going to streamline the efficiency of the government, provide better means of communication, and do away with upper-level bureaucracy. The Customs Office of Investigations was merged with the immigration service and became Immigration and Customs Enforcement (ICE). ICE was supposed to be the primary investigative division for the Department of Homeland Security. ICE functioned in constant crisis mode; everything was reactionary. The bosses above issued a gag order and ordered personnel that the only statement they could give was, "The office is in transition." To date, ICE is still in transition.

I was given the assignment of coordinator of special security events. This included the security at the Winter Olympics, the UN General Assembly, the G-8 summit, and the 2004 presidential campaign. I was now working directly with the Secret Service providing training, personnel, resources, and equipment for the various security details.

I stayed in touch with old friends. Joe had retired and moved to Wyoming, had bought a ranch there, and was happy teaching school. Layne was still teaching and coaching. He was enjoying retirement. Tom was assigned to the Nogales border patrol office and enjoyed the job to the end, when he retired in December 2004. Tom had signed on to work for the army at Fort Huachuca as an instructor for the new interrogation training for army personnel going to Afghanistan.

Ricardo, who had been the resident agent in charge in Nogales, took a position as the assistant attaché in Guadalajara, Mexico.

Rene was now the assistant special agent in charge (ASAC) in Tucson. He was the administrative ASAC in charge of shuffling paper; this job perfectly suited Rene. He handled all office purchases, record keeping, inventory, and a host of other jobs that would have made me wacko. Rene had done the math on retirement and had decided to work till the maximum age of fifty-seven. The government had long decided that special agents were useless after fifty-seven. That seems like a young age to most working stiffs in the civilian sector, who work until they're sixty-five.

As for me, I had decided that I wanted to retire in Arizona, so I requested a transfer back to either Tucson or Nogales. In the government, when they give you a paid move and buy your residence, they require that you work one full year of service. So my plan was to have the government pay for my relocation and after one year retire and walk away. The way the new Department of Homeland Security was established and implemented had left me pessimistic about the future of the agency.

THE BORDER AGAIN

AFTER my tour in Washington, D.C., I was in a state of disillusionment. The new Department of Homeland Security and ICE were dysfunctional. I had decided to get the hell out of the government and retire. The requirement for a paid final transfer was to work one year in the office I selected. I chose Arizona one last time.

When it was officially announced that I was returning to Arizona, the agents in the Nogales office called around to find out who the hell the new boss was. The response they received was scary. The agents in Arizona who had worked with me ten years earlier knew the younger me.

I received several telephone calls from an old buddy, Dave, who was now the intelligence research specialist in the Nogales office. Dave was an old cowboy who had worked as an inspector for twenty-five years before coming to work for ICE. Dave decided to add fuel to the fire and stir the pot by scaring the hell out of the agents by telling them I was the meanest, nastiest supervisor living. Dave referred to the guys in the office as a bunch of baby agents, since almost no one had more than two or three years on the job.

I was now fifty-three years old, twice the age of the agents in the Nogales office. Hell, I had been transferred so many times that when people asked me where I was from, I couldn't answer. I had been in my thirties when I started as a young supervisor in Nogales; the years had taken a toll on me. I thought to myself, *Of all the damn places I could have gone, why the hell did I decide to return to Nogales?* I guess this is where my history began and should end. The border was in my blood.

Nothing had changed in the office except the faces. The agents were still in the building next to Ryan's Pub, except that it was closed now. The agents now called the office "the crack house." My old Irish plaid couch was still there, looking no worse for wear. I couldn't help but stare at it and reflect on all the good times it had provided years earlier. I told the lads in the office that if that old couch could talk, I would be in real trouble.

My days of working the streets were all but over; I knew that I could still do everything, but that wasn't my position. I was finally comfortable with doing office work and was now working as the ASAC. I went out at night with the young agents in the office just to prove to myself that I still had what it takes. I joked and told the young agents, "Old age and treachery will overcome youth and skill."

The agents were eager to work, sometimes too eager. One morning I went to the garage to have my morning cigar, and Don showed me the Nogales newspaper. It seems that the sheriff's office had responded to a bomb threat. A woman went to leave her office and noticed a six-inch cylindrical tube with wires hanging from the bottom of her vehicle. The poor woman thought it was a pipe bomb and called the sheriff's office, who called the Arizona highway patrol bomb squad. As soon as DPS arrived, the bomb technician knew it was a tracking device.

The sheriff's office told the woman someone must have been playing a joke, and then they took the tracker and called the DEA and ICE. Of course it was ours. An agent suspected the lady of drug smuggling and wanted to monitor her activity hoping she would lead him to a stash house. The agent was pleased to have it returned, but no one had bothered to mention it to me.

I then had the pleasure of calling the young agent into my office and using the infamous Kirkpatrick stare. I left the lad standing there for a couple of minutes while I pretended to read the article again, and then I showed him the newspaper. I had learned to chew ass from the best old supervisory agents in the business. Hell, I had had my fair share of royal ass-chewings when I was a young agent. The agent, known as "Wild Bill," took it well and told the other agents that if the boss calls you in to chew your ass, you'd better take a roll of toilet paper with you. I wanted to laugh, but I enjoyed making the guy squirm; it was good to know I could intimidate the young agents.

The office had forty-two agents. As I walked around the office and talked to the lads, I realized why they called me "the old man"; these baby agents weren't even born when I started with Customs. From 1980 to 2005, the only thing that changed in the Nogales office was the technology. The cameras were smaller and high tech. The guys were now sending messages and e-mails via Black-Berrys. It was now a techy world.

The agents were still responding to the same areas: Short

Street, Escalada Drive, San Rafael Valley, Kino Springs, Summit Motorway, and hundreds of other locations that I had worked as a young agent. Nogales has always been a major drug corridor, and things in Nogales hadn't changed at all. The flow of narcotics was still flooding the area daily, and the agents did a good job of recruiting sources. A source I had recruited back in 1984 was still working for agents in the office. It was like old home week.

The various drug raids and undercover operations hadn't changed much in twenty-five years. The agents responded to the San Rafael Valley and the mountains to the west; the Crucero family was still living on Escalada Drive, only now the grandsons were moving the loads of dope. The two boys were caught and taken to the office; when the father entered and saw me, he told the young agents that I had arrested him years before and he did five years in prison. I smiled as he shook my hand. I remembered lying in the trash next to the hole in the fence and Rene chasing the vehicle when the driver ran the POE and was shot by the Mexican police.

I held a weekly all-hands meeting in the office and went around the room asking each agent to brief me on his cases or activity. Mario, the supervisor, told me about some drug smugglers getting shot and ripped off by other smugglers. These *bajadores* ("bandits") were working in the canyon around the Tumacacori Mountains, just to the south of Tubac, Arizona. This was almost twenty miles north of the border. I was surprised to learn that bandits were ambushing and attacking smuggling groups that far north of the border.

I had heard of bandits at the fence along the border on both sides, ripping off unsuspecting illegal aliens or smugglers and stealing their money and drugs. The violence and rape of illegal aliens had been going on for years. This new group of *bajadores* was working twenty-nine kilometers north of the border on remote mountain trails. With more than a hundred trails in these mountains, how did they know to choose this one? These border bandits were well informed and must have had inside knowledge to know the exact trail and time the smugglers would cross.

I began to wonder if it was a group of guys living in the Tumacacori area. Perhaps the bandits were rogue law enforcement officers stealing the loads. There is a border patrol checkpoint on Interstate 19; how were they getting the marijuana out of the canyon and past the checkpoint? Then another group of smugglers was ripped off and the load stolen, and another mule was shot and killed. These weren't isolated incidents; over the next year and a half, dozens more were reported. Six drug smugglers were shot and killed, and several others were wounded. Each incident took place within a four-to-five-kilometer area just west of Interstate 19, south of Tubac.

Every smuggler shot was from the same small town of Choix, Sinaloa. For every single victim to be from the same town in Sinaloa was more than a coincidence. Either someone had a vendetta against this particular smuggling group or they had good inside information. Someone had to be telling the *bajadores* exactly what night the smugglers would cross and what trail they would be using. The smugglers were armed as well with AK-47s and attempted to engage the *bajadores*, but the ambush laid out by the bandits was too good. The smugglers continued to lose a load about every three months.

I was briefed daily on all ongoing investigations. One night I decided to go out with the agents and rode with the most senior agent, Eddie. He had information about a load crossing near Patagonia, Arizona. I figured riding along would be a good way to get to know the agents better. Eddie picked a spot on a dirt road overlooking the highway, and the other agents picked surveillance locations around the area. Eddie's vehicle was meticulously clean. I asked him if he minded if I smoked my cigar; he hesitated slightly but told me to go ahead. He didn't smoke but decided what the hell, he wasn't going to say no. Rank has its privileges. I pulled out a large cigar and puffed away for the next two hours until the surveillance was called off.

The next day Eddie came to my office. He said he'd had a terrible fight with his wife when he got home. The wife accused him of being at a bar all night because he reeked of smoke. Eddie immediately took the defensive and said he was working, but his partner was smoking a cigar. The wife didn't buy it. She said, "You're lying, because you told me no one was allowed to smoke in your vehicle." The new agents, just like all the agents before, busted his balls all week, calling Eddie a kiss-ass and suck-up for letting me smoke in his vehicle.

Things were running smoothly; the guys in the office realized that I wasn't a two-headed monster who shot fire out of my ass. I provided some insight and guidance but mainly encouraged the agents to try new things; they were the future of the service. I'm sure they thought I was a rambling old fool, while I was thinking I was finally smart enough to do the job correctly. I realized that I wished I had paid more attention to the older agents who tried to tell me things.

In 2006, the newly elected president of Mexico, Felipe Calderón, made a campaign promise to take on the drug traffickers in Mexico. I had heard that bullshit speech before from President Fox of Mexico. Corruption in Mexico ran so deep that everyone was suspect. However, within a few months of President Calderón taking office, the MFJP arrested a few minor drug traffickers, and the traffickers retaliated by killing police and public officials who stood against them. The violence in Mexico took a dramatic turn for the worse. The traffickers declared war on anyone who stood against them.

Within the year, the Mexican newspapers reported that hundreds of top Mexican government officials were implicated as being corrupt by an informant. Supposedly the informant went directly to the Mexican embassy in Washington, D.C., and asked to talk to the DEA. He was debriefed by U.S. agents and placed in the Witness Protection Program. He provided some very high-level names. The list included thirty or more senior agents of CISEN and SIEDO, which are considered the Mexican government's equivalent of the U.S. Central Intelligence Agency. These were the agencies in charge of probing drug smuggling, weapons smuggling, kidnapping, and terrorism in Mexico. These corrupt officials were receiving monthly bribes of $150,000 to $500,000 from the Beltrán-Leyva and Chapo Guzman cartels.

I had met and worked with several CISEN agents along the border. They were thought to be uncorruptible and worked mainly on arms smuggling into Mexico. The Mexican government's biggest fear is that all the citizens will become armed and another revolution will take place.

The United States assists Mexico by funding $400 million a year to fight the war on drugs, and the Mexican government doesn't produce a single receipt to show accountability for its expenditures. The Mexican drug cartels' annual income is somewhere between $30 billion and $50 billon a year.

When President Calderón took office on December 1, 2006, he acted on his campaign promise to fight the major drug traffickers for control of Mexico. He realized that Mexico was being run by the traffickers, and if he didn't stop the takeover now Mexico would become a Narco Nation. With each cartel leader arrested or killed, the violence escalated more as new leaders stepped up to take power. Adversaries from other cartels tried to take advantage of their weakness and gain control of more territory. Territory and control of border towns in Mexico means more areas of distribution and smuggling routes to flood the United States with narcotics.

The violence was most prevalent in Ciudad Juarez, but I knew it was only a matter of time before it came to Nogales, Sonora. The office had established a Border Violence Group to gather intelligence on the groups and make sure that the violence didn't spread into the United States.

This increased violence was due to the killing of Arturo Beltrán-Leyva by the Mexican navy's special forces in a remote location south of Mexico City. Following Arturo's death, the Mexican government arrested his brother, Carlos Beltrán-Leyva. Then the organization fell to Ignacio Nacho Colonel, who was also arrested, and finally the fourth member of the Beltrán-Leyva organization, El Barbie, was arrested. The Chapo Guzman organization seized the moment; they decided to take advantage of the weakened Beltrán-Leyva cartel and began the takeover of the territory.

By 2007, the violence in Sonora had escalated and Chapo "Shorty" Guzman decided to take over the plaza in Nogales, Sonora. Control of Nogales would increase his smuggling routes and his ability to distribute more drugs into the United States. First, his group raided a police station in Cananea, Sonora, just south of Nogales and killed several police officers and kidnapped others.

The state police and military began a massive search for the officers and ended up in a major shootout with the cartel that left some thirty people dead.

The battle for the plaza in Nogales, Sonora, turned into a bloodbath; the remaining loyalists for Beltrán-Leyva tried to fight back but no longer had muscle. Gun battles took place in broad daylight in Nogales, Sonora, shopping centers and dozens of people were killed. Chapo Guzman's hit men killed members of the Beltrán-Leyva group at random. Automatic-weapon fire could be heard all day long. The traffickers threw hand grenades into bars and office buildings; the local police were helpless, and several were killed when they attempted to interfere.

I was in my office getting a briefing from an agent on the border violence task force, and he mentioned that sources said a narcotics trafficker called Quemado was sent by the Beltrán-Leyva cartel to take over the plaza of Nogales. I froze. Christ, I hadn't heard that name since 1988. I asked the agent, "Who did you say was sent to Nogales?"

He repeated the name: "Quemado." It sent a shiver down my spine.

Surely this must be a new trafficker; I had long thought that Quemado was dead. I had the agent contact his source for additional information. Could it be that the old psychopath had returned from the dead and was trying to take over the coveted plaza position?

To my surprise it was true. Quemado had reappeared as if resurrected from the dead. According to the source, Quemado had moved to Sinaloa and was ultimately arrested in Morelia, Michoacán, by the Mexican army. Quemado was sentenced to fifteen years in prison and released from prison around 2005. He was now about forty-eight years old; his time in prison had only made him more nasty. To survive fifteen years in a Mexican prison, you have to be the meanest bad-ass in existence.

After his release, Quemado went back to doing the only work he had ever known: drug smuggling for the Beltrán-Leyva organization. Apparently after Beltrán-Leyva was killed by the Mexican special forces, Quemado was sent to Nogales, Sonora, to run the distribution of narcotics. Who better than someone who had once been the most feared person in Nogales, Sonora, to regain control of the coveted plaza of Nogales, Sonora, Mexico?

I shuddered at the thought of Quemado taking over the plaza in Nogales. It meant more violence. I told the agents to expect the worst, because Quemado was known for his acts of violence and killing sprees.

Chapo Guzman's organization had other ideas for the plaza, and a bloody war broke out between the two factions for control of Nogales. Citizens were scared to go out, armed traffickers were patrolling the streets, and innocent people were caught in the crossfire as the turf battles raged through the area.

The Nogales, Sonora, deputy police chief, Padilla Molina, and his bodyguard were killed in a parking lot when a group of assailants pulled up beside their vehicle in a pickup truck and opened up with AK-47 assault rifles.

Then the director of the Sonora state police, Juan Manuel Pavon Felix, was ambushed in Nogales, Sonora, when he came to visit. He was ambushed by gunmen who threw hand grenades and opened up with automatic gunfire as he entered his hotel room with his bodyguard and other law enforcement officials. The chief of police in Agua Prieta, Sonora, the border town south of Douglas, Arizona, was shot and killed as he left his office.

Police officers throughout Sonora were being targeted and killed. The police were afraid to take any enforcement action for fear of reprisal. In Hermosillo, Sonora, a handwritten note was found attached to the blade of a knife stuck in the chest of one slain police officer. The note was quite specific: *Any judicial or municipal police working for the Beltrán-Leyva organization is going to die.*

One gun battle lasted more than four hours as the gunmen drove a caravan of three Chevrolet Tahoes from one neighborhood to another, raiding houses and businesses in an attempt to kill as many Beltrán-Leyva loyalists as possible. Ten individuals were killed in one morning alone. The traffickers waited for the police to respond and set up an ambush, killing several officers. This was followed by multiple individuals being beheaded and the body parts thrown into the street.

In the state of Durango, Mexico, the director of the Mexican prison was arrested when it was discovered that he had been paid by the drug cartels to carry out assassinations. The prison director had gathered a group of prisoners and formed his own hit squad of assassins. These prisoners were given targets, then released from prison equipped with weapons and vehicles belonging to the prison.

These prisoners' rampage of terror came to light when they went to the wrong residence and killed seventeen innocent teenagers having a party. The Mexican attorney general's office linked the prisoners to three mass killings: the teenagers and two more attacks on drug smugglers in bars where more than sixteen people were killed. The police traced the assault rifles found at the scene to the prison.

Then, just twelve miles south of Nogales, in the small town of Saric, the final showdown occurred. In the early-morning hours the Chapo Guzman cartel set up an ambush. A road cut through a small hill with about thirty-foot-high walls on both sides of the road allowed them to set up the perfect ambush.

They waited for the Beltrán-Leyva group to travel through the pass; the group drove right into the hands of the waiting ambushers. Like typical macho Mexicans, the traffickers were traveling in tandem, racing down the road, bumper to bumper, with about ten feet between the vehicles. If one stopped fast, every vehicle in the convoy would crash. The hit men were very professional, taking out the first vehicle and the last vehicle with their automatic weapons. The remaining six vehicles stuck in the middle of the pileup became sitting ducks in a shooting gallery. The hit men lobbed hand grenades down onto the road and continued firing away until twenty-one traffickers were killed.

When the Mexican police arrived, they found the bodies cut to ribbons, shot hundreds of times. Nine people were still alive, but they were severely wounded. The police recovered eight vehicles and seven weapons. I saw the pictures of the scene. It was a complete massacre, like Custer's last stand.

Following this massive gun battle, I inquired about Quemado. No one knew his whereabouts. He could be dead or in prison under a different name. Chapo's group had taken over the plaza; the violence subsided, and things became relatively calm again. The traffickers regrouped, and the locals resumed their smuggling operations.

The Mexican government estimates that approximately thirty-five thousand Mexican citizens have been killed in drug-related violence since 2006. The highest homicide rates have occurred along the border cites of Ciudad Juarez, Tijuana, Nuevo Laredo, and Nogales, Sonora. Nogales ranked number ten on a list of cities with the most homicides in Mexico. Ciudad Juarez, Mexico, across from El Paso, Texas, was number one on the list.

MY one year on the border had extended to three years. I felt a sense of satisfaction that the agents in the office had matured and the young supervisors had the office under control. I decided it was my time to let go and retire. I gave my notice that I was going to disappear into the sunset.

I have no idea what happened to Quemado; once again, no one knew anything, and he was never listed in the Mexican newspapers as one of the traffickers killed. I heard that people were seen at his mansion in Calle Kennedy. But once again, nothing; he had vanished in the night.

The original group I started my career with had all retired: Carlos, Layne, Joe, Ricardo, Rene, Tom, Louie, and Charlie. The change to Homeland Security in the government brought about a thirty percent increase in retirement of the old Customs special agents. Carlos had retired many years earlier to a ranch in Texas. Layne had also retired fifteen years earlier and begun a new career as a high school teacher. Tom had retired the year I returned from Washington, D.C., and had started a second career with the Department of Defense. Rene had had his fill of the politics in the Tucson, Arizona, office. Rene claims I persuaded him to retire, but I knew that in his mind, he had decided his time for retirement had come.

Ricardo had retired two years before and had stayed in Guadalajara, Mexico, to work as a private consultant for a high-powered Mexican attorney. However, he soon realized that this was not exactly what he'd expected, so he returned to the United

States. Ricardo then applied for a position with the Santa Cruz County Sheriff's Department. Ricardo loved being in uniform. He was sent to a training academy at age fifty-six with men half his age and was at the top of his graduating class. .

I later heard a rumor that Ricardo was being investigated by the DEA and had been arrested.

I was stunned by this. I could never believe Ricardo was crooked; there had to be something more to the story. I found out later that the attorney Ricardo worked for in Guadalajara had asked Ricardo to do a check on a defendant to see if he was wanted in the United States. Ricardo committed a cardinal sin for law enforcement; he lost the document, and somehow it ended up in the hands of the Mexican attorney. No one except other law enforcement is allowed the privilege of seeing these secure documents. Ricardo was not involved in any drug scheme as the DEA alleged, but once he was charged, the burden of proof fell upon him as well as costly attorney fees. Ricardo's attorney said they could win the case, but the cost would be at least another hundred thousand dollars. Ricardo had already drained his retirement, had taken a second mortgage on his house, and had borrowed money from his children. He decided to plea bargain and accepted a sentence of two years in a federal prison for losing the computer printout. I later learned that the attorney he worked for was a snitch for the DEA. The attorney had been arrested by the DEA before and was working off a charge: the first person he set up to save his ass was Ricardo. I have always preached to every agent who ever worked for me: never trust a fucking source.

The old crew was gone; it was my time to retire as well. I bid the agents farewell and stepped aside. I had given the service twenty-nine years of my life, and it was time to do something else.

I was asked to do contract work for the government. I no longer wanted to punch a clock or answer to anyone but myself. I had nothing to prove to anyone, so my answer was no.

I decided to follow a passion. I had begun smoking cigars as a young agent. During my travels around the world, I discovered that smoking cigars relaxed me, and during that thirty-minute or hour smoke, I had a little peace and tranquillity. I found that cigar smoking and good conversations go hand in hand at cigar lounges. As I watched the lingering trail of cigar smoke floating in the air, I knew I had found my new career.

So I followed my dreams and opened my own cigar shop in Tubac, Arizona, called Grumpy Gringo Fine Cigars. I now answer to the nickname "Grumpy," a fitting alias for a crotchety mean guy like myself. My patrons often asked me to tell stories about my rambling days as a rising young agent. One day a good friend of mine, Frank, suggested that I write a book so I would, as he politely said, "shut the hell up and stop telling stories." Frank held me on course to see this book finished.

The situation on the border remains volatile. An Arizona rancher was killed near Douglas, Arizona. Then a young border patrol agent was shot and killed by border bandits near Nogales, Arizona, just west of Interstate 19, a few kilometers south of the previous attacks on the smugglers.

The latest tragedy involved two ICE agents working TDY in Mexico City. They were followed and ambushed in San Luis Potosi, Mexico. One agent was killed and the other wounded when the notorious Zetas attacked their vehicle and fired more than eighty rounds from an AK-47. The ICE agents were forced off the road; a window of the armored vehicle was open and the traffickers shot one agent eight times and struck the other agent twice before he managed to get the window up.

I look back on the life I gave to the U.S. government and can say I have no regrets. Not many men get paid for doing something they love that challenges them and helps protect their country. I still hope that the governments of the United States and Mexico find a way to work together and put an end to the violence once and for all.

Mexico has always been a violent country. From conquest to rebellion, violence has been the answer to most issues. I have seen that violence grow in my years on the border, and now I worry about it spilling into U.S. cities. It is nothing short of a miracle that a town like El Paso, Texas, has only a few homicides a year when Ciudad Juarez, Mexico, separated by a river and a barely observed border, had three thousand homicides in 2010.

It has been said that law enforcement is the glue that holds society together, and there is no better example than Mexico. Once the people stopped trusting their own law enforcement officials, the traffickers knew they had won and could take over the country.

It's important that we, as Americans, recognize how special our country is. The laws and Constitution are valid only if the citizens believe in them. We must help our neighbors to the south until order is once again restored.